THE LETTERS OF ST. JEROME

Volume I

St. Jerome

Translated by:

W.H. Fremantle

G. Lewis

W.G. Martlcy

Edited by:

D.P. Curtin

THE LETTERS OF ST. JEROME

Library of Congress Cataloging-in-Publication Data

THE LETTERS OF ST. JEROME

S. HIERONYMVS.

LETTER I

To Innocent

Not only the first of the letters but probably the earliest extant composition of Jerome (c. 370 A.D.). Innocent, to whom it is addressed, was one of the little band of enthusiasts whom Jerome gathered round him in Aquileia. He followed his friend to Syria, where he died in 374 A.D. (See Letter III., 3.)

1. You have frequently asked me, dearest Innocent, not to pass over in silence the marvellous event which has happened in our own day. I have declined the task from modesty and, as I now feel, with justice, believing myself to be incapable of it, at once because human language is inadequate to the divine praise, and because inactivity, acting like rust upon the intellect, has dried up any little power of expression that I have ever had. You in reply urge that in the things of God we must look not at the work which we are able to accomplish, but at the spirit in which it is undertaken, and that he can never be at a loss for words who has believed on the Word.

2. What, then, must I do? The task is beyond me, and yet I dare not decline it. I am a mere unskilled passenger, and I find myself placed in charge of a freighted ship. I have not so much as handled a rowboat on a lake, and now I have to trust myself to the noise and turmoil of the Euxine. I see the shores sinking beneath the horizon, sky and sea on every side; darkness lowers over the water, the clouds are black as night, the waves only are white with foam. You urge me to hoist the swelling sails, to loosen the sheets, and to take the helm. At last I obey your commands, and as charity can do all things, I will trust in the Holy Ghost to guide my course, and I shall console myself, whatever the event. For, if our ship is wafted by the surf into the wished-for haven, I shall be content to be told that the pilotage was poor. But, if through my unpolished diction we run aground amid the rough cross-currents of language, you may blame my lack of power, but you will at least recognize my good intentions.

3. To begin, then: Vercellæ; is a Ligurian town, situated not far from the base of the Alps, once important, but now sparsely peopled and fallen into decay. When the consular was holding his visitation there, a poor woman and her paramour were brought before him— the charge of adultery had been fastened upon them by the husband— and were both consigned to the penal horrors of a prison. Shortly after an attempt was made to elicit the truth by torture, and when the blood-stained hook smote the young man's livid flesh and tore furrows in his side, the unhappy wretch sought to avoid prolonged pain by a speedy death. Falsely accusing his own passions, he involved another in the charge; and it appeared that he was of all men the most miserable, and that his execution was just inasmuch as he had left to an innocent woman no means of self-defence. But the woman, stronger in virtue if weaker in sex, though her frame was stretched upon the rack, and though her hands, stained with the filth of the prison, were tied behind her, looked up to

heaven with her eyes, which alone the torturer had been unable to bind, and while the tears rolled down her face, said: You are witness, Lord Jesus, to whom nothing is hid, who triest the reins and the heart. You are witness that it is not to save my life that I deny this charge. I refuse to lie because to lie is sin. And as for you, unhappy man, if you are bent on hastening your death, why must you destroy not one innocent person, but two? I also, myself, desire to die. I desire to put off this hated body, but not as an adulteress. I offer my neck; I welcome the shining sword without fear; yet I will take my innocence with me. He does not die who is slain while purposing so to live.

4. The consular, who had been feasting his eyes upon the bloody spectacle, now, like a wild beast, which after once tasting blood always thirsts for it, ordered the torture to be doubled, and cruelly gnashing his teeth, threatened the executioner with like punishment if he failed to extort from the weaker sex a confession which a man's strength had not been able to keep back.

5. Send help, Lord Jesus. For this one creature of Yours every species of torture is devised. She is bound by the hair to a stake, her whole body is fixed more firmly than ever on the rack; fire is brought and applied to her feet; her sides quiver beneath the executioner's probe; even her breasts do not escape. Still the woman remains unshaken; and, triumphing in spirit over the pain of the body, enjoys the happiness of a good conscience, round which the tortures rage in vain. The cruel judge rises, overcome with passion. She still prays to God. Her limbs are wrenched from their sockets; she only turns her eyes to heaven. Another confesses what is thought their common guilt. She, for the confessor's sake, denies the confession, and, in peril of her own life, clears one who is in peril of his.

6. Meantime she has but one thing to say: Beat me, burn me, tear me, if you will; I have not done it. If you will not believe my words, a day will come when this charge shall be carefully sifted. I have One who will judge me. Wearied out at last, the torturer sighed in response to her groans; nor could he find a spot on which to inflict a fresh wound. His cruelty overcome, he shuddered to see the body he had torn. Immediately the consular cried, in a fit of passion, Why does it surprise you, bystanders, that a woman prefers torture to death? It takes two people, most assuredly, to commit adultery; and I think it more credible that a guilty woman should deny a sin than that an innocent young man should confess one.

7. Like sentence, accordingly, was passed on both, and the condemned pair were dragged to execution. The entire people poured out to see the sight; indeed, so closely were the gates thronged by the out-rushing crowd, that you might have fancied the city itself to be migrating. At the very first stroke of the sword the head of the hapless youth was cut off, and the headless trunk rolled over in its blood. Then came the woman's turn. She knelt down upon the ground, and the shining sword was lifted over her quivering neck. But though the headsman summoned all his strength into his bared arm, the moment it touched her flesh the fatal blade stopped short, and, lightly glancing over the skin, merely grazed it sufficiently to draw blood. The striker saw, with terror, his hand unnerved, and, amazed at his defeated skill and at his drooping sword, he whirled it aloft for another stroke. Again the blade fell forceless on the woman, sinking harmlessly on her neck, as

though the steel feared to touch her. The enraged and panting officer, who had thrown open his cloak at the neck to give his full strength to the blow, shook to the ground the brooch which clasped the edges of his mantle, and not noticing this, began to poise his sword for a fresh stroke. See, cried the woman, a jewel has fallen from your shoulder. Pick up what you have earned by hard toil, that you may not lose it.

8. What, I ask, is the secret of such confidence as this? Death draws near, but it has no terrors for her. When smitten she exults, and the executioner turns pale. Her eyes see the brooch, they fail to see the sword. And, as if intrepidity in the presence of death were not enough, she confers a favor upon her cruel foe. And now the mysterious Power of the Trinity rendered even a third blow vain. The terrified soldier, no longer trusting the blade, proceeded to apply the point to her throat, in the idea that though it might not cut, the pressure of his hand might plunge it into her flesh. Marvel unheard of through all the ages! The sword bent back to the hilt, and in its defeat looked to its master, as if confessing its inability to slay.

9. Let me call to my aid the example of the three children, who, amid the cool, encircling fire, sang hymns, instead of weeping, and around whose turbans and holy hair the flames played harmlessly. Let me recall, too, the story of the blessed Daniel, Daniel vi in whose presence, though he was their natural prey, the lions crouched, with fawning tails and frightened mouths. Let Susannah also rise in the nobility of her faith before the thoughts of all; who, after she had been condemned by an unjust sentence, was saved through a youth inspired by the Holy Ghost. In both cases the Lord's mercy was alike shown; for while Susannah was set free by the judge, so as not to die by the sword, this woman, though condemned by the judge, was acquitted by the sword.

10. Now at length the populace rise in arms to defend the woman. Men and women of every age join in driving away the executioner, shouting round him in a surging crowd. Hardly a man dares trust his own eyes. The disquieting news reaches the city close at hand, and the entire force of constables is mustered. The officer who is responsible for the execution of criminals bursts from among his men, and

Staining his hoary hair with soiling dust,

exclaims: What! citizens, do you mean to seek my life? Do you intend to make me a substitute for her? However much your minds are set on mercy, and however much you wish to save a condemned woman, yet assuredly I— I who am innocent   ought not to perish. His tearful appeal tells upon the crowd, they are all benumbed by the influence of sorrow, and an extraordinary change of feeling is manifested. Before it had seemed a duty to plead for the woman's life, now it seemed a duty to allow her to be executed.

11. Accordingly a new sword is fetched, a new headsman appointed. The victim takes her place, once more strengthened only with the favor of Christ. The first blow makes her quiver, beneath the second she sways to and fro, by the third she falls wounded to the ground. Oh, majesty of the divine power highly to be

extolled! She who previously had received four strokes without injury, now, a few moments later, seems to die that an innocent man may not perish in her stead.

12. Those of the clergy whose duty it is to wrap the blood-stained corpse in a winding-sheet, dig out the earth and, heaping together stones, form the customary tomb. The sunset comes on quickly, and by God's mercy the night of nature arrives more swiftly than is its wont. Suddenly the woman's bosom heaves, her eyes seek the light, her body is quickened into new life. A moment after she sighs, she looks round, she gets up and speaks. At last she is able to cry: The Lord is on my side; I will not fear. What can man do unto me?

13. Meantime an aged woman, supported out of the funds of the church, gave back her spirit to heaven from which it came. Ecclesiastes 12:7 It seemed as if the course of events had been thus purposely ordered, for her body took the place of the other beneath the mound. In the gray dawn the devil comes on the scene in the form of a constable, asks for the corpse of her who had been slain, and desires to have her grave pointed out to him. Surprised that she could have died, he fancies her to be still alive. The clergy show him the fresh turf, and meet his demands by pointing to the earth lately heaped up, taunting him with such words as these: Yes, of course, tear up the bones which have been buried! Declare war anew against the tomb, and if even that does not satisfy you, pluck her limb from limb for birds and beasts to mangle! Mere dying is too good for one whom it took seven strokes to kill.

14. Before such opprobrious words the executioner retires in confusion, while the woman is secretly revived at home. Then, lest the frequency of the doctor's visits to the church might give occasion for suspicion, they cut her hair short and send her in the company of some virgins to a sequestered country house. There she changes her dress for that of a man, and scars form over her wounds. Yet even after the great miracles worked on her behalf, the laws still rage against her. So true is it that, where there is most law, there, there is also most injustice.

15. But now see whither the progress of my story has brought me; we come upon the name of our friend Evagrius. So great have his exertions been in the cause of Christ that, were I to suppose it possible adequately to describe them, I should only show my own folly; and were I minded deliberately to pass them by, I still could not prevent my voice from breaking out into cries of joy. Who can fittingly praise the vigilance which enabled him to bury, if I may so say, before his death Auxentius of Milan, that curse brooding over the church? Or who can sufficiently extol the discretion with which he rescued the Roman bishop from the toils of the net in which he was fairly entangled, and showed him the means at once of overcoming his opponents and of sparing them in their discomfiture? But

Such topics I must leave to other bards,
Shut out by envious straits of time and space.

I am satisfied now to record the conclusion of my tale. Evagrius seeks a special audience of the Emperor; importunes him with his entreaties, wins his favor by his services, and finally gains his cause through his earnestness. The Emperor restored to liberty the woman whom God had restored to life.

LETTER II

To Theodosius and the Rest of the Anchorites

Written from Antioch, 374 A.D., while Jerome was still in doubt as to his future course. Theodosius appears to have been the head of the solitaries in the Syrian Desert.

How I long to be a member of your company, and with uplifting of all my powers to embrace your admirable community! Though, indeed, these poor eyes are not worthy to look upon it. Oh! That I could behold the desert, lovelier to me than any city! Oh! That I could see those lonely spots made into a paradise by the saints that throng them! But since my sins prevent me from thrusting into your blessed company a head laden with every transgression, I adjure you (and I know that you can do it) by your prayers to deliver me from the darkness of this world. I spoke of this when I was with you, and now in writing to you I repeat anew the same request; for all the energy of my mind is devoted to this one object. It rests with you to give effect to my resolve. I have the will but not the power; this last can only come in answer to your prayers. For my part, I am like a sick sheep astray from the flock. Unless the good Shepherd shall place me on his shoulders and carry me back to the fold, Luke 15:3-5 my steps will totter, and in the very effort of rising I shall find my feet give way. I am the prodigal son Luke 15:11-32 who although I have squandered all the portion entrusted to me by my father, have not yet bowed the knee in submission to him; not yet have I commenced to put away from me the allurements of my former excesses. And because it is only a little while since I have begun not so much to abandon my vices as to desire to abandon them, the devil now ensnares me in new toils, he puts new stumbling-blocks in my path, he encompasses me on every side.

The seas around, and all around the main.

I find myself in mid-ocean, unwilling to retreat and unable to advance. It only remains that your prayers should win for me the gale of the Holy Spirit to waft me to the haven upon the desired shore.

LETTER III

To Rufinus the Monk.

Written from Antioch, 374 A.D., to Rufinus in Egypt. Jerome narrates his travels and the events which have taken place since his arrival in Syria, particularly the deaths of Innocent and Hylas (§3). He also describes the life of Bonosus, who was now a hermit on an island in the Adriatic (§4). The main object of the letter is to induce Rufinus to come to Syria.

1. That God gives more than we ask Him for, Ephesians 3:20 and that He often grants us things which eye has not seen nor ear heard, neither have they entered into the heart of man, 1 Corinthians 2:9 I knew indeed before from the mystic declaration of the sacred volumes; but now, dearest Rufinus, I have had proof of it in my own case. For I who fancied it too bold a wish to be allowed by an exchange of letters to counterfeit to myself your presence in the flesh, hear that you are penetrating the remotest parts of Egypt, visiting the monks and going round God's family upon earth. Oh, if only the Lord Jesus Christ would suddenly transport me to you as Philip was transported to the eunuch, Acts 8:26-30 and Habakkuk to Daniel, with what a close embrace would I clasp your neck, how fondly would I press kisses upon that mouth which has so often joined with me of old in error or in wisdom. But as I am unworthy (not that you should so come to me but) that I should so come to you, and because my poor body, weak even when well, has been shattered by frequent illnesses; I send this letter to meet you instead of coming myself, in the hope that it may bring you hither to me caught in the meshes of love's net.

2. My first joy at such unexpected good tidings was due to our brother, Heliodorus. I desired to be sure of it, but did not dare to feel sure, especially as he told me that he had only heard it from some one else, and as the strangeness of the news impaired the credit of the story. Once more my wishes hovered in uncertainty and my mind wavered, till an Alexandrian monk who had some time previously been sent over by the dutiful zeal of the people to the Egyptian confessors (in will already martyrs), impelled me by his presence to believe the tidings. Even then, I must admit I still hesitated. For on the one hand he knew nothing either of your name or country: yet on the other what he said seemed likely to be true, agreeing as it did with the hint which had already reached me. At last the truth broke upon me in all its fullness, for a constant stream of persons passing through brought the report: Rufinus is at Nitria, and has reached the abode of the blessed Macarius. At this point I cast away all that restrained my belief, and then first really grieved to find myself ill. Had it not been that my wasted and enfeebled frame fettered my movements, neither the summer heat nor the dangerous voyage should have had power to retard the rapid steps of affection. Believe me, brother, I look forward to seeing you more than the storm-tossed mariner looks for his haven, more than the thirsty fields long for the showers, more than the anxious mother sitting on the curving shore expects her son.

3. After that sudden whirlwind dragged me from your side, severing with its impious wrench the bonds of affection in which we were knit together,

The dark blue raincloud lowered o'er my head:
On all sides were the seas, on all the sky.

I wandered about, uncertain where to go. Thrace, Pontus, Bithynia, the whole of Galatia and Cappadocia, Cilicia also with its burning heat, one after another shattered my energies. At last Syria presented itself to me as a most secure harbor to a shipwrecked man. Here, after undergoing every possible kind of sickness, I lost one of my two eyes; for Innocent, the half of my soul, was taken away from me by a sudden attack of fever. The one eye which I now enjoy, and which is all in all to me, is our Evagrius, upon whom I with my constant infirmities have come as an additional burden. We had with us also Hylas, the servant of the holy Melanium, who by his stainless conduct had wiped out the taint of his previous servitude. His death opened afresh the wound which had not yet healed. But as the apostle's words forbid us to mourn for those who sleep, 1 Thessalonians 4:13 and as my excess of grief has been tempered by the joyful news that has since come to me, I recount this last, that, if you have not heard it, you may learn it; and that, if you know it already, you may rejoice over it with me.

4. Bonosus, your friend, or, to speak more truly, mine as well as yours, is now climbing the ladder foreshown in Jacob's dream. Genesis 28:12 He is bearing his cross, neither taking thought for the morrow Matthew 6:34 nor looking back at what he has left. Luke 9:62 He is sowing in tears that he may reap in joy. As Moses in a type so he in reality is lifting up the serpent in the wilderness. Numbers 21:9 This is a true story, and it may well put to shame the lying marvels described by Greek and Roman pens. For here you have a youth educated with us in the refining accomplishments of the world, with abundance of wealth, and in rank inferior to none of his associates; yet he forsakes his mother, his sisters, and his dearly loved brother, and settles like a new tiller of Eden on a dangerous island, with the sea roaring round its reefs; while its rough crags, bare rocks, and desolate aspect make it more terrible still. No peasant or monk is to be found there. Even the little Onesimus you know of, in whose kisses he used to rejoice as in those of a brother, in this tremendous solitude no longer remains at his side. Alone upon the island— or rather not alone, for Christ is with him— he sees the glory of God, which even the apostles saw not save in the desert. He beholds, it is true, no embattled towns, but he has enrolled his name in the new city. Garments of sackcloth disfigure his limbs, yet so clad he will be the sooner caught up to meet Christ in the clouds. 1 Thessalonians 4:17 No watercourse pleasant to the view supplies his wants, but from the Lord's side he drinks the water of life. Place all this before your eyes, dear friend, and with all the faculties of your mind picture to yourself the scene. When you realize the effort of the fighter then you will be able to praise his victory. Round the entire island roars the frenzied sea, while the beetling crags along its winding shores resound as the billows beat against them. No grass makes the ground green; there are no shady copses and no fertile fields. Precipitous cliffs surround his dreadful abode as if it were a prison. But he, careless, fearless, and armed from head to foot with the apostle's armor, Ephesians 6:13-17 now listens to God by reading the Scriptures, now speaks to

God as he prays to the Lord; and it may be that, while he lingers in the island, he sees some vision such as that once seen by John. Revelation 1:9-10

5. What snares, think you, is the devil now weaving? What stratagems is he preparing? Perchance, mindful of his old trick, he will try to tempt Bonosus with hunger. But he has been answered already: Man shall not live by bread alone. Matthew 4:4 Perchance he will lay before him wealth and fame. But it shall be said to him: They that desire to be rich fall into a trap and temptations, 1 Timothy 6:9 and For me all glorying is in Christ. 1 Corinthians 1:31 He will come, it may be, when the limbs are weary with fasting, and rack them with the pangs of disease; but the cry of the apostle will repel him: When I am weak, then am I strong, and My strength is made perfect in weakness. He will hold out threats of death; but the reply will be: I desire to depart and to be with Christ. Philippians 1:23 He will brandish his fiery darts, but they will be received on the shield of faith. Ephesians 6:16 In a word, Satan will assail him, but Christ will defend. Thanks be to You, Lord Jesus, that in Your day I have one able to pray to You for me. To You all hearts are open, You search the secrets of the heart, You see the prophet shut up in the fish's belly in the midst of the sea. Jonah 2:1-2 You know then how he and I grew up together from tender infancy to vigorous manhood, how we were fostered in the bosoms of the same nurses, and carried in the arms of the same bearers; and how after studying together at Rome we lodged in the same house and shared the same food by the half savage banks of the Rhine. You know, too, that it was I who first began to seek to serve You. Remember, I beseech You, that this warrior of Yours was once a raw recruit with me. I have before me the declaration of Your majesty: Whosoever shall teach and not do shall be called least in the kingdom of heaven. Matthew 5:19 May he enjoy the crown of virtue, and in return for his daily martyrdoms may he follow the Lamb robed in white raiment! Revelation 14:4 For in my Father's house are many mansions, John 14:2 and one star differs from another star in glory. 1 Corinthians 15:41 Give me strength to raise my head to a level with the saints' heels! I willed, but he performed. Therefore, pardon me for failing to keep my resolve, and reward him with the reward of his deserts.

I may perhaps have been tedious, and have said more than the short compass of a letter usually allows; but this, I find, is always the case with me when I have to say anything in praise of our dear Bonosus.

6. However, to return to the point from which I set out, I beseech you do not let me pass wholly out of sight and out of mind. A friend is long sought, hardly found, and with difficulty kept. Let those who will, allow gold to dazzle them and be borne along in splendor, their very baggage glittering with gold and silver. Love is not to be purchased, and affection has no price. The friendship which can cease has never been real. Farewell in Christ.

LETTER IV

To Florentius

Sent to Florentius along with the preceding letter, which Jerome requests him to deliver to Rufinus. This Florentius was a rich Italian who had retired to Jerusalem to pursue the monastic life. Jerome subsequently speaks of him as a distinguished monk so pitiful to the needy that he was generally known as the father of the poor. (Chron. ad A.D. 381.)

1. How much your name and sanctity are on the lips of the most different peoples you may gather from the fact that I commence to love you before I know you. For as, according to the apostle, Some men's sins are evident going before unto judgment, so contrariwise the report of your charity is so widespread that it is considered not so much praiseworthy to love you as criminal to refuse to do so. I pass over the countless instances in which you have supported Christ, Matthew 25:34-40 fed, clothed, and visited Him. The aid you rendered to our brother Heliodorus in his need may well loose the utterance of the dumb. With what gratitude, with what commendation, does he speak of the kindness with which you smoothed a pilgrim's path. I am, it is true, the most sluggish of men, consumed by an unendurable sickness; yet keen affection and desire have winged my feet, and I have come forward to salute and embrace you. I wish you every good thing, and pray that the Lord may establish our nascent friendship.

2. Our brother, Rufinus, is said to have come from Egypt to Jerusalem with the de vout lady, Melanium. He is inseparably bound to me in brotherly love; and I beg you to oblige me by delivering to him the annexed letter. You must not, however, judge of me by the virtues that you find in him. For in him you will see the clearest tokens of holiness, while I am but dust and vile dirt, and even now, while still living, nothing but ashes. It is enough for me if my weak eyes can bear the brightness of his excellence. He has but now washed himself and is clean, yea, is made white as snow; while I, stained with every sin, wait day and night with trembling to pay the uttermost farthing. Matthew 5:26 But since the Lord looses the prisoners, and rests upon him who is of a contrite spirit, and that trembles at His words, Isaiah 66:2 perchance he may say even to me who lie in the grave of sin: Jerome, come forth. John 11:43

The reverend presbyter, Evagrius, warmly salutes you. We both with united respect salute the brother, Martinianus. I desire much to see him, but I am impeded by the chain of sickness. Farewell in Christ.

LETTER V

To Florentius

Written a few months after the preceding (about the end of 374 A.D.) from the Syrian Desert. After dilating on his friendship for Florentius, and making a passing allusion to Rufinus, Jerome mentions certain books, copies of which he desires to be sent to him. He also speaks of a runaway slave about whom Florentius had written to him.

1. Your letter, dear friend, finds me dwelling in that quarter of the desert which is nearest to Syria and the Saracens. And the reading of it rekindles in my mind so keen a desire to set out for Jerusalem that I am almost ready to violate my monastic vow in order to gratify my affection. Wishing to do the best I can, as I cannot come in person I send you a letter instead; and thus, though absent in the body, I come to you in love and in spirit. Colossians 2:5 For my earnest prayer is that our infant friendship, firmly cemented as it is in Christ, may never be rent asunder by time or distance. We ought rather to strengthen the bond by an interchange of letters. Let these pass between us, meet each other on the way, and converse with us. Affection will not lose much if it keeps up an intercourse of this kind.

2. You write that our brother, Rufinus, has not yet come to you. Even if he does come it will do little to satisfy my longing, for I shall not now be able to see him. He is too far away to come hither, and the conditions of the lonely life that I have adopted forbid me to go to him. For I am no longer free to follow my own wishes. I entreat you, therefore, to ask him to allow you to have the commentaries of the reverend Rhetitius, bishop of Augustodunum, copied, in which he has so eloquently explained the Song of Songs. A countryman of the aforesaid brother Rufinus, the old man Paul, writes that Rufinus has his copy of Tertullian, and urgently requests that this may be returned. Next I have to ask you to get written on paper by a copyist certain books which the subjoined list will show you that I do not possess. I beg also that you will send me the explanation of the Psalms of David, and the copious work on Synods of the reverend Hilary, which I copied for him at Trêves with my own hand. Such books, you know, must be the food of the Christian soul if it is to meditate in the law of the Lord day and night.

Others you welcome beneath your roof, you cherish and comfort, you help out of your own purse; but so far as I am concerned, you have given me everything when once you have granted my request. And since, through the Lord's bounty, I am rich in volumes of the sacred library, you may command me in turn. I will send you what you please; and do not suppose that an order from you will give me trouble. I have pupils devoted to the art of copying. Nor do I merely promise a favor because I am asking one. Our brother, Heliodorus, tells me that there are many parts of the

Scriptures which you seek and cannot find. But even if you have them all, affection is sure to assert its rights and to seek for itself more than it already has.

3. As regards the present master of your slave— of whom you have done me the honor to write— I have no doubt but that he is his kidnapper. While I was still at Antioch the presbyter, Evagrius, often reproved him in my presence. To whom he made this answer: I have nothing to fear. He declares that his master has dismissed him. If you both wanthim,

he is here; send him whither you will. I think I am not wrong in refusing to allow a runaway to stray farther. Here in the wilderness I cannot myself execute your orders; and therefore I have asked my dear friend Evagrius to push the affair vigorously, both for your sake and for mine. I desire your welfare in Christ.

LETTER VI

To Julian, a Deacon of Antioch

This letter, written in 374 A.D., is chiefly interesting for its mention of Jerome's sister. It would seem that she had fallen into sin and had been restored to a life of virtue by the deacon, Julian. Jerome speaks of her again in the next letter (§4).

It is an old saying, Liars are disbelieved even when they speak the truth. And from the way in which you reproach me for not having written, I perceive that this has been my lot with you. Shall I say, I wrote often, but the bearers of my letters were negligent? You will reply, Your excuse is the old one of all who fail to write. Shall I say, I could not find any one to take my letters? You will say that numbers of persons have gone from my part of the world to yours. Shall I contend that I have actually given them letters? They not having delivered them, will deny that they have received them. Moreover, so great a distance separates us that it will be hard to come at the truth. What shall I do then? Though really not to blame, I ask your forgiveness, for I think it better to fall back and make overtures for peace than to keep my ground and offer battle. The truth is that constant sickness of body and vexation of mind have so weakened me that with death so close at hand I have not been as collected as usual. And lest you should account this plea a false one, now that I have stated my case, I shall, like a pleader, call witnesses to prove it. Our reverend brother, Heliodorus, has been here; but in spite of his wish to dwell in the desert with me, he has been frightened away by my crimes. But my present wordiness will atone for my past remissness; for, as Horace says in his satire:

All singers have one fault among their friends:
They never sing when asked, unasked they never cease.

Henceforth I shall overwhelm you with such bundles of letters that you will take the opposite line and beg me not to write.

I rejoice that my sister — to you a daughter in Christ— remains steadfast in her purpose, a piece of news which I owe in the first instance to you. For here where I now am I am ignorant not only as to what goes on in my native land, but even as to its continued existence. Even though the Iberian viper shall rend me with his baneful fangs, I will not fear men's judgment, seeing that I shall have God to judge me. As one puts it:

Shatter the world to fragments if you will:
'Twill fall upon a head which knows not fear.

Bear in mind, then, I pray you, the apostle's precept 1 Corinthians 3:14 that we should make our work abiding; prepare for yourself a reward from the Lord in my sister's salvation; and by frequent letters increase my joy in that glory in Christ which we share together.

LETTER VII

To Chromatius, Jovinus, and Eusebius.

This letter (written like the preceding in 374 A.D.) is addressed by Jerome to three of his former companions in the religious life. It commends Bonosus (§3), asks guidance for the writer's sister (§4), and attacks the conduct of Lupicinus, Bishop of Stridon (§5).

1. Those whom mutual affection has joined together, a written page ought not to sunder. I must not, therefore, distribute my words some to one and some to another. For so strong is the love that binds you together that affection unites all three of you in a bond no less close than that which naturally connects two of your number. Indeed, if the conditions of writing would only admit of it, I should amalgamate your names and express them under a single symbol. The very letter which I have received from you challenges me in each of you to see all three, and in all three to recognize each. When the reverend Evagrius transmitted it to me in the corner of the desert which stretches between the Syrians and the Saracens, my joy was intense. It wholly surpassed the rejoicings felt at Rome when the defeat of Cannæ; was retrieved, and Marcellus at Nola cut to pieces the forces of Hannibal. Evagrius frequently comes to see me, and cherishes me in Christ as his own bowels. Yet as he is separated from me by a long distance, his departure has gener ally left me as much regret as his arrival has brought me joy.

2. I converse with your letter, I embrace it, it talks to me; it alone of those here speaks Latin. For hereabout you must either learn a barbarous jargon or else hold your tongue. As often as the lines— traced in a well-known hand— bring back to me the faces which I hold so dear, either I am no longer here, or else you are here with me. If you will credit the sincerity of affection, I seem to see you all as I write this.

Now at the outset I should like to ask you one petulant question. Why is it that, when we are separated by so great an interval of land and sea, you have sent me so short a letter? Is it that I have deserved no better treatment, not having first written to you? I cannot believe that paper can have failed you while Egypt continues to supply its wares. Even if a Ptolemy had closed the seas, King Attalus would still have sent you parchments from Pergamum, and so by his skins you could have made up for the want of paper. The very name parchment is derived from a historical incident of the kind which occurred generations ago. What then? Am I to suppose the messenger to have been in haste? No matter how long a letter may be, it can be written in the course of a night. Or had you some business to attend to which prevented you from writing? No claim is prior to that of affection. Two suppositions remain, either that you felt disinclined to write or else that I did not deserve a letter. Of the two I prefer to charge you with sloth than to condemn myself as undeserving. For it is easier to mend neglect than to quicken love.

3. You tell me that Bonosus, like a true son of the Fish, has taken to the water. As for me who am still foul with my old stains, like the basilisk and the scorpion I haunt the dry places. Deuteronomy 8:15 Bonosus has his heel already on the serpent's head, while I am still as food to the same serpent which by divine appointment devours the earth. Genesis 3:14 He can scale already that ladder of which the psalms of degrees are a type; while I, still weeping on its first step, hardly know whether I shall ever be able to say: I will lift up my eyes unto the hills, from whence comes my help. Amid the threatening billows of the world he is sitting in the safe shelter of his island, that is, of the church's pale, and it may be that even now, like John, he is being called to eat God's book; Revelation 10:9-10 while I, still lying in the sepulchre of my sins and bound with the chains of my iniquities, wait for the Lord's command in the Gospel: Jerome, come forth. John 11:43 But Bonosus has done more than this. Like the prophet Jeremiah 13:4-5 he has carried his girdle across the Euphrates (for all the devil's strength is in the loins), and has hidden it there in a hole of the rock. Then, afterwards finding it rent, he has sung: O Lord, you have possessed my reins. You have broken my bonds in sunder. I will offer to you the sacrifice of thanksgiving. But as for me, Nebuchadnezzar has brought me in chains to Babylon, to the babel that is of a distracted mind. There he has laid upon me the yoke of captivity; there inserting in my nostrils a ring of iron, 2 Kings 19:28 he has commanded me to sing one of the songs of Zion. To whom I have said, The Lord looses the prisoners; the Lord opens the eyes of the blind. To complete my contrast in a single sentence, while I pray for mercy Bonosus looks for a crown.

4. My sister's conversion is the fruit of the efforts of the saintly Julian. He has planted, it is for you to water, and the Lord will give the increase. 1 Corinthians 3:6 Jesus Christ has given her to me to console me for the wound which the devil has inflicted on her. He has restored her from death to life. But in the words of the pagan poet, for her

There is no safety that I do not fear.

You know yourselves how slippery is the path of youth— a path on which I have myself fallen, and which you are now traversing not without fear. She, as she enters upon it, must have the advice and the encouragement of all, she must be aided by frequent letters from you, my reverend brothers. And— for charity endures all things, 1 Corinthians 13:7 — I beg you to get from Pope Valerian a letter to confirm her resolution. A girl's courage, as you know, is strengthened when she realizes that persons in high place are interested in her.

5. The fact is that my native land is a prey to barbarism, that in it men's only God is their belly, that they live only for the present, and that the richer a man is the holier he is held to be. Moreover, to use a well-worn proverb, the dish has a cover worthy of it; for Lupicinus is their priest. Like lips like lettuce, as the saying goes— the only one, as Lucilius tells us, at which Crassus ever laughed— the reference being to a donkey eating thistles. What I mean is that an unstable pilot steers a leaking ship, and that the blind is leading the blind straight to the pit. The ruler is like the ruled.

6. I salute your mother and mine with the respect which, as you know, I feel towards her. Associated with you as she is in a holy life, she has the start of you, her holy children, in that she is your mother. Her womb may thus be truly called golden. With her I salute your sisters, who ought all to be welcomed wherever they go, for they have triumphed over their sex and the world, and await the Bridegroom's coming, Matthew 25:4 their lamps replenished with oil. O happy the house which is a home of a widowed Anna, of virgins that are prophetesses, and of twin Samuels bred in the Temple! Fortunate the roof which shelters the martyr-mother of the Maccabees, with her sons around her, each and all wearing the martyr's crown! 2 Maccabbees vii For although you confess Christ every day by keeping His commandments, yet to this private glory you have added the public one of an open confession; for it was through you that the poison of the Arian heresy was formerly banished from your city.

You are surprised perhaps at my thus making a fresh beginning quite at the close of my letter. But what am I to do? I cannot refuse expression to my feelings. The brief limits of a letter compel me to be silent; my affection for you urges me to speak. I write in haste, my language is confused and ill-arranged; but love knows nothing of order.

LETTER VIII

To Niceas, Sub-Deacon of Aquileia

Niceas, the sub-deacon, had accompanied Jerome to the East but had now returned home. In after-years he became bishop of Aquileia in succession to Chromatius. The date of the letter is 374 A.D.

The comic poet Turpilius says of the exchange of letters that it alone makes the absent present. The remark, though occurring in a work of fiction, is not untrue. For what more real presence— if I may so speak— can there be between absent friends than speaking to those whom they love in letters, and in letters hearing their reply? Even those Italian savages, the Cascans of Ennius, who— as Cicero tells us in his books on rhetoric— hunted their food like beasts of prey, were wont, before paper and parchment came into use, to exchange letters written on tablets of wood roughly planed, or on strips of bark torn from the trees. For this reason men called letter-carriers tablet-bearers, and letter-writers bark-users, because they used the bark of trees. How much more then are we, who live in a civilized age, bound not to omit a social duty performed by men who lived in a state of gross savagery, and were in some respects entirely ignorant of the refinements of life. The saintly Chromatius, look you, and the reverend Eusebius, brothers as much by compatibility of disposition as by the ties of nature, have challenged me to diligence by the letters which they have showered upon me. You, however, who have but just left me, have not merely unknit our new-made friendship; you have torn it asunder— a process which Lælius, in Cicero's treatise, wisely forbids. Can it be that the East is so hateful to you that you dread the thought of even your letters coming hither? Wake up, wake up, arouse yourself from sleep, give to affection at least one sheet of paper. Amid the pleasures of life at home sometimes heave a sigh over the journeys which we have made together. If you love me, write in answer to my prayer. If you are angry with me, though angry still write. I find my longing soul much comforted when I receive a letter from a friend, even though that friend be out of temper with me.

LETTER IX

To Chrysogonus, a Monk of Aquileia

A bantering letter to an indifferent correspondent. Of the same date as the preceding.

Heliodorus, who is so dear to us both, and who loves you with an affection no less deep than my own, may have given you a faithful account of my feelings towards you; how your name is always on my lips, and how in every conversation which I have with him I begin by recalling my pleasant intercourse with you, and go on to marvel at your lowliness, to extol your virtue, and to proclaim your holy love.

Lynxes, they say, when they look behind them, forget what they have just seen, and lose all thought of what their eyes have ceased to behold. And so it seems to be with you. For so entirely have you forgotten our joint attachment that you have not merely blurred but erased the writing of that epistle which, as the apostle tells us, 2 Corinthians 3:2 is written in the hearts of Christians. The creatures that I have mentioned lurk on branches of leafy trees and pounce on fleet roes or frightened stags. In vain their victims fly, for they carry their tormentors with them, and these rend their flesh as they run. Lynxes, however, only hunt when an empty belly makes their mouths dry. When they have satisfied their thirst for blood, and have filled their stomachs with food, satiety induces forgetfulness, and they bestow no thought on future prey till hunger recalls them to a sense of their need.

Now in your case it cannot be that you have already had enough of me. Why then do you bring to a premature close a friendship which is but just begun? Why do you let slip what you have hardly as yet fully grasped? But as such remissness as yours is never at a loss for an excuse, you will perhaps declare that you had nothing to write. Had this been so, you should still have written to inform me of the fact.

LETTER X

To Paul, an Old Man of Concordia

Jerome writes to Paul of Concordia, a centenarian (§2), and the owner of a good theological library (§3), to lend him some commentaries. In return he sends him his life (newly written) of Paul the hermit. The date of the letter is 374 A.D.

1. The shortness of man's life is the punishment for man's sin; and the fact that even on the very threshold of the light death constantly overtakes the new-born child proves that the times are continually sinking into deeper depravity. For when the first tiller of paradise had been entangled by the serpent in his snaky coils, and had been forced in consequence to migrate earthwards, although his deathless state was changed for a mortal one, yet the sentence of man's curse was put off for nine hundred years, or even more, a period so long that it may be called a second immortality. Afterwards sin gradually grew more and more virulent, till the ungodliness of the giants Genesis 6:4 brought in its train the shipwreck of the whole world. Then when the world had been cleansed by the baptism— if I may so call it— of the deluge, human life was contracted to a short span. Yet even this we have almost altogether wasted, so continually do our iniquities fight against the divine purposes. For how few there are, either who go beyond their hundredth year, or who, going beyond it, do not regret that they have done so; according to that which the Scripture witnesses in the book of Psalms: the days of our years are threescore years and ten; and if by reason of strength they be fourscore years, yet is their strength labor and sorrow.

2. Why, say you, these opening reflections so remote and so far fetched that one might use against them the Horatian witticism:

Back to the eggs which Leda laid for Zeus,
The bard is fain to trace the war of Troy?

Simply that I may describe in fitting terms your great age and hoary head as white as Christ's. Revelation 1:14 For see, the hundredth circling year is already passing over you, and yet, always keeping the commandments of the Lord, amid the circumstances of your present life you think over the blessedness of that which is to come. Your eyes are bright and keen, your steps steady, your hearing good, your teeth are white, your voice musical, your flesh firm and full of sap; your ruddy cheeks belie your white hairs, your strength is not that of your age. Advancing years have not, as we too often see them do, impaired the tenacity of your memory; the coldness of your blood has not blunted an intellect at once warm and wary. Your face is not wrinkled nor your brow furrowed. Lastly, no tremors palsy your hand or cause it to travel in crooked pathways over the wax on which you write. The Lord shows us in you the bloom of the resurrection that is to be ours; so that whereas in others who die by inches while yet living, we recognize the results of sin, in your case we ascribe it to righteousness that you still simulate youth at an age to which it is foreign. And although we see the like haleness of body in many even of those who are sinners, in their case it is a grant of the devil to lead them into sin, while in yours it is a gift of God to make you rejoice.

3. Tully in his brilliant speech on behalf of Flaccus describes the learning of the Greeks as innate frivolity and accomplished vanity.

Certainly their ablest literary men used to receive money for pronouncing eulogies upon their kings or princes. Following their example, I set a price upon my praise. Nor must you suppose my demand a small one. You are asked to give me the pearl of the Gospel, Matthew 13:46 the words of the Lord, pure words, even as the silver which from the earth is tried, and purified seven times in the fire, I mean the commentaries of Fortunatian and— for its account of the persecutors— the History of Aurelius Victor, and with these the Letters of Novatian; so that, learning the poison set forth by this schismatic, we may the more gladly drink of the antidote supplied by the holy martyr Cyprian. In the mean time I have sent to you, that is to say, to Paul the aged, a Paul that is older still. I have taken great pains to bring my language down to the level of the simpler sort. But, somehow or other, though you fill it with water,

the jar retains the odor which it acquired when first used. If my little gift should please you, I have others also in store which (if the Holy Spirit shall breathe favorably), shall sail across the sea to you with all kinds of eastern merchandise.

LETTER XI

To the Virgins of Æmona

Æmona was a Roman colony not far from Stridon, Jerome's birthplace. The virgins to whom the note is addressed had omitted to answer his letters, and he now writes to upbraid them for their remissness. The date of the letter is 374 A.D.

This scanty sheet of paper shows in what a wilderness I live, and because of it I have to say much in few words. For, desirous though I am to speak to you more fully, this miserable scrap compels me to leave much unsaid. Still ingenuity makes up for lack of means, and by writing small I can say a great deal. Observe, I beseech you, how I love you, even in the midst of my difficulties, since even the want of materials does not stop me from writing to you.

Pardon, I beseech you, an aggrieved man: if I speak in tears and in anger it is because I have been injured. For in return for my regular letters you have not sent me a single syllable. Light, I know, has no communion with darkness, 2 Corinthians 6:14 and God's handmaidens no fellowship with a sinner, yet a harlot was allowed to wash the Lord's feet with her tears, and dogs are permitted to eat of their masters' crumbs. Matthew 15:27 It was the Saviour's mission to call sinners and not the righteous; for, as He said Himself, they that be whole need not a physician. Matthew 9:12-13 He wills the repentance of a sinner rather than his death, Ezekiel 33:11 and carries home the poor stray sheep on His own shoulders. Luke 15:5 So, too, when the prodigal son returns, his father receives him with joy. Luke 15:20 Nay more, the apostle says: Judge nothing before the time. 1 Corinthians 4:5 For who are you that judgest another man's servant? To his own master he stands or falls. Romans 14:4 And let him that stands take heed lest he fall. 1 Corinthians 10:12 Bear ye one another's burdens. Galatians 6:2

Dear sisters, man's envy judges in one way, Christ in another; and the whisper of a corner is not the same as the sentence of His tribunal. Many ways seem right to men which are afterwards found to be wrong. Proverbs 14:12 And a treasure is often stowed in earthen vessels. 2 Corinthians 4:7 Peter thrice denied his Lord, yet his bitter tears restored him to his place. To whom much is forgiven, the same loves much. Luke 7:47 No word is said of the flock as a whole, yet the angels joy in heaven over the safety of one sick ewe. Luke 15:7, 10 And if any one demurs to this reasoning, the Lord Himself has said: Friend, is your eye evil because I am good? Matthew 20:15

LETTER XII

To Antony, Monk

The subject of this letter is similar to that of the preceding. Of Antony nothing is known except that some manuscripts describe him as of Æmona. The date of the letter is 374 A.D.

While the disciples were disputing concerning precedence our Lord, the teacher of humility, took a little child and said: Unless you are converted and become as little children ye cannot enter the kingdom of heaven. Matthew 18:3 And lest He should seem to preach more than he practised, He fulfilled His own precept in His life. For He washed His disciples' feet, John 13:5 he received the traitor with a kiss, Luke 22:47 He conversed with the woman of Samaria, John 4:7 He spoke of the kingdom of heaven with Mary at His feet, and when He rose again from the dead He showed Himself first to some poor women. Pride is opposed to humility, and through it Satan lost his eminence as an archangel. The Jewish people perished in their pride, for while they claimed the chief seats and salutations in the market place, Matthew 23:6-7 they were superseded by the Gentiles, who had before been counted as a drop of a bucket. Isaiah 40:15 Two poor fishermen, Peter and James, were sent to confute the sophists and the wise men of the world. As the Scripture says: God resists the proud and gives grace to the humble. 1 Peter 5:5 Think, brother, what a sin it must be which has God for its opponent. In the Gospel the Pharisee is rejected because of his pride, and the publican is accepted because of his humility.

Now, unless I am mistaken, I have already sent you ten letters, affectionate and earnest, while you have not deigned to give me even a single line. The Lord speaks to His servants, but you, my brother servant, refuse to speak to me. Believe me, if reserve did not check my pen, I could show my annoyance in such invective that you would have to reply— even though it might be in anger. But since anger is human, and a Christian must not act injuriously, I fall back once more on entreaty, and beg you to love one who loves you, and to write to him as a servant should to his fellow-servant. Farewell in the Lord.

LETTER XIII

To Castorina, His Maternal Aunt

An interesting letter, as throwing some light on Jerome's family relations. Castorina, his maternal aunt, had, for some reason, become estranged from him, and he now writes to her to effect a reconciliation. Whether he succeeded in doing so, we do not know. The date of the letter is 374 A.D.

The apostle and evangelist John rightly says, in his first epistle, that whosoever hates his brother is a murderer. 1 John 3:15 For, since murder often springs from hate, the hater, even though he has not yet slain his victim, is at heart a murderer. Why, you ask, do I begin in this style? Simply that you and I may both lay aside past ill feeling and cleanse our hearts to be a habitation for God. Be angry, David says, and sin not, or, as the apostle more fully expresses it, let not the sun go down upon your wrath. What then shall *we* do in the day of judgment, upon whose wrath the sun has gone down not one day but many years? The Lord says in the Gospel: If you bring your gift to the altar, and there rememberest that your brother has anything against you; leave there your gift before the altar, and go your way; first be reconciled to your brother, and then come and offer your gift. Matthew 5:23-24 Woe to me, wretch that I am; woe, I had almost said, to you also. This long time past we have either offered no gift at the altar or have offered it while cherishing anger without a cause. How have we been able in our daily prayers to say Forgive us our debts as we forgive our debtors, Matthew 6:12 while our feelings have been at variance with our words, and our petition inconsistent with our conduct? Therefore I renew the prayer which I made a year ago in a previous letter, that the Lord's legacy of peace John 14:27 may be indeed ours, and that my desires and your feelings may find favor in His sight. Soon we shall stand before His judgment seat to receive the reward of harmony restored or to pay the penalty for harmony broken. In case you shall prove unwilling— I hope that it may not be so— to accept my advances, I for my part shall be free. For this letter, when it is read, will insure my acquittal.

LETTER XIV

To Heliodorus, Monk

Heliodorus, originally a soldier, but now a presbyter of the Church, had accompanied Jerome to the East, but, not feeling called to the solitary life of the desert, had returned to Aquileia. Here he resumed his clerical duties, and in course of time was raised to the episcopate as bishop of Altinum.

The letter was written in the first bitterness of separation and reproaches Heliodorus for having gone back from the perfect way of the ascetic life. The description given of this is highly colored and seems to have produced a great impression in the West. Fabiola was so much enchanted by it that she learned the letter by heart. The date is 373 or 374 A.D.

1. So conscious are you of the affection which exists between us that you cannot but recognize the love and passion with which I strove to prolong our common sojourn in the desert. This very letter— blotted, as you see, with tears— gives evidence of the lamentation and weeping with which I accompanied your departure. With the pretty ways of a child you then softened your refusal by soothing words, and I, being off my guard, knew not what to do. Was I to hold my peace? I could not conceal my eagerness by a show of indifference. Or was I to entreat you yet more earnestly? You would have refused to listen, for your love was not like mine. Despised affection has taken the one course open to it. Unable to keep you when present, it goes in search of you when absent. You asked me yourself, when you were going away, to invite you to the desert when I took up my quarters there, and I for my part promised to do so. Accordingly I invite you now; come, and come quickly. Do not call to mind old ties; the desert is for those who have left all. Nor let the hardships of our former travels deter you. You believe in Christ, believe also in His words: Seek ye first the kingdom of God and all these things shall be added unto you. Matthew 6:33 Take neither scrip nor staff. He is rich enough who is poor— with Christ.

2. But what is this, and why do I foolishly importune you again? Away with entreaties, an end to coaxing words. Offended love does well to be angry. You have spurned my petition; perhaps you will listen to my remonstrance. What keeps you, effeminate soldier, in your father's house? Where are your ramparts and trenches? When have you spent a winter in the field? Lo, the trumpet sounds from heaven! Lo, the Leader comes with clouds! Revelation 1:7 He is armed to subdue the world, and out of His mouth proceeds a two-edged sword Revelation 1:16 to mow down all that encounters it. But as for you, what will you do? Pass straight from your chamber to the battlefield, and from the cool shade into the burning sun? Nay, a body used to a tunic cannot endure a buckler; a head that has worn a cap refuses a helmet; a hand made tender by disuse is galled by a sword-hilt. Hear the proclamation of your King: He that is not with me is against me, and he that gathers not with me scatters. Matthew 12:30 Remember the day on which you enlisted, when, buried with Christ in baptism, you swore fealty to Him, declaring that for His sake you would spare neither father nor mother. Lo, the enemy is

striving to slay Christ in your breast. Lo, the ranks of the foe sigh over that bounty which you received when you entered His service. Should your little nephew hang on your neck, pay no regard to him; should your mother with ashes on her hair and garments rent show you the breasts at which she nursed you, heed her not; should your father prostrate himself on the threshold, trample him under foot and go your way. With dry eyes fly to the standard of the cross. In such cases cruelty is the only true affection.

3. Hereafter there shall come— yes, there shall come— a day when you will return a victor to your true country, and will walk through the heavenly Jerusalem crowned with the crown of valor. Then will you receive the citizenship thereof with Paul. Then will you seek the like privilege for your parents. Then will you intercede for me who have urged you forward on the path of victory.

I am not ignorant of the fetters which you may plead as hindrances. My breast is not of iron nor my heart of stone. I was not born of flint or suckled by a tigress. I have passed through troubles like yours myself. Now it is a widowed sister who throws her caressing arms around you. Now it is the slaves, your foster-brothers, who cry, To what master are you leaving us? Now it is a nurse bowed with age, and a body-servant loved only less than a father, who exclaim: Only wait till we die and follow us to our graves. Perhaps, too, an aged mother, with sunken bosom and furrowed brow, recalling the lullaby with which she once soothed you, adds her entreaties to theirs. The learned may call you, if they please,

The sole support and pillar of your house.

The love of God and the fear of hell will easily break such bonds.

Scripture, you will argue, bids us obey our parents. Ephesians 6:1 Yes, but whoso loves them more than Christ loses his own soul. Matthew 10:37 The enemy takes sword in hand to slay me, and shall I think of a mother's tears? Or shall I desert the service of Christ for the sake of a father to whom, if I am Christ's servant, I owe no rites of burial, Luke 9:59-60 albeit if I am Christ's true servant I owe these to all? Peter with his cowardly advice was an offense to the Lord on the eve of His passion; Matthew 16:23 and to the brethren who strove to restrain him from going up to Jerusalem, Paul's one answer was: What mean ye to weep and to break my heart? For I am ready not to be bound only, but also to die at Jerusalem for the name of the Lord Jesus. Acts 21:13 The battering-ram of natural affection which so often shatters faith must recoil powerless from the wall of the Gospel. My mother and my brethren are these whosoever do the will of my Father which is in heaven. If they believe in Christ let them bid me God-speed, for I go to fight in His name. And if they do not believe, let the dead bury their dead. Matthew 8:22

4. But all this, you argue, only touches the case of martyrs. Ah! My brother, you are mistaken, you are mistaken, if you suppose that there is ever a time when the Christian does not suffer persecution. Then are you most hardly beset when you know not that you are beset at all. Our adversary as a roaring lion walks about seeking whom he may devour, 1 Peter 5:8 and do you think of peace? He sits in the lurking-places of the villages: in the secret places does he murder the innocent;

his eyes are privily set against the poor. He lies in wait secretly as a lion in his den; he lies in wait to catch the poor; and do you slumber under a shady tree, so as to fall an easy prey? On one side self-indulgence presses me hard; on another covetousness strives to make an inroad; my belly wishes to be a God to me, in place of Christ, and lust would fain drive away the Holy Spirit that dwells in me and defile His temple. 1 Corinthians 3:17 I am pursued, I say, by an enemy

Whose name is Legion and his wiles untold;
and, hapless wretch that I am, how shall I hold myself a victor when I am being led away a captive?

5. My dear brother, weigh well the various forms of transgression, and think not that the sins which I have mentioned are less flagrant than that of idolatry. Nay, hear the apostle's view of the matter. For this ye know, he writes, that no whore-monger or unclean person, nor covetous man, who is an idolater, has any inheritance in the kingdom of Christ and of God. Ephesians 5:5 In a general way all that is of the devil savors of enmity to God, and what is of the devil is idolatry, since all idols are subject to him. Yet Paul elsewhere lays down the law in express and unmistakable terms, saying: Mortify your members, which are upon the earth, laying aside fornication, uncleanness, evil concupiscence and covetousness, which are idolatry, for which things' sake the wrath of God comes. Colossians 3:5-6

Idolatry is not confined to casting incense upon an altar with finger and thumb, or to pouring libations of wine out of a cup into a bowl. Covetousness is idolatry, or else the selling of the Lord for thirty pieces of silver was a righteous act. Matthew 26:15 Lust involves profanation, or else men may defile with common harlots those members of Christ which should be a living sacrifice acceptable to God. Romans 12:1 Fraud is idolatry, or else they are worthy of imitation who, in the Acts of the Apostles, sold their inheritance, and because they kept back part of the price, perished by an instant doom. Consider well, my brother; nothing is yours to keep. Whosoever he be of you, the Lord says, that forsakes not all that he has, he cannot be my disciple. Luke 14:33 Why are you such a half-hearted Christian?

6. See how Peter left his net; Matthew 4:18-20 see how the publican rose from the receipt of custom. Matthew 9:9 In a moment he became an apostle. The Son of man has not where to lay his head, Matthew 8:20 and do you plan wide porticos and spacious halls? If you look to inherit the good things of the world you can no longer be a joint-heir with Christ. Romans 8:17 You are called a monk, and has the name no meaning? What brings you, a solitary, into the throng of men? The advice that I give is that of no inexperienced mariner who has never lost either ship or cargo, and has never known a gale. Lately shipwrecked as I have been myself, my warnings to other voyagers spring from my own fears. On one side, like Charybdis, self-indulgence sucks into its vortex the soul's salvation. On the other, like Scylla, lust, with a smile on her girl's face, lures it on to wreck its chastity. The coast is savage, and the devil with a crew of pirates carries irons to fetter his captives. Be not credulous, be not over-confident. The sea may be as smooth and smiling as a pond, its quiet surface may be scarcely ruffled by a breath of air, yet sometimes its waves are as high as mountains. There is danger in its depths, the foe is lurking there. Ease your sheets, spread your sails, fasten the cross as an

ensign on your prow. The calm that you speak of is itself a tempest. Why so? you will perhaps argue; are not all my fellow-townsmen Christians? Your case, I reply, is not that of others. Listen to the words of the Lord: If you will be perfect go and sell that you have, and give to the poor, and come and follow me. Matthew 19:21 You have already promised to be perfect. For when you forsook the army and made yourself an eunuch for the kingdom of heaven's sake, Matthew 19:12 you did so that you might follow the perfect life. Now the perfect servant of Christ has nothing beside Christ. Or if he have anything beside Christ he is not perfect. And if he be not perfect when he has promised God to be so, his profession is a lie. But the mouth that lies slays the soul. Wisdom 1:11 To conclude, then, if you are perfect you will not set your heart on your father's goods; and if you are not perfect you have deceived the Lord. The Gospel thunders forth its divine warning: You cannot serve two masters, Luke 16:13 and does any one dare to make Christ a liar by serving at once both God and Mammon? Repeatedly does He proclaim, If any one will come after me let him deny himself and take up his cross and follow me. Luke 9:23 If I load myself with gold can I think that I am following Christ? Surely not. He that says he abides in Him ought himself also so to walk even as He walked. 1 John 2:6

7. I know you will rejoin that you possess nothing. Why, then, if you are so well prepared for battle, do you not take the field? Perhaps you think that *you* can wage war in your own country, although the Lord could do no signs in His? Matthew 13:58 Why not? You ask. Take the answer which comes to you with his authority: No prophet is accepted in his own country. Luke 4:24 But, you will say, I do not seek honor; the approval of my conscience is enough for me. Neither did the Lord seek it; for when the multitudes would have made Him a king he fled from them. John 6:15 But where there is no honor there is contempt; and where there is contempt there is frequent rudeness; and where there is rudeness there is vexation; and where there is vexation there is no rest; and where there is no rest the mind is apt to be diverted from its purpose. Again, where, through restlessness, earnestness loses any of its force, it is lessened by what it loses, and that which is lessened cannot be called perfect. The upshot of all which is that a monk cannot be perfect in his own country. Now, not to aim at perfection is itself a sin.

8. Driven from this line of defence you will appeal to the example of the clergy. These, you will say, remain in their cities, and yet they are surely above criticism. Far be it from me to censure the successors of the apostles, who with holy words consecrate the body of Christ, and who make us Christians. Having the keys of the kingdom of heaven, they judge men to some extent before the day of judgment, and guard the chastity of the bride of Christ. But, as I have before hinted, the case of monks is different from that of the clergy. The clergy feed Christ's sheep; I as a monk am fed by them. They live of the altar: 1 Corinthians 9:13-14 I, if I bring no gift to it, have the axe laid to my root as to that of a barren tree. Matthew 3:10 Nor can I plead poverty as an excuse, for the Lord in the gospel has praised an aged widow for casting into the treasury the last two coins that she had. Luke 21:1-4 I may not sit in the presence of a presbyter; he, if I sin, may deliver me to Satan, for the destruction of the flesh that the spirit may be saved. 1 Corinthians 5:5 Under the old law he who disobeyed the priests was put outside the camp and stoned by

the people, or else he was beheaded and expiated his contempt with his blood. Deuteronomy 17:5, 12 But now the disobedient person is cut down with the spiritual sword, or he is expelled from the church and torn to pieces by ravening demons. Should the entreaties of your brethren induce you to take orders, I shall rejoice that you are lifted up, and fear lest you may be cast down. You will say: If a man desire the office of a bishop, he desires a good work. 1 Timothy 3:1 I know that; but you should add what follows: such an one must be blameless, the husband of one wife, vigilant, sober, chaste, of good behavior, given to hospitality, apt to teach, not given to wine, no striker but patient. 1 Timothy 3:2-3 After fully explaining the qualifications of a bishop the apostle speaks of ministers of the third degree with equal care. Likewise must the deacons be grave, he writes, not double-tongued, not given to much wine, not greedy of filthy lucre, holding the mystery of the faith in a pure conscience. And let these also first be proved; then, let them minister, being found blameless. 1 Timothy 3:8-10 Woe to the man who goes in to the supper without a wedding garment. Nothing remains for him but the stern question, Friend, how did you come in hither? And when he is speechless the order will be given, Bind him hand and foot, and take him away, and cast him into outer darkness; there shall be weeping and gnashing of teeth. Matthew 22:11-13 Woe to him who, when he has received a talent, has bound it in a napkin; and, while others make profits, only preserves what he has received. His angry lord shall rebuke him in a moment. Thou wicked servant, he will say, wherefore gavest thou not my money into the bank that at my coming I might have required my own with usury? Luke 19:23 That is to say, you should have laid before the altar what you were not able to bear. For while you, a slothful trader, keep a penny in your hands, you occupy the place of another who might double the money. Wherefore, as he who ministers well purchases to himself a good degree, 1 Timothy 3:13 so he who approaches the cup of the Lord unworthily shall be guilty of the body and blood of the Lord. 1 Corinthians 11:27

9. Not all bishops are bishops indeed. You consider Peter; mark Judas as well. You notice Stephen; look also on Nicolas, sentenced in the Apocalypse by the Lord's own lips, Revelation 2:6 whose shameful imaginations gave rise to the heresy of the Nicolaitans. Let a man examine himself and so let him come. 1 Corinthians 11:28 For it is not ecclesiastical rank that makes a man a Christian. The centurion Cornelius was still a heathen when he was cleansed by the gift of the Holy Spirit. Daniel was but a child when he judged the elders. Amos was stripping mulberry bushes when, in a moment, he was made a prophet. Amos 7:14 David was only a shepherd when he was chosen to be king. And the least of His disciples was the one whom Jesus loved the most. My brother, sit down in the lower room, that when one less honorable comes you may be bidden to go up higher. Luke 14:10 Upon whom does the Lord rest but upon him that is lowly and of a contrite spirit, and that trembles at His word? Isaiah 66:2 To whom God has committed much, of him He will ask the more. Luke 12:48 Mighty men shall be mightily tormented. Wisdom 6:6 No man need pride himself in the day of judgment on merely physical chastity, for then shall men give account for every idle word, Matthew 12:36 and the reviling of a brother shall be counted as the sin of murder. Matthew 5:21-22 Paul and Peter now reign with Christ, and it is not easy to take the place of the one or to hold the office of the other. There may come

an angel to rend the veil of your temple, Matthew 27:51 and to remove your candlestick out of its place. Revelation 2:5 If you intend to build the tower, first count the cost. Luke 14:28 Salt that has lost its savor is good for nothing but to be cast out and to be trodden under foot of swine. Matthew 5:13 If a monk fall, a priest shall intercede for him; but who shall intercede for a fallen priest?

10. At last my discourse is clear of the reefs: at last this frail bark has passed from the breakers into deep water. I may now spread my sails to the breeze; and, as I leave the rocks of controversy astern, my epilogue will be like the joyful shout of mariners. O desert, bright with the flowers of Christ! O solitude whence come the stones of which, in the Apocalypse, the city of the great king is built! Revelation 21:19-20 O wilderness, gladdened with God's special presence! What keeps you in the world, my brother, you who are above the world? How long shall gloomy roofs oppress you? How long shall smoky cities immure you? Believe me, I have more light than you. Sweet it is to lay aside the weight of the body and to soar into the pure bright ether. Do you dread poverty? Christ calls the poor blessed. Luke 6:20 Does toil frighten you? No athlete is crowned but in the sweat of his brow. Are you anxious as regards food? Faith fears no famine. Do you dread the bare ground for limbs wasted with fasting? The Lord lies there beside you. Do you recoil from an unwashed head and uncombed hair? Christ is your true head. Does the boundless solitude of the desert terrify you? In the spirit you may walk always in paradise. Do but turn your thoughts there and you will be no more in the desert. Is your skin rough and scaly because you no longer bathe? He that is once washed in Christ needs not to wash again. John 13:10 To all your objections the apostle gives this one brief answer: The sufferings of this present time are not worthy to be compared with the glory which shall come after them, which shall be revealed in us. Romans 8:18 You are too greedy of enjoyment, my brother, if you wish to rejoice with the world here, and to reign with Christ hereafter.

11. It shall come, it shall come, that day when this corruptible shall put on incorruption , and this mortal shall put on immortality. 1 Corinthians 15:53 Then shall that servant be blessed whom the Lord shall find watching. Matthew 24:46 Then at the sound of the trumpet 1 Thessalonians 4:16 the earth and its peoples shall tremble, but you shall rejoice. The world shall howl at the Lord who comes to judge it, and the tribes of the earth shall smite the breast. Once mighty kings shall tremble in their nakedness. Venus shall be exposed, and her son too. Jupiter with his fiery bolts will be brought to trial; and Plato, with his disciples, will be but a fool. Aristotle's arguments shall be of no avail. You may seem a poor man and country bred, but then you shall exult and laugh, and say: Behold my crucified Lord, behold my judge. This is He who was once an infant wrapped in swaddling clothes and crying in a manger. Luke 2:7 This is He whose parents were a workingman and a working-woman. This is He, who, carried into Egypt in His mother's bosom, though He was God, fled before the face of man. This is He who was clothed in a scarlet robe and crowned with thorns. Matthew 27:28-29 This is He who was called a sorcerer and a man with a devil and a Samaritan. John 8:48 Jew, behold the hands which you nailed to the cross. Roman, behold the side which you pierced with the spear. See both of you whether it was this body that

the disciples stole secretly and by night. Matthew 27:64 For this you profess to believe.

My brother, it is affection which has urged me to speak thus; that you who now find the Christian life so hard may have your reward in that day.

LETTER XV

To Pope Damasus

This letter, written in 376 or 377 A.D., illustrates Jerome's attitude towards the see of Rome at this time held by Damasus, afterwards his warm friend and admirer. Referring to Rome as the scene of his own baptism and as a church where the true faith has remained unimpaired (§1), and laying down the strict doctrine of salvation only within the pale of the church (§2), Jerome asks the successor of the fisherman two questions, viz.: (1) who is the true bishop of the three claimants of the see of Antioch, and (2) which is the correct terminology, to speak of three hypostases in the Godhead, or of one? On the latter question he expresses fully his own opinion.

1. Since the East, shattered as it is by the long-standing feuds, subsisting between its peoples, is bit by bit tearing into shreds the seamless vest of the Lord, woven from the top throughout, John 19:23 since the foxes are destroying the vineyard of Christ, Song of Songs 2:15 and since among the broken cisterns that hold no water it is hard to discover the sealed fountain and the garden inclosed, Song of Songs 4:12 I think it my duty to consult the chair of Peter, and to turn to a church whose faith has been praised by Paul. I appeal for spiritual food to the church whence I have received the garb of Christ. The wide space of sea and land that lies between us cannot deter me from searching for the pearl of great price. Matthew 13:46 Wheresoever the body is, there will the eagles be gathered together. Matthew 24:28 Evil children have squandered their patrimony; you alone keep your heritage intact. The fruitful soil of Rome, when it receives the pure seed of the Lord, bears fruit an hundredfold; but here the seed grain is choked in the furrows and nothing grows but darnel or oats. Matthew 13:22-23 In the West the Sun of righteousness Malachi 4:2 is even now rising; in the East, Lucifer, who fell from heaven, Luke 10:18 has once more set his throne above the stars. Isaiah 14:12 You are the light of the world, Matthew 5:14 you are the salt of the earth, Matthew 5:13 you are vessels of gold and of silver. Here are vessels of wood or of earth, 2 Timothy 2:20 which wait for the rod of iron, Revelation 2:27 and eternal fire.

2. Yet, though your greatness terrifies me, your kindness attracts me. From the priest I demand the safe-keeping of the victim, from the shepherd the protection due to the sheep. Away with all that is overweening; let the state of Roman majesty withdraw. My words are spoken to the successor of the fisherman, to the disciple of the cross. As I follow no leader save Christ, so I communicate with none but your blessedness, that is with the chair of Peter. For this, I know, is the rock on which the church is built! Matthew 16:18 This is the house where alone the paschal lamb can be rightly eaten. Exodus 12:22 This is the ark of Noah, and he who is not found in it shall perish when the flood prevails. Genesis 7:23 But since by reason of my sins I have betaken myself to this desert which lies between Syria and the uncivilized waste, I cannot, owing to the great distance between us, always ask of your sanctity the holy thing of the Lord. Consequently I here follow the Egyptian confessors who share your faith, and anchor my frail craft under the

shadow of their great argosies. I know nothing of Vitalis; I reject Meletius; I have nothing to do with Paulinus. He that gathers not with you scatters; Matthew 12:30 he that is not of Christ is of Antichrist.

3. Just now, I am sorry to say, those Arians, the Campenses, are trying to extort from me, a Roman Christian, their unheard-of formula of three hypostases. And this, too, after the definition of Nicæa and the decree of Alexandria, in which the West has joined. Where, I should like to know, are the apostles of these doctrines? Where is their Paul, their new doctor of the Gentiles? I ask them what three hypostases are supposed to mean. They reply three persons subsisting. I rejoin that this is my belief. They are not satisfied with the meaning, they demand the term. Surely some secret venom lurks in the words. If any man refuse, I cry, to acknowledge three hypostases in the sense of three things hypostatized, that is three persons subsisting, let him be anathema. Yet, because I do not learn their words, I am counted a heretic. But, if any one, understanding by hypostasis essence, deny that in the three persons there is one hypostasis, he has no part in Christ. Because this is my confession I, like you, am branded with the stigma of Sabellianism.

4. If you think fit enact a decree; and then I shall not hesitate to speak of three hypostases. Order a new creed to supersede the Nicene; and then, whether we are Arians or orthodox, one confession will do for us all. In the whole range of secular learning hypostasis never means anything but essence. And can any one, I ask, be so profane as to speak of three essences or substances in the Godhead? There is one nature of God and one only; and this, and this alone, truly *is.* For absolute being is derived from no other source but is all its own. All things besides, that is all things created, although they appear to be, are not. For there was a time when they were not, and that which once was not may again cease to be. God alone who is eternal, that is to say, who has no beginning, really deserves to be called an essence. Therefore also He says to Moses from the bush, I am that I am, and Moses says of Him, I am has sent me. Exodus 3:14 As the angels, the sky, the earth, the seas, all existed at the time, it must have been as the absolute being that God claimed for himself that name of essence, which apparently was common to all. But because His nature alone is perfect, and because in the three persons there subsists but one Godhead, which truly is and is one nature; whosoever in the name of religion declares that there are in the Godhead three elements, three hypostases, that is, or essences, is striving really to predicate three natures of God. And if this is true, why are we severed by walls from Arius, when in dishonesty we are one with him? Let Ursicinus be made the colleague of your blessedness; let Auxentius be associated with Ambrose. But may the faith of Rome never come to such a pass! May the devout hearts of your people never be infected with such unholy doctrines! Let us be satisfied to speak of one substance and of three subsisting persons— perfect, equal, coeternal. Let us keep to one hypostasis, if such be your pleasure, and say nothing of three. It is a bad sign when those who mean the same thing use different words. Let us be satisfied with the form of creed which we have hitherto used. Or, if you think it right that I should speak of three hypostases, explaining what I mean by them, I am ready to submit. But, believe me, there is poison hidden under their honey; the angel of Satan has transformed himself into

an angel of light. 2 Corinthians 11:14 They give a plausible explanation of the term hypostasis; yet when I profess to hold it in the same sense they count me a heretic. Why are they so tenacious of a word? Why do they shelter themselves under ambiguous language? If their belief corresponds to their explanation of it, I do not condemn them for keeping it. On the other hand, if my belief corresponds to their expressed opinions, they should allow me to set forth their meaning in my own words.

5. I implore your blessedness, therefore, by the crucified Saviour of the world, and by the consubstantial trinity, to authorize me by letter either to use or to refuse this formula of three hypostases. And lest the obscurity of my present abode may baffle the bearers of your letter, I pray you to address it to Evagrius, the presbyter, with whom you are well acquainted. I beg you also to signify with whom I am to communicate at Antioch. Not, I hope, with the Campenses; for they— with their allies the heretics of Tarsus — only desire communion with you to preach with

greater authority their traditional doctrine of three hypostases.

LETTER XVI

To Pope Damasus

This letter, written a few months after the preceding, is another appeal to Damasus to solve the writer's doubts. Jerome once more refers to his baptism at Rome, and declares that his one answer to the factions at Antioch is, He who clings to the chair of Peter is accepted by me. Written from the desert in the year 377 or 378.

1. By her importunity the widow in the gospel at last gained a hearing, Matthew 15:28 and by the same means one friend induced another to give him bread at midnight, when his door was shut and his servants were in bed. Luke 11:7-8 The publican's prayers overcame God, Luke 18:10-14 although God is invincible. Nineveh was saved by its tears from the impending ruin caused by its sin. Jonah 3:5, 10 To what end, you ask, these far-fetched references? To this end, I make answer; that you in your greatness should look upon me in my littleness; that you, the rich shepherd, should not despise me, the ailing sheep. Christ Himself brought the robber from the cross to paradise, Luke 23:43 and, to show that repentance is never too late, He turned a murderer's death into a martyrdom. Gladly does Christ embrace the prodigal son when he returns to Him; Luke 15:20 and, leaving the ninety and nine, the good shepherd carries home on His shoulders the one poor sheep that is left. Luke 15:5 From a persecutor Paul becomes a preacher. His bodily eyes are blinded to clear the eyes of his soul, Acts 9:8 and he who once haled Christ's servants in chains before the council of the Jews, Acts 8:3 lives afterwards to glory in the bonds of Christ. 2 Corinthians 12:10

2. As I have already written to you, I, who have received Christ's garb in Rome, am now detained in the waste that borders Syria. No sentence of banishment, however, has been passed upon me; the punishment which I am undergoing is self-inflicted. But, as the heathen poet says:

They change not mind but sky who cross the sea.

The untiring foe follows me closely, and the assaults that I suffer in the desert are severer than ever. For the Arian frenzy raves, and the powers of the world support it. The church is rent into three factions, and each of these is eager to seize me for its own. The influence of the monks is of long standing, and it is directed against me. I meantime keep crying: He who clings to the chair of Peter is accepted by me. Meletius, Vitalis, and Paulinus all profess to cleave to you, and I could believe the assertion if it were made by one of them only. As it is, either two of them or else all three are guilty of falsehood. Therefore I implore your blessedness, by our Lord's cross and passion, those necessary glories of our faith, as you hold an apostolic office, to give an apostolic decision. Only tell me by letter with whom I am to communicate in Syria, and I will pray for you that you may sit in judgment enthroned with the twelve; Matthew 19:28 that when you grow old, like Peter, you may be girded not by yourself but by another, John 21:18 and that, like Paul, you may be made a citizen of the heavenly kingdom. Do not despise a soul for which Christ died.

LETTER XVII

To the Presbyter Marcus

In this letter, addressed to one who seems to have had some pre-eminence among the monks of the Chalcidian desert, Jerome complains of the hard treatment meted out to him because of his refusal to take any part in the great theological dispute then raging in Syria. He protests his own orthodoxy, and begs permission to remain where he is until the return of spring, when he will retire from the inhospitable desert. Written in A.D. 378 or 379.

1. I had made up my mind to use the words of the psalmist: While the wicked was before me I was dumb with silence; I was humbled, and I held my peace even from good and I, as a deaf man, heard not; and I was as a dumb man that opens not his mouth. Thus I was as a man that hears not. But charity overcomes all things, 1 Corinthians 13:7 and my regard for you defeats my determination. I am, indeed, less careful to retaliate upon my assailants than to comply with your request. For among Christians, as one has said, not he who endures an outrage is unhappy, but he who commits it.

2. And first, before I speak to you of my belief (which you know full well), I am forced to cry out against the inhumanity of this country. A hackneyed quotation best expresses my meaning:

What savages are these who will not grant
A rest to strangers, even on their sands!
They threaten war and drive us from their coasts.

I take this from a Gentile poet that one who disregards the peace of Christ may at least learn its meaning from a heathen. I am called a heretic, although I preach the consubstantial trinity. I am accused of the Sabellian impiety although I proclaim with unwearied voice that in the Godhead there are three distinct, real, whole, and perfect persons. The Arians do right to accuse me, but the orthodox forfeit their orthodoxy when they assail a faith like mine. They may, if they like, condemn me as a heretic; but if they do they must also condemn Egypt and the West, Damasus and Peter. Why do they fasten the guilt on one and leave his companions uncensured? If there is but little water in the stream, it is the fault, not of the channel, but of the source. I blush to say it, but from the caves which serve us for cells we monks of the desert condemn the world. Rolling in sack-cloth and ashes, we pass sentence on bishops. What use is the robe of a penitent if it covers the pride of a king? Chains, squalor, and long hair are by right tokens of sorrow, and not ensigns of royalty. I merely ask leave to remain silent. Why do they torment a man who does not deserve their ill-will? I am a heretic, you say. What is it to you if I am? Stay quiet, and all is said. You are afraid, I suppose, that, with my fluent knowledge of Syriac and Greek, I shall make a tour of the churches, lead the people into error, and form a schism! I have robbed no man of anything; neither have I taken what I have not earned. With my own hand 1 Corinthians 4:12 daily and in the sweat of my brow Genesis 3:19 I labor for my food, knowing that it is

written by the apostle: If any will not work, neither shall he eat.
2 Thessalonians 3:10

3. Reverend and holy father, Jesus is my witness with what groans and tears I have written all this. I have kept silence, says the Lord, but shall I always keep silence? Surely not. I cannot have so much as a corner of the desert. Every day I am asked for my confession of faith; as though when I was regenerated in baptism I had made none. I accept their formulas, but they are still dissatisfied. I sign my name to them, but they still refuse to believe me. One thing only will content them, that I should leave the country. I am on the point of departure. They have already torn away from me my dear brothers, who are a part of my very life. They are, as you see, anxious to depart— nay, they are actually departing; it is preferable, they say, to live among wild beasts rather than with Christians such as these. I myself, too, would be at this moment a fugitive were I not withheld by physical infirmity and by the severity of the winter. I ask to be allowed the shelter of the desert for a few months till spring returns; or if this seems too long a delay, I am ready to depart now. The earth is the Lord's and the fullness thereof. Let them climb up to heaven alone; for them alone Christ died; they possess all things and glory in all. Be it so. But God forbid that I should glory save in the cross of our Lord Jesus Christ, by whom the world is crucified unto me and I unto the world. Galatians 6:14

4. As regards the questions which you have thought fit to put to me concerning the faith, I have given to the reverend Cyril a written confession which sufficiently answers them. He who does not so believe has no part in Christ. My faith is attested both by your ears and by those of your blessed brother, Zenobius, to whom, as well as to yourself, we all of us here send our best greeting.

LETTER XVIII

To Pope Damasus.

This (written from Constantinople in A.D. 381) is the earliest of Jerome's expository letters. In it he explains at length the vision recorded in the sixth chapter of Isaiah, and enlarges upon its mystical meaning. Some of my predecessors, he writes, make 'the Lord sitting upon a throne' God the Father, and suppose the seraphim to represent the Son and the Holy Spirit. I do not agree with them, for John expressly tells us John 12:41 that it was Christ and not the Father whom the prophet saw. And again, The word seraphim means either 'glow' or 'beginning of speech,' and the two seraphim thus stand for the Old and New Testaments. 'Did not our heart burn within us,' said the disciples, 'while he opened to us the Scriptures?' Luke 24:32 Moreover, the Old Testament is written in Hebrew, and this unquestionably was man's original language. Jerome then speaks of the unity of the sacred books. Whatever, he asserts, we read in the Old Testament we find also in the Gospel; and what we read in the Gospel is deduced from the Old Testament. There is no discord between them, no disagreement. In both Testaments the Trinity is preached.

The letter is noticeable for the evidence it affords of the thoroughness of Jerome's studies. Not only does he cite the several Greek versions of Isaiah in support of his argument, but he also reverts to the Hebrew original. So far as the West was concerned he may be said to have discovered this anew. Even educated men like Augustine had ceased to look beyond the LXX., and were more or less aghast at the boldness with which Jerome rejected its time-honored but inaccurate renderings.

The letter also shows that independence of judgment which always marked Jerome's work. At the time when he wrote it he was much under the sway of Origen. But great as was his admiration for the master, he was not afraid to discard his exegesis when, **To Eustochium**

Perhaps the most famous of all the letters. In it Jerome lays down at great length (1) the motives which ought to actuate those who devote themselves to a life of virginity, and (2) the rules by which they ought to regulate their daily conduct. The letter contains a vivid picture of Roman society as it then was— the luxury, profligacy, and hypocrisy prevalent among both men and women, besides some graphic autobiographical details (§§7, 30), and concludes with a full account of the three kinds of monasticism then practised in Egypt (§§34-36). Thirty years later Jerome wrote a similar letter to Demetrias (CXXX.), with which this ought to be compared. Written at Rome 384 A.D.

1. Hear, O daughter, and consider, and incline your ear; forget also your own people and your father's house, and the king shall desire your beauty. In this forty-fourth psalm God speaks to the human soul that, following the example of Abraham, it should go out from its own land and from its kindred, and should leave the Chaldeans, that is the demons, and should dwell in the country of the living, for which elsewhere the prophet sighs: I think to see the good things of the Lord in the land of the living. But it is not enough for you to go out from your own land unless you forget your people and your father's house; unless you scorn the flesh and cling to the bridegroom in a close embrace. Look not behind you, he says, neither stay thou in all the plain; escape to the mountain lest you be consumed. Genesis 19:17 He who has grasped the plough must not look behind him Luke 9:62 or return home from the field, or having Christ's garment, descend from the roof to fetch other raiment. Matthew 24:17-18 Truly a marvellous thing, a father charges his daughter not to remember her father. You are of your father the devil, and the lusts of your father it is your will to do. So it was said to the Jews.

And in another place, He that commits sin is of the devil. 1 John 3:8 Born, in the first instance, of such parentage we are naturally black, and even when we have repented, so long as we have not scaled the heights of virtue, we may still say: I am black but comely, O you daughters of Jerusalem. Song of Songs 1:5 But you will say to me, I have left the home of my childhood; I have forgotten my father, I am born anew in Christ. What reward do I receive for this? The context shows— The king shall desire your beauty. This, then, is the great mystery. For this cause shall a man leave his father and his mother and shall be joined unto his wife, and they two shall be not as is there said, of one flesh, Ephesians 5:31-32 but of one spirit. Your bridegroom is not haughty or disdainful; He has married an Ethiopian woman. Numbers 12:1 When once you desire the wisdom of the true Solomon and come to Him, He will avow all His knowledge to you; He will lead you into His chamber with His royal hand; Song of Songs 1:4 He will miraculously change your complexion so that it shall be said of you, Who is this that goes up and has been made white?

2. I write to you thus, Lady Eustochium (I am bound to call my Lord's bride lady), to show you by my opening words that my object is not to praise the virginity which you follow, and of which you have proved the value, or yet to recount the drawbacks of marriage, such as pregnancy, the crying of infants, the torture caused by a rival, the cares of household management, and all those fancied blessings which death at last cuts short. Not that married women are as such outside the pale; they have their own place, the marriage that is honorable and the bed undefiled. Hebrews 13:4 My purpose is to show you that you are fleeing from Sodom and should take warning by Lot's wife. Genesis 19:26 There is no flattery, I can tell you, in these pages. A flatterer's words are fair, but for all that he is an enemy. You need expect no rhetorical flourishes setting you among the angels, and while they extol virginity as blessed, putting the world at your feet.

3. I would have you draw from your monastic vow not pride but fear. Romans 11:20 You walk laden with gold; you must keep out of the robber's way. To us men this life is a race-course: we contend here, we are crowned elsewhere. No man can lay aside fear while serpents and scorpions beset his path. The Lord says: My sword has drunk its fill in heaven, and do you expect to find peace on the earth? No, the earth yields only thorns and thistles, and its dust is food for the serpent. For our wrestling is not against flesh and blood, but against the principalities, against the powers, against the world rulers of this darkness, against the spiritual hosts of wickedness in the heavenly places. We are hemmed in by hosts of foes, our enemies are upon every side. The weak flesh will soon be ashes: one against many, it fights against tremendous odds. Not till it has been dissolved, not till the Prince of this world has come and found no sin therein, not till then may you safely listen to the prophet's words: You shall not be afraid for the terror by night nor for the arrow that flies by day; nor for the trouble which haunts you in darkness; nor for the demon and his attacks at noonday. A thousand shall fall at your side and ten thousand at your right hand; but it shall not come near you. When the hosts of the enemy distress you, when your frame is fevered and your passions roused, when you say in your heart, What shall I do? Elisha's words shall give you your answer, Fear not, for they that be with us are more than they that be

with them. 2 Kings 6:16 He shall pray, Lord, open the eyes of your handmaid that she may see. And then when your eyes have been opened you shall see a fiery chariot like Elijah's waiting to carry you to heaven, and shall joyfully sing: Our soul is escaped as a bird out of the snare of the fowlers: the snare is broken and we are escaped.

4. So long as we are held down by this frail body, so long as we have our treasure in earthen vessels; 2 Corinthians 4:7 so long as the flesh lusts against the spirit and the spirit against the flesh, Galatians 5:17 there can be no sure victory. Our adversary the devil goes about as a roaring lion seeking whom he may devour. 1 Peter 5:8 You make darkness, David says, and it is night: wherein all the beasts of the forest do creep forth. The young lions roar after their prey and seek their meat from God. The devil looks not for unbelievers, for those who are without, whose flesh the Assyrian king roasted in the furnace. Jeremiah 29:22 It is the church of Christ that he makes haste to spoil. According to Habakkuk, His food is of the choicest. A Job is the victim of his machinations, and after devouring Judas he seeks power to sift the [other] apostles. Luke 22:31 The Saviour came not to send peace upon the earth but a sword. Matthew 10:34 Lucifer fell, Lucifer who used to rise at dawn; Isaiah 14:12 and he who was bred up in a paradise of delight had the well-earned sentence passed upon him, Though thou exalt yourself as the eagle, and though thou set your nest among the stars, thence will I bring you down, says the Lord. Obadiah 4 For he had said in his heart, I will exalt my throne above the stars of God, and I will be like the Most High. Isaiah 14:13-14 Wherefore God says every day to the angels, as they descend the ladder that Jacob saw in his dream, Genesis 28:12 I have said you are Gods and all of you are children of the Most High. But you shall die like men and fall like one of the princes. The devil fell first, and since God stands in the congregation of the Gods and judges among the Gods, the apostle writes to those who are ceasing to be Gods— Whereas there is among you envying and strife, are you not carnal and walk as men? 1 Corinthians 3:3

5. If, then, the apostle, who was a chosen vessel Acts 9:15 separated unto the gospel of Christ, Galatians 1:15 by reason of the pricks of the flesh and the allurements of vice keeps under his body and brings it into subjection, lest when he has preached to others he may himself be a castaway; 1 Corinthians 9:27 and yet, for all that, sees another law in his members warring against the law of his mind, and bringing him into captivity to the law of sin; Romans 7:23 if after nakedness, fasting, hunger, imprisonment, scourging and other torments, he turns back to himself and cries Oh, wretched man that I am, who shall deliver me from the body of this death? Romans 7:24 do you fancy that you ought to lay aside apprehension? See to it that God say not some day of you: The virgin of Israel is fallen and there is none to raise her up. Amos 5:2 I will say it boldly, though God can do all things He cannot raise up a virgin when once she has fallen. He may indeed relieve one who is defiled from the penalty of her sin, but He will not give her a crown. Let us fear lest in us also the prophecy be fulfilled, Good virgins shall faint. Amos 8:13 Notice that it is good virgins who are spoken of, for there are bad ones as well. Whosoever looks on a woman, the Lord says, to lust after her has committed adultery with her already in his heart. Matthew 5:28 So that virginity

may be lost even by a thought. Such are evil virgins, virgins in the flesh, not in the spirit; foolish virgins, who, having no oil, are shut out by the Bridegroom.

6. But if even real virgins, when they have other failings, are not saved by their physical virginity, what shall become of those who have prostituted the members of Christ, and have changed the temple of the Holy Ghost into a brothel? Straightway shall they hear the words: Come down and sit in the dust, O virgin daughter of Babylon, sit on the ground; there is no throne, O daughter of the Chaldæans: for you shall no more be called tender and delicate. Take the millstone and grind meal; uncover your locks, make bare the legs, pass over the rivers; your nakedness shall be uncovered, yea, your shame shall be seen. Isaiah 47:1-3 And shall she come to this after the bridal-chamber of God the Son, after the kisses of Him who is to her both kinsman and spouse? Yes, she of whom the prophetic utterance once sang, Upon your right hand stood the queen in a vesture of gold wrought about with various colours, shall be made naked, and her skirts shall be discovered upon her face. Jeremiah 13:26 She shall sit by the waters of loneliness, her pitcher laid aside; and shall open her feet to every one that passes by, and shall be polluted to the crown of her head. Ezekiel 16:25 Better had it been for her to have submitted to the yoke of marriage, to have walked in level places, than thus, aspiring to loftier heights, to fall into the deep of hell. I pray you, let not Zion the faithful city become a harlot: Isaiah 1:21 let it not be that where the Trinity has been entertained, there demons shall dance and owls make their nests, and jackals build. Let us not loose the belt that binds the breast. When lust tickles the sense and the soft fire of sensual pleasure sheds over us its pleasing glow, let us immediately break forth and cry: The Lord is on my side: I will not fear what the flesh can do unto me. When the inner man shows signs for a time of wavering between vice and virtue, say: Why art you cast down, O my soul, and why are you disquieted within me? Hope thou in God, for I shall yet praise Him who is the health of my countenance and my God. You must never let suggestions of evil grow on you, or a babel of disorder win strength in your breast. Slay the enemy while he is small; and, that you may not have a crop of tares, nip the evil in the bud. Bear in mind the warning words of the Psalmist: Hapless daughter of Babylon, happy shall he be that rewards you as you have served us. Happy shall he be that takes and dashes your little ones against the stones. Because natural heat inevitably kindles in a man sensual passion, he is praised and accounted happy who, when foul suggestions arise in his mind, gives them no quarter, but dashes them instantly against the rock. Now the Rock is Christ. 1 Corinthians 10:4

7. How often, when I was living in the desert, in the vast solitude which gives to hermits a savage dwelling-place, parched by a burning sun, how often did I fancy myself among the pleasures of Rome! I used to sit alone because I was filled with bitterness. Sackcloth disfigured my unshapely limbs and my skin from long neglect had become as black as an Ethiopian's. Tears and groans were every day my portion; and if drowsiness chanced to overcome my struggles against it, my bare bones, which hardly held together, clashed against the ground. Of my food and drink I say nothing: for, even in sickness, the solitaries have nothing but cold water, and to eat one's food cooked is looked upon as self-indulgence. Now, although in my fear of hell I had consigned myself to this prison, where I had no

companions but scorpions and wild beasts, I often found myself amid bevies of girls. My face was pale and my frame chilled with fasting; yet my mind was burning with desire, and the fires of lust kept bubbling up before me when my flesh was as good as dead. Helpless, I cast myself at the feet of Jesus, I watered them with my tears, I wiped them with my hair: and then I subdued my rebellious body with weeks of abstinence. I do not blush to avow my abject misery; rather I lament that I am not now what once I was. I remember how I often cried aloud all night till the break of day and ceased not from beating my breast till tranquillity returned at the chiding of the Lord. I used to dread my very cell as though it knew my thoughts; and, stern and angry with myself, I used to make my way alone into the desert. Wherever I saw hollow valleys, craggy mountains, steep cliffs, there I made my oratory, there the house of correction for my unhappy flesh. There, also— the Lord Himself is my witness— when I had shed copious tears and had strained my eyes towards heaven, I sometimes felt myself among angelic hosts, and for joy and gladness sang: because of the savour of your good ointments we will run after you. Song of Songs 1:3-4

8. Now, if such are the temptations of men who, since their bodies are emaciated with fasting, have only evil thoughts to fear, how must it fare with a girl whose surroundings are those of luxury and ease? Surely, to use the apostle's words, She is dead while she lives. 1 Timothy 5:6 Therefore, if experience gives me a right to advise, or clothes my words with credit, I would begin by urging you and warning you as Christ's spouse to avoid wine as you would avoid poison. For wine is the first weapon used by demons against the young. Greed does not shake, nor pride puff up, nor ambition infatuate so much as this. Other vices we easily escape, but this enemy is shut up within us, and wherever we go we carry him with us. Wine and youth between them kindle the fire of sensual pleasure. Why do we throw oil on the flame— why do we add fresh fuel to a miserable body which is already ablaze. Paul, it is true, says to Timothy drink no longer water, but use a little wine for your stomach's sake, and for your frequent infirmities. 1 Timothy 5:23 But notice the reasons for which the permission is given, to cure an aching stomach and a frequent infirmity. And lest we should indulge ourselves too much on the score of our ailments, he commands that but little shall be taken; advising rather as a physician than as an apostle (though, indeed, an apostle is a spiritual physician). He evidently feared that Timothy might succumb to weakness, and might prove unequal to the constant moving to and fro involved in preaching the Gospel. Besides, he remembered that he had spoken of wine wherein is excess, Ephesians 5:18 and had said, it is good neither to eat flesh nor to drink wine. Romans 14:21 Noah drank wine and became intoxicated; but living as he did in the rude age after the flood, when the vine was first planted, perhaps he did not know its power of inebriation. And to let you see the hidden meaning of Scripture in all its fullness (for the word of God is a pearl and may be pierced on every side) after his drunkenness came the uncovering of his body; self-indulgence culminated in lust. Genesis 9:20-21 First the belly is crammed; then the other members are roused. Similarly, at a later period, The people sat down to eat and to drink and rose up to play. Exodus 32:6 Lot also, God's friend, whom He saved upon the mountain, who was the only one found righteous out of so many thousands, was intoxicated by his daughters. And, although they may have acted as they did more

from a desire of offspring than from love of sinful pleasure— for the human race seemed in danger of extinction— yet they were well aware that the righteous man would not abet their design unless intoxicated. In fact he did not know what he was doing, and his sin was not wilful. Still his error was a grave one, for it made him the father of Moab and Ammon, Genesis 19:30-38 Israel's enemies, of whom it is said: Even to the fourteenth generation they shall not enter into the congregation of the Lord forever.

9. When Elijah, in his flight from Jezebel, lay weary and desolate beneath the oak, there came an angel who raised him up and said, Arise and eat. And he looked, and behold there was a cake and a cruse of water at his head. 1 Kings 19:4-6 Had God willed it, might He not have sent His prophet spiced wines and dainty dishes and flesh basted into tenderness? When Elisha invited the sons of the prophets to dinner, he only gave them field-herbs to eat; and when all cried out with one voice: There is death in the pot, the man of God did not storm at the cooks (for he was not used to very sumptuous fare), but caused meal to be brought, and casting it in, sweetened the bitter mess 2 Kings 4:38-41 with spiritual strength as Moses had once sweetened the waters of Mara. Exodus 15:23-25 Again, when men were sent to arrest the prophet, and were smitten with physical and mental blindness, that he might bring them without their own knowledge to Samaria, notice the food with which Elisha ordered them to be refreshed. Set bread and water, he said, before them, that they may eat and drink and go to their master. 2 Kings 6:18-23 And Daniel, who might have had rich food from the king's table, Daniel 1:8 preferred the mower's breakfast, brought to him by Habakkuk, which must have been but country fare. He was called a man of desires, because he would not eat the bread of desire or drink the wine of concupiscence.

10. There are, in the Scriptures, countless divine answers condemning gluttony and approving simple food. But as fasting is not my present theme and an adequate discussion of it would require a treatise to itself, these few observations must suffice of the many which the subject suggests. By them you will understand why the first man, obeying his belly and not God, was cast down from paradise into this vale of tears; and why Satan used hunger to tempt the Lord Himself in the wilderness; Matthew 4:2-3 and why the apostle cries: Meats for the belly and the belly for meats, but God shall destroy both it and them; 1 Corinthians 6:13 and why he speaks of the self-indulgent as men whose God is their belly. Philippians 3:19 For men invariably worship what they like best. Care must be taken, therefore, that abstinence may bring back to Paradise those whom satiety once drove out.

11. You will tell me, perhaps, that, high-born as you are, reared in luxury and used to lie softly, you cannot do without wine and dainties, and would find a stricter rule of life unendurable. If so, I can only say: Live, then, by your own rule, since God's rule is too hard for you. Not that the Creator and Lord of all takes pleasure in a rumbling and empty stomach, or in fevered lungs; but that these are indispensable as means to the preservation of chastity. Job was dear to God, perfect and upright before Him; Job 2:3 yet hear what he says of the devil: His strength is in the loins, and his force is in the navel.

The terms are chosen for decency's sake, but the reproductive organs of the two sexes are meant. Thus, the descendant of David, who, according to the promise is to sit upon his throne, is said to come from his loins. And the seventy-five souls descended from Jacob who entered Egypt are said to come out of his thigh. Genesis 46:26 So, also, when his thigh shrank after the Lord had wrestled with him, Genesis 32:24-25 he ceased to beget children. The Israelites, again, are told to celebrate the passover with loins girded and mortified. Exodus 12:11 God says to Job: Gird up your loins as a man. Job 38:3 John wears a leathern girdle. Matthew 3:4 The apostles must gird their loins to carry the lamps of the Gospel. Luke 12:35 When Ezekiel tells us how Jerusalem is found in the plain of wandering, covered with blood, he uses the words: Your navel has not been cut. Ezekiel 16:4-6 In his assaults on men, therefore, the devil's strength is in the loins; in his attacks on women his force is in the navel.

12. Do you wish for proof of my assertions? Take examples. Sampson was braver than a lion and tougher than a rock; alone and unprotected he pursued a thousand armed men; and yet, in Delilah's embrace, his resolution melted away. David was a man after God's own heart, and his lips had often sung of the Holy One, the future Christ; and yet as he walked upon his housetop he was fascinated by Bathsheba's nudity, and added murder to adultery. 2 Samuel xi Notice here how, even in his own house, a man cannot use his eyes without danger. Then repenting, he says to the Lord: Against you, you only, have I sinned and done this evil in Your sight. Being a king he feared no one else. So, too, with Solomon. Wisdom used him to sing her praise, and he treated of all plants from the cedar tree that is in Lebanon even unto the hyssop that springs out of the wall; 1 Kings 4:33 and yet he went back from God because he was a lover of women. 1 Kings 11:1-4 And, as if to show that near relationship is no safeguard, Amnon burned with illicit passion for his sister Tamar. 2 Samuel xiii

13. I cannot bring myself to speak of the many virgins who daily fall and are lost to the bosom of the church, their mother: stars over which the proud foe sets up his throne, Isaiah 14:13 and rocks hollowed by the serpent that he may dwell in their fissures. You may see many women widows before wedded, who try to conceal their miserable fall by a lying garb. Unless they are betrayed by swelling wombs or by the crying of their infants, they walk abroad with tripping feet and heads in the air. Some go so far as to take potions, that they may insure barrenness, and thus murder human beings almost before their conception. Some, when they find themselves with child through their sin, use drugs to procure abortion, and when (as often happens) they die with their offspring, they enter the lower world laden with the guilt not only of adultery against Christ but also of suicide and child murder. Yet it is these who say: 'Unto the pure all things are pure;' Titus 1:15 my conscience is sufficient guide for me. A pure heart is what God looks for. Why should I abstain from meats which God has created to be received with thanksgiving? 1 Timothy 4:3 And when they wish to appear agreeable and entertaining they first drench themselves with wine, and then joining the grossest profanity to intoxication, they say Far be it from me to abstain from the blood of Christ. And when they see another pale or sad they call her wretch or Manichæan; quite logically, indeed, for on their principles fasting involves heresy. When they

go out they do their best to attract notice, and with nods and winks encourage troops of young fellows to follow them. Of each and all of these the prophet's words are true: You have a whore's forehead; you refuse to be ashamed. Jeremiah 3:3 Their robes have but a narrow purple stripe, it is true; and their head-dress is somewhat loose, so as to leave the hair free. From their shoulders flutters the lilac mantle which they call ma-forte; they have their feet in cheap slippers and their arms tucked up tight-fitting sleeves. Add to these marks of their profession an easy gait, and you have all the virginity that they possess. Such may have eulogizers of their own, and may fetch a higher price in the market of perdition, merely because they are called virgins. But to such virgins as these I prefer to be displeasing.

14. I blush to speak of it, it is so shocking; yet though sad, it is true. How comes this plague of the agapetæ to be in the church? Whence come these unwedded wives, these novel concubines, these harlots, so I will call them, though they cling to a single partner? One house holds them and one chamber. They often occupy the same bed, and yet they call us suspicious if we fancy anything amiss. A brother leaves his virgin sister; a virgin, slighting her unmarried brother, seeks a brother in a stranger. Both alike profess to have but one object, to find spiritual consolation from those not of their kin; but their real aim is to indulge in sexual intercourse. It is on such that Solomon in the book of proverbs heaps his scorn. Can a man take fire in his bosom, he says, and his clothes not be burned? Can one go upon hot coals and his feet not be burned? Proverbs 6:27-28

15. We cast out, then, and banish from our sight those who only wish to seem and not to be virgins. Henceforward I may bring all my speech to bear upon you who, as it is your lot to be the first virgin of noble birth in Rome, have to labor the more diligently not to lose good things to come, as well as those that are present. You have at least learned from a case in your own family the troubles of wedded life and the uncertainties of marriage. Your sister, Blæsilla, before you in age but behind you in declining the vow of virginity, has become a widow but seven months after she has taken a husband. Hapless plight of us mortals who know not what is before us! She has lost, at once, the crown of virginity and the pleasures of wedlock. And, although, as a widow, the second degree of chastity is hers, still can you not imagine the continual crosses which she has to bear, daily seeing in her sister what she has lost herself; and, while she finds it hard to go without the pleasures of wedlock, having a less reward for her present continence? Still she, too, may take heart and rejoice. The fruit which is an hundredfold and that which is sixtyfold both spring from one seed, and that seed is chastity. Matthew 13:8

16. Do not court the company of married ladies or visit the houses of the high-born. Do not look too often on the life which you despised to become a virgin. Women of the world, you know, plume themselves because their husbands are on the bench or in other high positions. And the wife of the emperor always has an eager throng of visitors at her door. Why do you, then, wrong your husband? Why do you, God's bride, hasten to visit the wife of a mere man? Learn in this respect a holy pride; know that you are better than they. And not only must you avoid intercourse with those who are puffed up by their husbands' honors, who are hedged in with troops of eunuchs, and who wear robes inwrought with threads of

gold. You must also shun those who are widows from necessity and not from choice. Not that they ought to have desired the death of their husbands; but that they have not welcomed the opportunity of continence when it has come. As it is, they only change their garb; their old self-seeking remains unchanged. To see them in their capacious litters, with red cloaks and plump bodies, a row of eunuchs walking in front of them, you would fancy them not to have lost husbands but to be seeking them. Their houses are filled with flatterers and with guests. The very clergy, who ought to inspire them with respect by their teaching and authority, kiss these ladies on the forehead, and putting forth their hands (so that, if you knew no better, you might suppose them in the act of blessing), take wages for their visits. They, meanwhile, seeing that priests cannot do without them, are lifted up into pride; and as, having had experience of both, they prefer the license of widowhood to the restraints of marriage, they call themselves chaste livers and nuns. After an immoderate supper they retire to rest to dream of the apostles.

17. Let your companions be women pale and thin with fasting, and approved by their years and conduct; such as daily sing in their hearts: Tell me where you feed your flock, where you make it to rest at noon, and say, with true earnestness, I have a desire to depart and to be with Christ. Philippians 1:23 Be subject to your parents, imitating the example of your spouse. Luke 2:51 Rarely go abroad, and if you wish to seek the aid of the martyrs seek it in your own chamber. For you will never need a pretext for going out if you always go out when there is need. Take food in moderation, and never overload your stomach. For many women, while temperate as regards wine, are intemperate in the use of food. When you rise at night to pray, let your breath be that of an empty and not that of an overfull stomach. Read often, learn all that you can. Let sleep overcome you, the roll still in your hands; when your head falls, let it be on the sacred page. Let your fasts be of daily occurrence and your refreshment such as avoids satiety. It is idle to carry an empty stomach if, in two or three days' time, the fast is to be made up for by repletion. When cloyed the mind immediately grows sluggish, and when the ground is watered it puts forth the thorns of lust. If ever you feel the outward man sighing for the flower of youth, and if, as you lie on your couch after a meal, you are excited by the alluring train of sensual desires; then seize the shield of faith, for it alone can quench the fiery darts of the devil. Ephesians 6:16 They are all adulterers, says the prophet; they have made ready their heart like an oven. But do you keep close to the footsteps of Christ, and, intent upon His words, say: Did not our heart burn within us by the way while Jesus opened to us the Scriptures? Luke 24:32 and again: Your word is tried to the uttermost, and your servant loves it. It is hard for the human soul to avoid loving something, and our mind must of necessity give way to affection of one kind or another. The love of the flesh is overcome by the love of the spirit. Desire is quenched by desire. What is taken from the one increases the other. Therefore, as you lie on your couch, say again and again: By night have I sought Him whom my soul loves. Song of Songs 3:1 Mortify, therefore, says the apostle, your members which are upon the earth. Colossians 3:5 Because he himself did so, he could afterwards say with confidence: I live, yet not I, but Christ, lives in me. Galatians 2:20 He who mortifies his members, and feels that he is walking in a vain show, is not afraid to say: I have become like a bottle in the frost. Whatever there was in me of the

moisture of lust has been dried out of me. And again: My knees are weak through fasting; I forget to eat my bread. By reason of the voice of my groaning my bones cleave to my skin.

18. Be like the grasshopper and make night musical. Nightly wash your bed and water your couch with your tears. Watch and be like the sparrow alone upon the housetop. Sing with the spirit, but sing with the understanding also.
1 Corinthians 14:15 And let your song be that of the psalmist: Bless the Lord, O my soul; and forget not all his benefits; who forgives all your iniquities; who heals all your diseases; who redeems your life from destruction. Can we, any of us, honestly make his words our own: I have eaten ashes like bread and mingled my drink with weeping? Yet, should we not weep and groan when the serpent invites us, as he invited our first parents, to eat forbidden fruit, and when after expelling us from the paradise of virginity he desires to clothe us with mantles of skins such as that which Elijah, on his return to paradise, left behind him on earth?
2 Kings 2:13 Say to yourself: What have I to do with the pleasures of sense that so soon come to an end? What have I to do with the song of the sirens so sweet and so fatal to those who hear it? I would not have you subject to that sentence whereby condemnation has been passed upon mankind. When God says to Eve, In pain and in sorrow you shall bring forth children, say to yourself, That is a law for a married woman, not for me. And when He continues, Your desire shall be to your husband, Genesis 3:16 say again: Let her desire be to her husband who has not Christ for her spouse. And when, last of all, He says, You shall surely die, Genesis 2:17 once more, say, Marriage indeed must end in death; but the life on which I have resolved is independent of sex. Let those who are wives keep the place and the time that properly belong to them. For me, virginity is consecrated in the persons of Mary and of Christ.

19. Some one may say, Do you dare detract from wedlock, which is a state blessed by God? I do not detract from wedlock when I set virginity before it. No one compares a bad thing with a good. Wedded women may congratulate themselves that they come next to virgins. Be fruitful, God says, and multiply, and replenish the earth. Genesis 1:28 He who desires to replenish the earth may increase and multiply if he will. But the train to which you belong is not on earth, but in heaven. The command to increase and multiply first finds fulfilment after the expulsion from paradise, after the nakedness and the fig-leaves which speak of sexual passion. Let them marry and be given in marriage who eat their bread in the sweat of their brow; whose land brings forth to them thorns and thistles, Genesis 3:18-19 and whose crops are choked with briars. My seed produces fruit a hundredfold. All men cannot receive God's saying, but they to whom it is given.

Some people may be eunuchs from necessity; I am one of free will.
Matthew 19:11-12 There is a time to embrace and a time to refrain from embracing. There is a time to cast away stones, and a time to gather stones together. Ecclesiastes 3:5 Now that out of the hard stones of the Gentiles God has raised up children unto Abraham, Matthew 3:9 they begin to be holy stones rolling upon the earth. They pass through the whirlwinds of the world, and roll on in God's chariot on rapid wheels. Let those stitch coats to themselves who have lost the coat woven from the top throughout; John 19:23 who delight in the cries of

infants which, as soon as they see the light, lament that they are born. In paradise Eve was a virgin, and it was only after the coats of skins that she began her married life. Now paradise is your home too. Keep therefore your birthright and say: Return unto your rest, O my soul. To show that virginity is natural while wedlock only follows guilt, what is born of wedlock is virgin flesh, and it gives back in fruit what in root it has lost. There shall come forth a rod out of the stem of Jesse, and a flower shall grow out of his roots. The rod is the mother of the Lord— simple, pure, unsullied; drawing no germ of life from without but fruitful in singleness like God Himself. The flower of the rod is Christ, who says of Himself: I am the rose of Sharon and the lily of the valleys. Song of Songs 2:1 In another place He is foretold to be a stone cut out of the mountain without hands, Daniel 2:45 a figure by which the prophet signifies that He is to be born a virgin of a virgin. For the hands are here a figure of wedlock as in the passage: His left hand is under my head and his right hand does embrace me. Song of Songs 2:6 It agrees, also, with this interpretation that the unclean animals are led into Noah's ark in pairs, while of the clean an uneven number is taken. Genesis 7:2 Similarly, when Moses and Joshua were bidden to remove their shoes because the ground on which they stood was holy, the command had a mystical meaning. So, too, when the disciples were appointed to preach the gospel they were told to take with them neither shoe nor shoe-latchet; and when the soldiers came to cast lots for the garments of Jesus John 19:23-24 they found no boots that they could take away. For the Lord could not Himself possess what He had forbidden to His servants.

20. I praise wedlock, I praise marriage, but it is because they give me virgins. I gather the rose from the thorns, the gold from the earth, the pearl from the shell. Does the plowman plow all day to sow? Isaiah 28:24 Shall he not also enjoy the fruit of his labor? Wedlock is the more honored, the more what is born of it is loved. Why, mother, do you grudge your daughter her virginity? She has been reared on your milk, she has come from your womb, she has grown up in your bosom. Your watchful affection has kept her a virgin. Are you angry with her because she chooses to be a king's wife and not a soldier's? She has conferred on you a high privilege; you are now the mother-in-law of God. Concerning virgins, says the apostle, I have no commandment of the Lord. 1 Corinthians 7:25 Why was this? Because his own virginity was due, not to a command, but to his free choice. For they are not to be heard who feign him to have had a wife; for, when he is discussing continence and commending perpetual chastity, he uses the words, I would that all men were even as I myself. And farther on, I say, therefore, to the unmarried and widows, it is good for them if they abide even as I. 1 Corinthians 7:7-8 And in another place, have we not power to lead about wives even as the rest of the apostles? 1 Corinthians 9:5 Why then has he no commandment from the Lord concerning virginity? Because what is freely offered is worth more than what is extorted by force, and to command virginity would have been to abrogate wedlock. It would have been a hard enactment to compel opposition to nature and to extort from men the angelic life; and not only so, it would have been to condemn what is a divine ordinance.

21. The old law had a different ideal of blessedness, for therein it is said: Blessed is he who has seed in Zion and a family in Jerusalem: and Cursed is the barren

who bears not: and Your children shall be like olive-plants round about your table. Riches too are promised to the faithful and we are told that there was not one feeble person among their tribes. But now even to eunuchs it is said, Say not, behold I am a dry tree, Isaiah 56:3 for instead of sons and daughters you have a place forever in heaven. Now the poor are blessed, now Lazarus is set before Dives in his purple. Now he who is weak is counted strong. But in those days the world was still unpeopled: accordingly, to pass over instances of childlessness meant only to serve as types, those only were considered happy who could boast of children. It was for this reason that Abraham in his old age married Keturah; Genesis 25:1 that Leah hired Jacob with her son's mandrakes, Genesis 30:14-16 and that fair Rachel— a type of the church— complained of the closing of her womb. Genesis 30:1-2 But gradually the crop grew up and then the reaper was sent forth with his sickle. Elijah lived a virgin life, so also did Elisha and many of the sons of the prophets. To Jeremiah the command came: You shall not take you a wife. Jeremiah 16:2 He had been sanctified in his mother's womb, Jeremiah 1:5 and now he was forbidden to take a wife because the captivity was near. The apostle gives the same counsel in different words. I think, therefore, that this is good by reason of the present distress, namely that it is good for a man to be as he is. What is this distress which does away with the joys of wedlock? The apostle tells us, in a later verse: The time is short: it remains that those who have wives be as though they had none. 1 Corinthians 7:29 Nebuchadnezzar is hard at hand. The lion is bestirring himself from his lair. What good will marriage be to me if it is to end in slavery to the haughtiest of kings? What good will little ones be to me if their lot is to be that which the prophet sadly describes: The tongue of the sucking child cleaves to the roof of his mouth for thirst; the young children ask for bread and no man breaks it unto them? Lamentations 4:4 In those days, as I have said, the virtue of continence was found only in men: Eve still continued to travail with children. But now that a virgin has conceived Isaiah 7:14 in the womb and has borne to us a child of which the prophet says that Government shall be upon his shoulder, and his name shall be called the mighty God, the everlasting Father, Isaiah 9:6 now the chain of the curse is broken. Death came through Eve, but life has come through Mary. And thus the gift of virginity has been bestowed most richly upon women, seeing that it has had its beginning from a woman. As soon as the Son of God set foot upon the earth, He formed for Himself a new household there; that, as He was adored by angels in heaven, angels might serve Him also on earth. Then chaste Judith once more cut off the head of Holofernes. Judith xiii Then Haman— whose name means iniquity— was once more burned in fire of his own kindling. Esther 7:10 Then James and John forsook father and net and ship and followed the Saviour: neither kinship nor the world's ties, nor the care of their home could hold them back. Then were the words heard: Whosoever will come after me, let him deny himself and take up his cross and follow me. Mark 8:34 For no soldier goes with a wife to battle. Even when a disciple would have buried his father, the Lord forbade him, and said: Foxes have holes and the birds of the air have nests, but the Son of Man has not where to lay His head. Matthew 8:20-22 So you must not complain if you have but scanty house-room. In the same strain, the apostle writes: He that is unmarried cares for the things that belong to the Lord, how he may please the Lord: but he that is married cares for the things that are of the world how he may please his wife. There is difference also between a wife and a virgin. The unmarried woman cares for the things of the Lord that she may be holy both in body and in spirit. But she that is married cares for the things of the world how she may please her husband. 1 Corinthians 7:32-34

22. How great inconveniences are involved in wedlock and how many anxieties encompass it I have, I think, described shortly in my treatise— published against Helvidius — on the perpetual virginity of the blessed Mary. It would be tedious to go over the same ground now; and any one who pleases may draw from that fountain. But lest I should seem wholly to have passed over the matter, I will just say now that the apostle bids us pray without ceasing, 1 Thessalonians 5:17 and that he who in the married state renders his wife her due cannot so pray. Either we pray always and are virgins, or we cease to pray that we may fulfil the claims of marriage. Still he says: If a virgin marry she has not sinned. Nevertheless such shall have trouble in the flesh. 1 Corinthians 7:28 At the outset I promised that I should say little or nothing of the embarrassments of wedlock, and now I give you notice to the same effect. If you want to know from how many vexations a virgin is free and by how many a wife is fettered you should read Tertullian to a philosophic friend, and his other treatises on virginity, the blessed Cyprian's noble volume, the writings of Pope Damasus in prose and verse, and the treatises recently written for his sister by our own Ambrose. In these he has poured forth his soul with such a flood of eloquence that he has sought out, set forth, and put in order all that bears on the praise of virgins.

23. We must proceed by a different path, for our purpose is not the praise of virginity but its preservation. To know that it is a good thing is not enough: when we have chosen it we must guard it with jealous care. The first only requires judgment, and we share it with many; the second calls for toil, and few compete with us in it. He that shall endure unto the end, the Lord says, the same shall be saved, Matthew 24:13 and many are called but few are chosen. Therefore I conjure you before God and Jesus Christ and His elect angels to guard that which you have received, not readily exposing to the public gaze the vessels of the Lord's temple (which only the priests are by right allowed to see), that no profane person may look upon God's sanctuary. Uzzah, when he touched the ark which it was not lawful to touch, was struck down suddenly by death. 2 Samuel 6:6-7 And assuredly no gold or silver vessel was ever so dear to God as is the temple of a virgin's body. The shadow went before, but now the reality has come. You indeed may speak in all simplicity, and from motives of amiability may treat with courtesy the veriest strangers, but unchaste eyes see nothing aright. They fail to appreciate the beauty of the soul, and only value that of the body. Hezekiah showed God's treasure to the Assyrians, 2 Kings 20:12-13 who ought never to have seen what they were sure to covet. The consequence was that Judæa was torn by continual wars, and that the very first things carried away to Babylon were these vessels of the Lord. We find Belshazzar at his feast and among his concubines (vice always glories in defiling what is noble) drinking out of these sacred cups. Daniel 5:1-3

24. Never incline your ear to words of mischief. For men often say an improper word to make trial of a virgin's steadfastness, to see if she hears it with pleasure, and if she is ready to unbend at every silly jest. Such persons applaud whatever

you affirm and deny whatever you deny; they speak of you as not only holy but accomplished, and say that in you there is no guile. Behold, say they, a true handmaid of Christ; behold entire singleness of heart. How different from that rough, unsightly, countrified fright, who most likely never married because she could never find a husband. Our natural weakness induces us readily to listen to such flatterers; but, though we may blush and reply that such praise is more than our due, the soul within us rejoices to hear itself praised.

Like the ark of the covenant Christ's spouse should be overlaid with gold within and without; Exodus 25:11 she should be the guardian of the law of the Lord. Just as the ark contained nothing but the tables of the covenant, 1 Kings 8:9 so in you there should be no thought of anything that is outside. For it pleases the Lord to sit in your mind as He once sat on the mercy-seat and the cherubims. Exodus 25:22 As He sent His disciples to loose Him the foal of an ass that he might ride on it, so He sends them to release you from the cares of the world, that leaving the bricks and straw of Egypt, you may follow Him, the true Moses, through the wilderness and may enter the land of promise. Let no one dare to forbid you, neither mother nor sister nor kinswoman nor brother: The Lord has need of you. Matthew 21:1-3 Should they seek to hinder you, let them fear the scourges that fell on Pharaoh, who, because he would not let God's people go that they might serve Him, Exodus 7:16 suffered the plagues described in Scripture. Jesus entering into the temple cast out those things which belonged not to the temple. For God is jealous and will not allow the father's house to be made a den of robbers. Where money is counted, where doves are sold, where simplicity is stifled where, that is, a virgin's breast glows with cares of this world; straightway the veil of the temple is rent, Matthew 27:51 the bridegroom rises in anger, he says: Your house is left unto you desolate. Matthew 23:38 Read the gospel and see how Mary sitting at the feet of the Lord is set before the zealous Martha. In her anxiety to be hospitable Martha was preparing a meal for the Lord and His disciples; yet Jesus said to her: Martha, Martha, you are careful and troubled about many things. But few things are needful or one. And Mary has chosen that good part which shall not be taken away from her. Luke 10:41-42 Be then like Mary; prefer the food of the soul to that of the body. Leave it to your sisters to run to and fro and to seek how they may fitly welcome Christ. But do you, having once for all cast away the burden of the world, sit at the Lord's feet and say: I have found him whom my soul loves; I will hold him, I will not let him go. Song of Songs 3:4 And He will answer: My dove, my undefiled is but one; she is the only one of her mother, she is the choice one of her that bare her. Song of Songs 6:9 Now the mother of whom this is said is the heavenly Jerusalem. Galatians 4:26

25. Ever let the privacy of your chamber guard you; ever let the Bridegroom sport with you within. Genesis 26:8 Do you pray? You speak to the Bridegroom. Do you read? He speaks to you. When sleep overtakes you He will come behind and put His hand through the hole of the door, and your heart shall be moved for Him; and you will awake and rise up and say: I am sick of love. Then He will reply: A garden inclosed is my sister, my spouse; a spring shut up, a fountain sealed. Song of Songs 4:12

Go not from home nor visit the daughters of a strange land, though you have patriarchs for brothers and Israel for a father. Dinah went out and was seduced. Genesis xxxiv Do not seek the Bridegroom in the streets; do not go round the corners of the city. For though you may say: I will rise now and go about the city: in the streets and in the broad ways I will seek Him whom my soul loves, and though you may ask the watchmen: Saw ye Him whom my soul loves? Song of Songs 3:2-3 no one will deign to answer you. The Bridegroom cannot be found in the streets: Strait and narrow is the way which leads unto life. Matthew 7:14 So the Song goes on: I sought him but I could not find him: I called him but he gave me no answer. And would that failure to find Him were all. You will be wounded and stripped, you will lament and say: The watchmen that went about the city found me: they smote me, they wounded me, they took away my veil from me. Song of Songs 5:7 Now if one who could say: I sleep but my heart wakes, Song of Songs 5:2 and A bundle of myrrh is my well beloved unto me; he shall lie all night between my breasts; Song of Songs 1:13 if one who could speak thus suffered so much because she went abroad, what shall become of us who are but young girls; of us who, when the bride goes in with the Bridegroom, still remain without? Jesus is jealous. He does not choose that your face should be seen of others. You may excuse yourself and say: I have drawn close my veil, I have covered my face and I have sought You there and have said: 'Tell me, O Thou whom my soul loves, where You feed Your flock, where You make it to rest at noon. For why should I be as one that is veiled beside the flocks of Your companions?' Yet in spite of your excuses He will be angry, He will swell with anger and say: If you know not yourself, O you fairest among women, go your way forth by the footsteps of the flock and feed your goats beside the shepherd's tents. You may be fair, and of all faces yours may be the dearest to the Bridegroom; yet, unless you know yourself, and keep your heart with all diligence, Proverbs 4:23 unless also you avoid the eyes of the young men, you will be turned out of My bride-chamber to feed the goats, which shall be set on the left hand. Matthew 25:33

26. These things being so, my Eustochium, daughter, lady, fellow-servant, sister— these names refer the first to your age, the second to your rank, the third to your religious vocation, the last to the place which you hold in my affection— hear the words of Isaiah: Come, my people, enter thou into your chambers, and shut your doors about you: hide yourself as it were for a little moment, until the indignation of the Lord be overpast. Isaiah 26:20 Let foolish virgins stray abroad, but for your part stay at home with the Bridegroom; for if you shut your door, and, according to the precept of the Gospel, Matthew 6:6 pray to your Father in secret, He will come and knock, saying: Behold, I stand at the door and knock; if any man...open the door, I will come in to him, and will sup with him, and he with me. Revelation 3:20 Then straightway you will eagerly reply: It is the voice of my beloved that knocks, saying, Open to me, my sister, my love, my dove, my undefiled. It is impossible that you should refuse, and say: I have put off my coat; how shall I put it on? I have washed my feet; how shall I defile them? Song of Songs 5:2-3 Arise immediately and open. Otherwise while you linger He may pass on and you may have mournfully to say: I opened to my beloved, but my beloved had gone. Song of Songs 5:6 Why need the doors of your heart be closed

to the Bridegroom? Let them be open to Christ but closed to the devil according to the saying: If the spirit of him who has power rise up against you, leave not your place. Daniel, in that upper story to which he withdrew when he could no longer continue below, had his windows open toward Jerusalem. Do you too keep your windows open, but only on the side where light may enter and whence you may see the eye of the Lord. Open not those other windows of which the prophet says: Death has come up into our windows. Jeremiah 9:21

27. You must also be careful to avoid the snare of a passion for vainglory. How, Jesus says, can you believe which receive glory one from another? What an evil that must be the victim of which cannot believe! Let us rather say: You are my glorying, Jeremiah 9:24 and He that glories, let him glory in the Lord, 1 Corinthians 1:31 and If I yet pleased men I should not be the servant of Christ, Galatians 1:10 and Far be it from me to glory save in the cross of our Lord Jesus Christ, through whom the world has been crucified unto me and I unto the world; and once more: In God we boast all the day long; my soul shall make her boast in the Lord. When you do alms, let God alone see you. When you fast, be of a cheerful countenance. Let your dress be neither too neat nor too slovenly; neither let it be so remarkable as to draw the attention of passers-by, and to make men point their fingers at you. Is a brother dead? Has the body of a sister to be carried to its burial? Take care lest in too often performing such offices you die yourself. Do not wish to seem very devout nor more humble than need be, lest you seek glory by shunning it. For many, who screen from all men's sight their poverty, charity, and fasting, desire to excite admiration by their very disdain of it, and strangely seek for praise while they profess to keep out of its way. From the other disturbing influences which make men rejoice, despond, hope, and fear I find many free; but this is a defect which few are without, and he is best whose character, like a fair skin, is disfigured by the fewest blemishes. I do not think it necessary to warn you against boasting of your riches, or against priding yourself on your birth, or against setting yourself up as superior to others. I know your humility; I know that you can say with sincerity: Lord, my heart is not haughty nor my eyes lofty; I know that in your breast as in that of your mother the pride through which the devil fell has no place. It would be time wasted to write to you about it; for there is no greater folly than to teach a pupil what he knows already. But now that you have despised the boastfulness of the world, do not let the fact inspire you with new boastfulness. Harbor not the secret thought that having ceased to court attention in garments of gold you may begin to do so in mean attire. And when you come into a room full of brothers and sisters, do not sit in too low a place or plead that you are unworthy of a footstool. Do not deliberately lower your voice as though worn out with fasting; nor, leaning on the shoulder of another, mimic the tottering gait of one who is faint. Some women, it is true, disfigure their faces, that they may appear unto men to fast. Matthew 6:16 As soon as they catch sight of any one they groan, they look down; they cover up their faces, all but one eye, which they keep free to see with. Their dress is sombre, their girdles are of sackcloth, their hands and feet are dirty; only their stomachs— which cannot be seen— are hot with food. Of these the psalm is sung daily: The Lord will scatter the bones of them that please themselves. Others change their garb and assume the mien of men, being ashamed of being what they were born to

be— women. They cut off their hair and are not ashamed to look like eunuchs. Some clothe themselves in goat's hair, and, putting on hoods, think to become children again by making themselves look like so many owls.

28. But I will not speak only of women. Avoid men, also, when you see them loaded with chains and wearing their hair long like women, contrary to the apostle's precept, 1 Corinthians 11:14 not to speak of beards like those of goats, black cloaks, and bare feet braving the cold. All these things are tokens of the devil. Such an one Rome groaned over some time back in Antimus; and Sophronius is a still more recent instance. Such persons, when they have once gained admission to the houses of the high-born, and have deceived silly women laden with sins, ever learning and never able to come to the knowledge of the truth, 2 Timothy 3:6-7 feign a sad mien and pretend to make long fasts while at night they feast in secret. Shame forbids me to say more, for my language might appear more like invective than admonition. There are others— I speak of those of my own order— who seek the presbyterate and the diaconate simply that they may be able to see women with less restraint. Such men think of nothing but their dress; they use perfumes freely, and see that there are no creases in their leather shoes. Their curling hair shows traces of the tongs; their fingers glisten with rings; they walk on tiptoe across a damp road, not to splash their feet. When you see men acting in this way, think of them rather as bridegrooms than as clergymen. Certain persons have devoted the whole of their energies and life to the single object of knowing the names, houses, and characters of married ladies. I will here briefly describe the head of the profession, that from the master's likeness you may recognize the disciples. He rises and goes forth with the sun; he has the order of his visits duly arranged; he takes the shortest road; and, troublesome old man that he is, forces his way almost into the bedchambers of ladies yet asleep. If he sees a pillow that takes his fancy or an elegant table-cover— or indeed any article of household furniture— he praises it, looks admiringly at it, takes it into his hand, and, complaining that he has nothing of the kind, begs or rather extorts it from the owner. All the women, in fact, fear to cross the news-carrier of the town. Chastity and fasting are alike distasteful to him. What he likes is a savory breakfast— say off a plump young crane such as is commonly called a cheeper. In speech he is rude and forward, and is always ready to bandy reproaches. Wherever you turn he is the first man that you see before you. Whatever news is noised abroad he is either the originator of the rumor or its magnifier. He changes his horses every hour; and they are so sleek and spirited that you would take him for a brother of the Thracian king.

29. Many are the stratagems which the wily enemy employs against us. The serpent, we are told, was more subtle than any beast of the field which the Lord God had made. Genesis 3:1 And the apostle says: We are not ignorant of his devices. 2 Corinthians 2:11 Neither an affected shabbiness nor a stylish smartness becomes a Christian. If there is anything of which you are ignorant, if you have any doubt about Scripture, ask one whose life commends him, whose age puts him above suspicion, whose reputation does not belie him; one who may be able to say: I have espoused you to one husband that I may present you as a chaste virgin to Christ. Or if there should be none such able to explain, it is better to avoid

danger at the price of ignorance than to court it for the sake of learning. Remember that you walk in the midst of snares, and that many veteran virgins, of a chastity never called in question, have, on the very threshold of death, let their crowns fall from their hands.

If any of your handmaids share your vocation, do not lift up yourself against them or pride yourself because you are their mistress. You have all chosen one Bridegroom; you all sing the same psalms; together you receive the Body of Christ. Why then should your thoughts be different? You must try to win others, and that you may attract the more readily you must treat the virgins in your train with the greatest respect. If you find one of them weak in the faith, be attentive to her, comfort her, caress her, and make her chastity your treasure. But if a girl pretends to have a vocation simply because she desires to escape from service, read aloud to her the words of the apostle: It is better to marry than to burn. 1 Corinthians 7:9

Idle persons and busybodies, whether virgins or widows; such as go from house to house calling on married women and displaying an unblushing effrontery greater than that of a stage parasite, cast from you as you would the plague. For evil communications corrupt good manners, 1 Corinthians 15:33 and women like these care for nothing but their lowest appetites. They will often urge you, saying, My dear creature, make the best of your advantages, and live while life is yours, and Surely you are not laying up money for your children. Given to wine and wantonness, they instill all manner of mischief into people's minds, and induce even the most austere to indulge in enervating pleasures. And when they have begun to wax wanton against Christ they will marry, having condemnation because they have rejected their first faith. 1 Timothy 5:11-12

Do not seek to appear over-eloquent, nor trifle with verse, nor make yourself gay with lyric songs. And do not, out of affectation, follow the sickly taste of married ladies who, now pressing their teeth together, now keeping their lips wide apart, speak with a lisp, and purposely clip their words, because they fancy that to pronounce them naturally is a mark of country breeding. Accordingly they find pleasure in what I may call an adultery of the tongue. For what communion has light with darkness? And what concord has Christ with Belial? 2 Corinthians 6:14-15 How can Horace go with the psalter, Virgil with the gospels, Cicero with the apostle? Is not a brother made to stumble if he sees you sitting at meat in an idol's temple? 1 Corinthians 8:10 Although unto the pure all things are pure, Titus 1:15 and nothing is to be refused if it be received with thanksgiving, 1 Timothy 4:4 still we ought not to drink the cup of Christ, and, at the same time, the cup of devils. 1 Corinthians 10:21 Let me relate to you the story of my own miserable experience.

30. Many years ago, when for the kingdom of heaven's sake I had cut myself off from home, parents, sister, relations, and— harder still— from the dainty food to which I had been accustomed; and when I was on my way to Jerusalem to wage my warfare, I still could not bring myself to forego the library which I had formed for myself at Rome with great care and toil. And so, miserable man that I was, I would fast only that I might afterwards read Cicero. After many nights spent in

vigil, after floods of tears called from my inmost heart, after the recollection of my past sins, I would once more take up Plautus. And when at times I returned to my right mind, and began to read the prophets, their style seemed rude and repellent. I failed to see the light with my blinded eyes; but I attributed the fault not to them, but to the sun. While the old serpent was thus making me his plaything, about the middle of Lent a deep-seated fever fell upon my weakened body, and while it destroyed my rest completely— the story seems hardly credible— it so wasted my unhappy frame that scarcely anything was left of me but skin and bone. Meantime preparations for my funeral went on; my body grew gradually colder, and the warmth of life lingered only in my throbbing breast. Suddenly I was caught up in the spirit and dragged before the judgment seat of the Judge; and here the light was so bright, and those who stood around were so radiant, that I cast myself upon the ground and did not dare to look up. Asked who and what I was I replied: I am a Christian. But He who presided said: Thou liest, you are a follower of Cicero and not of Christ. For 'where your treasure is, there will your heart be also.' Matthew 6:21 Instantly I became dumb, and amid the strokes of the lash— for He had ordered me to be scourged— I was tortured more severely still by the fire of conscience, considering with myself that verse, In the grave who shall give you thanks? Yet for all that I began to cry and to bewail myself, saying: Have mercy upon me, O Lord: have mercy upon me. Amid the sound of the scourges this cry still made itself heard. At last the bystanders, falling down before the knees of Him who presided, prayed that He would have pity on my youth, and that He would give me space to repent of my error. He might still, they urged, inflict torture on me, should I ever again read the works of the Gentiles. Under the stress of that awful moment I should have been ready to make even still larger promises than these. Accordingly I made oath and called upon His name, saying: Lord, if ever again I possess worldly books, or if ever again I read such, I have denied You. Dismissed, then, on taking this oath, I returned to the upper world, and, to the surprise of all, I opened upon them eyes so drenched with tears that my distress served to convince even the incredulous. And that this was no sleep nor idle dream, such as those by which we are often mocked, I call to witness the tribunal before which I lay, and the terrible judgment which I feared. May it never, hereafter, be my lot to fall under such an inquisition! I profess that my shoulders were black and blue, that I felt the bruises long after I awoke from my sleep, and that thenceforth I read the books of God with a zeal greater than I had previously given to the books of men.

31. You must also avoid the sin of covetousness, and this not merely by refusing to seize upon what belongs to others, for that is punished by the laws of the state, but also by not keeping your own property, which has now become no longer yours. If have not been faithful, the Lord says, in that which is another man's, who shall give you that which is your own? Luke 16:12 That which is another man's is a quantity of gold or of silver, while that which is our own is the spiritual heritage of which it is elsewhere said: The ransom of a man's life is his riches. No man can serve two masters, for either he will hate the one and love the other; or else he will hold to the one and despise the other. You cannot serve God and Mammon. Matthew 6:24 Riches, that is; for in the heathen tongue of the Syrians riches are called mammon. The thorns which choke our faith Matthew 13:7, 22 are the taking

thought for our life. Matthew 6:25 Care for the things which the Gentiles seek after Matthew 6:32 is the root of covetousness.

But you will say: I am a girl delicately reared, and I cannot labor with my hands. Suppose that I live to old age and then fall sick, who will take pity on me? Hear Jesus speaking to the apostles: Take no thought what you shall eat; nor yet for your body what you shall put on. Is not the life more than meat, and the body than raiment? Behold the fowls of the air: for they sow not, neither do they reap nor gather into barns; yet your heavenly Father feeds them. Matthew 6:25-26 Should clothing fail you, set the lilies before your eyes. Should hunger seize you, think of the words in which the poor and hungry are blessed. Should pain afflict you, read Therefore I take pleasure in infirmities, and There was given to me a thorn in the flesh, the messenger of Satan to buffet me, lest I should be exalted above measure. Rejoice in all God's judgments; for does not the psalmist say: The daughters of Judah rejoiced because of your judgments, O Lord? Let the words be ever on your lips: Naked came I out of my mother's womb, and naked shall I return there; Job 1:21 and We brought nothing into this world, and it is certain we can carry nothing out. 1 Timothy 6:7

32. Today you may see women cramming their wardrobes with dresses, changing their gowns from day to day, and for all that unable to vanquish the moths. Now and then one more scrupulous wears out a single dress; yet, while she appears in rags, her boxes are full. Parchments are dyed purple, gold is melted into lettering, manuscripts are decked with jewels, while Christ lies at the door naked and dying. When they hold out a hand to the needy they sound a trumpet; Matthew 6:2 when they invite to a love-feast they engage a crier. I lately saw the noblest lady in Rome— I suppress her name, for I am no satirist— with a band of eunuchs before her in the basilica of the blessed Peter. She was giving money to the poor, a coin apiece; and this with her own hand, that she might be accounted more religious. Hereupon a by no means uncommon incident occurred. An old woman, full of years and rags, ran forward to get a second coin, but when her turn came she received not a penny but a blow hard enough to draw blood from her guilty veins.

The love of money is the root of all evil, 1 Timothy 6:10 and the apostle speaks of covetousness as being idolatry. Colossians 3:5 Seek ye first the kingdom of God and all these things shall be added unto you. Matthew 6:33 The Lord will never allow a righteous soul to perish of hunger. I have been young, the psalmist says, and now am old, yet have I not seen the righteous forsaken nor his seed begging bread. Elijah is fed by ministering ravens. 1 Kings 17:4, 6 The widow of Zarephath, who with her sons expected to die the same night, went without food herself that she might feed the prophet. He who had come to be fed then turned feeder, for, by a miracle, he filled the empty barrel. 1 Kings 17:9-16 The apostle Peter says: Silver and gold have I none, but such as I have give I you. In the name of Jesus Christ rise up and walk. Acts 3:6 But now many, while they do not say it in words, by their deeds declare: Faith and pity have I none; but such as I have, silver and gold, these I will not give you. Having food and raiment let us be therewith content. 1 Timothy 6:8 Hear the prayer of Jacob: If God will be with me and will keep me in this way that I go, and will give me bread to eat and raiment to put on, then shall the Lord be my God. Genesis 28:20-21 He prayed only for things necessary; yet, twenty years afterwards, he returned to the land of Canaan rich in substance and richer still in children. Genesis 32:5, 10 Numberless are the instances in Scripture which teach men to Beware of covetousness. Luke 12:15

33. As I have been led to touch to the subject— it shall have a treatise to itself if Christ permit— I will relate what took place not very many years ago at Nitria. A brother, more thrifty than covetous, and ignorant that the Lord had been sold for thirty pieces of silver, Matthew 26:15 left behind him at his death a hundred pieces of money which he had earned by weaving linen. As there were about five thousand monks in the neighborhood, living in as many separate cells, a council was held as to what should be done. Some said that the coins should be distributed among the poor; others that they should be given to the church, while others were for sending them back to the relatives of the deceased. However, Macarius, Pambo, Isidore and the rest of those called fathers, speaking by the Spirit, decided that they should be interred with their owner, with the words: Your money perish with you. Acts 8:20 Nor was this too harsh a decision; for so great fear has fallen upon all throughout Egypt, that it is now a crime to leave after one a single shilling.

34. As I have mentioned the monks, and know that you like to hear about holy things, lend an ear to me for a few moments. There are in Egypt three classes of monks. First, there are the cœnobites, called in their Gentile language Sauses, or, as we should say, men living in a community. Secondly, there are the anchorites, who live in the desert, each man by himself, and are so called because they have withdrawn from human society. Thirdly, there is the class called Remoboth, a very inferior and little regarded type, peculiar to my own province, or, at least, originating there. These live together in twos and threes, but seldom in larger numbers, and are bound by no rule; but do exactly as they choose. A portion of their earnings they contribute to a common fund, out of which food is provided for all. In most cases they reside in cities and strongholds; and, as though it were their workmanship which is holy, and not their life, all that they sell is extremely dear. They often quarrel because they are unwilling, while supplying their own food, to be subordinate to others. It is true that they compete with each other in fasting; they make what should be a private concern an occasion for a triumph. In everything they study effect: their sleeves are loose, their boots bulge, their garb is of the coarsest. They are always sighing, or visiting virgins, or sneering at the clergy; yet when a holiday comes, they make themselves sick— they eat so much.

35. Having then rid ourselves of these as of so many plagues, let us come to that more numerous class who live together, and who are, as we have said, called Cœnobites. Among these the first principle of union is to obey superiors and to do whatever they command. They are divided into bodies of ten and of a hundred, so that each tenth man has authority over nine others, while the hundredth has ten of these officers under him. They live apart from each other, in separate cells. According to their rule, no monk may visit another before the ninth hour; except the deans above mentioned, whose office is to comfort, with soothing words, those whose thoughts disquiet them. After the ninth hour they meet together to sing psalms and read the Scriptures according to usage. Then when the prayers have ended and all have sat down, one called the father stands up among them and

begins to expound the portion of the day. While he is speaking the silence is profound; no man ventures to look at his neighbor or to clear his throat. The speaker's praise is in the weeping of his hearers. Silent tears roll down their cheeks, but not a sob escapes from their lips. Yet when he begins to speak of Christ's kingdom, and of future bliss, and of the glory which is to come, every one may be noticed saying to himself, with a gentle sigh and uplifted eyes: Oh, that I had wings like a dove! For then would I fly away and be at rest. After this the meeting breaks up and each company of ten goes with its father to its own table. This they take in turns to serve each for a week at a time. No noise is made over the food; no one talks while eating. Bread, pulse and greens form their fare, and the only seasoning that they use is salt. Wine is given only to the old, who with the children often have a special meal prepared for them to repair the ravages of age and to save the young from premature decay. When the meal is over they all rise together, and, after singing a hymn, return to their dwellings. There each one talks till evening with his comrade thus: Have you noticed so-and-so? What grace he has! How silent he is! How soberly he walks! If any one is weak they comfort him; or if he is fervent in love to God, they encourage him to fresh earnestness. And because at night, besides the public prayers, each man keeps vigil in his own chamber, they go round all the cells one by one, and putting their ears to the doors, carefully ascertain what their occupants are doing. If they find a monk slothful, they do not scold him; but, dissembling what they know, they visit him more frequently, and at first exhort rather than compel him to pray more. Each day has its allotted task, and this being given in to the dean, is by him brought to the steward. This latter, once a month, gives a scrupulous account to their common father. He also tastes the dishes when they are cooked, and, as no one is allowed to say, I am without a tunic or a cloak or a couch of rushes, he so arranges that no one need ask for or go without what he wants. In case a monk falls ill, he is moved to a more spacious chamber, and there so attentively nursed by the old men, that he misses neither the luxury of cities nor a mother's kindness. Every Lord's day they spend their whole time in prayer and reading; indeed, when they have finished their tasks, these are their usual occupations. Every day they learn by heart a portion of Scripture. They keep the same fasts all the year round, but in Lent they are allowed to live more strictly. After Whitsuntide they exchange their evening meal for a midday one; both to satisfy the tradition of the church and to avoid overloading their stomachs with a double supply of food.

A similar description is given of the Essenes by Philo, Plato's imitator; also by Josephus, the Greek Livy, in his narrative of the Jewish captivity.

36. As my present subject is virgins, I have said rather too much about monks. I will pass on, therefore, to the third class, called anchorites, who go from the monasteries into the deserts, with nothing but bread and salt. Paul introduced this way of life; Antony made it famous, and— to go farther back still— John the Baptist set the first example of it. The prophet Jeremiah describes one such in the words: It is good for a man that he bear the yoke in his youth. He sits alone and keeps silence, because he has borne it upon him. He gives his cheek to him that smites him, he is filled full with reproach. For the Lord will not cast off forever. The struggle of the anchorites and their life— in the flesh, yet not of the flesh— I

will, if you wish, explain to you at some other time. I must now return to the subject of covetousness, which I left to speak of the monks. With them before your eyes you will despise, not only gold and silver in general, but earth itself and heaven. United to Christ, you will sing, The Lord is my portion.

37. Farther, although the apostle bids us to pray without ceasing, 1 Thessalonians 5:17 and although to the saints their very sleep is a supplication, we ought to have fixed hours of prayer, that if we are detained by work, the time may remind us of our duty. Prayers, as every one knows, ought to be said at the third, sixth and ninth hours, at dawn and at evening. No meal should be begun without prayer, and before leaving table thanks should be returned to the Creator. We should rise two or three times in the night, and go over the parts of Scripture which we know by heart. When we leave the roof which shelters us, prayer should be our armor; and when we return from the street we should pray before we sit down, and not give the frail body rest until the soul is fed. In every act we do, in every step we take, let our hand trace the Lord's cross. Speak against nobody, and do not slander your mother's son. Who are you that judgest the servant of another? To his own lord he stands or falls; yea, he shall be made to stand, for the Lord has power to make him stand. If you have fasted two or three days, do not think yourself better than others who do not fast. You fast and are angry; another eats and wears a smiling face. You work off your irritation and hunger in quarrels. He uses food in moderation and gives God thanks. Daily Isaiah cries: Is it such a fast that I have chosen, says the Lord? Isaiah 58:5 and again: In the day of your fast ye find your own pleasure, and oppress all your laborers. Behold ye fast for strife and contention, and to smite with the fist of wickedness. How fast ye unto me? What kind of fast can his be whose wrath is such that not only does the night go down upon it, but that even the moon's changes leave it unchanged?

38. Look to yourself and glory in your own success and not in others' failure. Some women care for the flesh and reckon up their income and daily expenditure: such are no fit models for you. Judas was a traitor, but the eleven apostles did not waver. Phygellus and Alexander made shipwreck; but the rest continued to run the race of faith. Say not: So-and-so enjoys her own property, she is honored of men, her brothers and sisters come to see her. Has she then ceased to be a virgin? In the first place, it is doubtful if she is a virgin. For the Lord sees not as man sees; for man looks upon the outward appearance, but the Lord looks on the heart. 1 Samuel 16:7 Again, she may be a virgin in body and not in spirit. According to the apostle, a true virgin is holy both in body and in spirit. 1 Corinthians 7:34 Lastly, let her glory in her own way. Let her override Paul's opinion and live in the enjoyment of her good things. But you and I must follow better examples.

Set before you the blessed Mary, whose surpassing purity made her meet to be the mother of the Lord. When the angel Gabriel came down to her, in the form of a man, and said: Hail, you that are highly favored; the Lord is with you, Luke 1:28 she was terror-stricken and unable to reply, for she had never been saluted by a man before. But, on learning who he was, she spoke, and one who had been afraid of a man conversed fearlessly with an angel. Now you, too, may be the Lord's mother. Take you a great roll and write in it with a man's pen Maher-shalal-hash-baz. And when you have gone to the prophetess, and have conceived in the womb, and have brought forth a son, say: Lord, we have been with child by your fear, we have been in pain, we have brought forth the spirit of your salvation, which we have wrought upon the earth. Then shall your Son reply: Behold my mother and my brethren. Matthew 12:49 And He whose name you have so recently inscribed upon the table of your heart, and have written with a pen upon its renewed surface — He, after He has recovered the spoil from the enemy, and has spoiled principalities and powers, nailing them to His cross Colossians 2:14-15 — having been miraculously conceived, grows up to manhood; and, as He becomes older, regards you no longer as His mother, but as His bride. To be as the martyrs, or as the apostles, or as Christ, involves a hard struggle, but brings with it a great reward.

All such efforts are only of use when they are made within the church's pale; we must celebrate the passover in the one house, Exodus 12:46 we must enter the ark with Noah, 1 Peter 3:20-21 we must take refuge from the fall of Jericho with the justified harlot, Rahab. James 2:25 Such virgins as there are said to be among the heretics and among the followers of the infamous Manes must be considered, not virgins, but prostitutes. For if— as they allege— the devil is the author of the body, how can they honor that which is fashioned by their foe? No; it is because they know that the name virgin brings glory with it, that they go about as wolves in sheep's clothing. Matthew 7:15 As antichrist pretends to be Christ, such virgins assume an honorable name, that they may the better cloak a discreditable life. Rejoice, my sister; rejoice, my daughter; rejoice, my virgin; for you have resolved to be, in reality, that which others insincerely feign.

39. The things that I have here set forth will seem hard to her who loves not Christ. But one who has come to regard all the splendor of the world as off-scourings, and to hold all things under the sun as vain, that he may win Christ; Philippians 3:8 one who has died with his Lord and risen again, and has crucified the flesh with its affections and lusts; he will boldly cry out: Who shall separate us from the love of Christ? Shall tribulation, or distress, or persecution, or famine, or nakedness, or peril, or sword? and again: I am persuaded that neither death nor life, nor angels, nor principalities nor powers, nor things present, nor things to come, nor height, nor depth, nor any other creature shall be able to separate us from the love of God which is in Christ Jesus, our Lord.

For our salvation the Son of God is made the Son of Man. Nine months He awaits His birth in the womb, undergoes the most revolting conditions, and comes forth covered with blood, to be swathed in rags and covered with caresses. He who shuts up the world in His fist is contained in the narrow limits of a manger. I say nothing of the thirty years during which he lives in obscurity, satisfied with the poverty of his parents. Luke 2:51-52 When He is scourged He holds His peace; when He is crucified, He prays for His crucifiers. What shall I render unto the Lord for all His benefits towards me? I will take the cup of salvation and call upon the name of the Lord. Precious in the sight of the Lord is the death of His saints. The only fitting return that we can make to Him is to give blood for blood; and, as we are redeemed by the blood of Christ, gladly to lay down our lives for our Redeemer. What saint has ever won his crown without first contending for it? Righteous Abel is murdered. Abraham is in danger of losing his wife. And, as I must not enlarge my book unduly, seek for yourself: you will find that all holy men have suffered adversity. Solomon alone lived in luxury and perhaps it was for this reason that he fell. For whom the Lord loves, He chastens, and scourges every son whom He receives. Hebrews 12:6 Which is best— for a short time to do battle, to carry stakes for the palisades, to bear arms, to faint under heavy bucklers, that ever afterwards we may rejoice as victors? Or to become slaves forever, just because we cannot endure for a single hour?

40. Love finds nothing hard; no task is difficult to the eager. Think of all that Jacob bore for Rachel, the wife who had been promised to him. Jacob, the Scripture says, served seven years for Rachel. And they seemed unto him but a few days for the love he had to her. Genesis 29:20 Afterwards he himself tells us what he had to undergo. In the day the drought consumed me and the frost by night. Genesis 31:40 So we must love Christ and always seek His embraces. Then everything difficult will seem easy; all things long we shall account short; and smitten with His arrows, we shall say every moment: Woe is me that I have prolonged my pilgrimage. For the sufferings of this present time are not worthy to be compared with the glory which shall be revealed in us. Romans 8:18 For tribulation works patience, and patience experience, and experience hope; and hope makes not ashamed. Romans 5:3-5 When your lot seems hard to bear read Paul's second epistle to the Corinthians: In labors more abundant; in stripes above measure; in prisons more frequent; in deaths oft. Of the Jews five times received I forty stripes save one; thrice was I beaten with rods; once was I stoned; thrice I suffered shipwreck; a night and a day I have been in the deep; in journeyings often, in perils of waters, in perils of robbers, in perils by my own countrymen, in perils by the heathen, in perils in the city, in perils in the wilderness, in perils in the sea, in perils among false brethren, in weariness and painfulness, in watchings often, in hunger and thirst, in fastings often, in cold and nakedness.
2 Corinthians 11:23-27 Which of us can claim the veriest fraction of the virtues here enumerated? Yet it was these which afterwards made him bold to say: I have finished my course, I have kept the faith. Henceforth there is laid up for me a crown of righteousness which the Lord, the righteous Judge, shall give me at that day. 2 Timothy 4:7-8

But we, if our food is less appetizing than usual, get sullen, and fancy that we do God a favor by drinking watered wine. And if the water brought to us is a trifle too warm, we break the cup and overturn the table and scourge the servant in fault until blood comes. The kingdom of heaven suffers violence and the violent take it by force. Matthew 11:12 Still, unless you use force you will never seize the kingdom of heaven. Unless you knock importunately you will never receive the sacramental bread. Luke 11:5-8 Is it not truly violence, think you, when the flesh desires to be as God and ascends to the place whence angels have fallen Isaiah 14:12-13 to judge angels?

41. Emerge, I pray you, for a while from your prison-house, and paint before your eyes the reward of your present toil, a reward which eye has not seen, nor ear heard, neither has it entered into the heart of man. 1 Corinthians 2:9 What will be the glory of that day when Mary, the mother of the Lord, shall come to meet you, accompanied by her virgin choirs! When, the Red Sea past and Pharaoh drowned

with his host, Miriam, Aaron's sister, her timbrel in her hand, shall chant to the answering women: Sing ye unto the Lord, for he has triumphed gloriously; the horse and his rider has he thrown into the sea. Exodus 15:20-21 Then shall Thecla fly with joy to embrace you. Then shall your Spouse himself come forward and say: Rise up, my love, my fair one, and come away, for lo! The winter is past, the rain is over and gone. Song of Songs 2:10-11 Then shall the angels say with wonder: Who is she that looks forth as the morning, fair as the moon, clear as the sun? Song of Songs 6:10 The daughters shall see you and bless you; yea, the queens shall proclaim and the concubines shall praise you. Song of Songs 6:9 And, after these, yet another company of chaste women will meet you. Sarah will come with the wedded; Anna, the daughter of Phanuel, with the widows. In the one band you will find your natural mother and in the other your spiritual. The one will rejoice in having borne, the other will exult in having taught you. Then truly will the Lord ride upon his ass, and thus enter the heavenly Jerusalem. Then the little ones (of whom, in Isaiah, the Saviour says: Behold, I and the children whom the Lord has given me Isaiah 8:18) shall lift up palms of victory and shall sing with one voice: Hosanna in the highest, blessed is he that comes in the name of the Lord, hosanna in the highest. Matthew 21:9 Then shall the hundred and forty and four thousand hold their harps before the throne and before the elders and shall sing the new song. And no man shall have power to learn that song save those for whom it is appointed. These are they which were not defiled with women; for they are virgins. These are they which follow the Lamb wherever he goes.
Revelation 14:1-4 As often as this life's idle show tries to charm you; as often as you see in the world some vain pomp, transport yourself in mind to Paradise, essay to be now what you will be hereafter, and you will hear your Spouse say: Set me as a sunshade in your heart and as a seal upon your arm. And then, strengthened in body as well as in mind, you, too, will cry aloud and say: Many waters cannot quench love, neither can the floods drown it. Song of Songs 8:7 as in the case of the seraphim, he believed it to be erroneous.

LETTER XIX

From Pope Damasus

A letter from Damasus to Jerome, in which he asks for an explanation of the word Hosanna (A.D. 383).

LETTER XX

To Pope Damasus

Jerome's reply to the foregoing. Exposing the error of Hilary of Poitiers, who supposed the expression to signify redemption of the house of David, he goes on to show that in the gospels it is a quotation from Psa. cxviii. 25 and that its true meaning is save now (so A.V.). Let us, he writes, leave the streamlets of conjecture and return to the fountain-head. It is from the Hebrew writings that the truth is to be drawn. Written at Rome A.D. 383.

LETTER XXI

To Damasus

In this letter Jerome, at the request of Damasus, gives a minutely detailed explanation of the parable of the prodigal son.

LETTER XXII

To Eustochium

Perhaps the most famous of all the letters. In it Jerome lays down at great length (1) the motives which ought to actuate those who devote themselves to a life of virginity, and (2) the rules by which they ought to regulate their daily conduct. The letter contains a vivid picture of Roman society as it then was— the luxury, profligacy, and hypocrisy prevalent among both men and women, besides some graphic autobiographical details (§§7, 30), and concludes with a full account of the three kinds of monasticism then practised in Egypt (§§34-36). Thirty years later Jerome wrote a similar letter to Demetrias (CXXX.), with which this ought to be compared. Written at Rome 384 A.D.

1. Hear, O daughter, and consider, and incline your ear; forget also your own people and your father's house, and the king shall desire your beauty. In this forty-fourth psalm God speaks to the human soul that, following the example of Abraham, it should go out from its own land and from its kindred, and should leave the Chaldeans, that is the demons, and should dwell in the country of the living, for which elsewhere the prophet sighs: I think to see the good things of the Lord in the land of the living. But it is not enough for you to go out from your own land unless you forget your people and your father's house; unless you scorn the flesh and cling to the bridegroom in a close embrace. Look not behind you, he says, neither stay thou in all the plain; escape to the mountain lest you be consumed. Genesis 19:17 He who has grasped the plough must not look behind him Luke 9:62 or return home from the field, or having Christ's garment, descend from the roof to fetch other raiment. Matthew 24:17-18 Truly a marvellous thing, a father charges his daughter not to remember her father. You are of your father the devil, and the lusts of your father it is your will to do. So it was said to the Jews. And in another place, He that commits sin is of the devil. 1 John 3:8 Born, in the first instance, of such parentage we are naturally black, and even when we have repented, so long as we have not scaled the heights of virtue, we may still say: I am black but comely, O you daughters of Jerusalem. Song of Songs 1:5 But you will say to me, I have left the home of my childhood; I have forgotten my father, I am born anew in Christ. What reward do I receive for this? The context shows— The king shall desire your beauty. This, then, is the great mystery. For this cause shall a man leave his father and his mother and shall be joined unto his wife, and they two shall be not as is there said, of one flesh, Ephesians 5:31-32 but of one spirit. Your bridegroom is not haughty or disdainful; He has married an Ethiopian woman. Numbers 12:1 When once you desire the wisdom of the true Solomon and come to Him, He will avow all His knowledge to you; He will lead you into His chamber with His royal hand; Song of Songs 1:4 He will miraculously change your complexion so that it shall be said of you, Who is this that goes up and has been made white?

2. I write to you thus, Lady Eustochium (I am bound to call my Lord's bride lady), to show you by my opening words that my object is not to praise the virginity which you follow, and of which you have proved the value, or yet to recount the

drawbacks of marriage, such as pregnancy, the crying of infants, the torture caused by a rival, the cares of household management, and all those fancied blessings which death at last cuts short. Not that married women are as such outside the pale; they have their own place, the marriage that is honorable and the bed undefiled. Hebrews 13:4 My purpose is to show you that you are fleeing from Sodom and should take warning by Lot's wife. Genesis 19:26 There is no flattery, I can tell you, in these pages. A flatterer's words are fair, but for all that he is an enemy. You need expect no rhetorical flourishes setting you among the angels, and while they extol virginity as blessed, putting the world at your feet.

3. I would have you draw from your monastic vow not pride but fear. Romans 11:20 You walk laden with gold; you must keep out of the robber's way. To us men this life is a race-course: we contend here, we are crowned elsewhere. No man can lay aside fear while serpents and scorpions beset his path. The Lord says: My sword has drunk its fill in heaven, and do you expect to find peace on the earth? No, the earth yields only thorns and thistles, and its dust is food for the serpent. For our wrestling is not against flesh and blood, but against the principalities, against the powers, against the world rulers of this darkness, against the spiritual hosts of wickedness in the heavenly places. We are hemmed in by hosts of foes, our enemies are upon every side. The weak flesh will soon be ashes: one against many, it fights against tremendous odds. Not till it has been dissolved, not till the Prince of this world has come and found no sin therein, not till then may you safely listen to the prophet's words: You shall not be afraid for the terror by night nor for the arrow that flies by day; nor for the trouble which haunts you in darkness; nor for the demon and his attacks at noonday. A thousand shall fall at your side and ten thousand at your right hand; but it shall not come near you. When the hosts of the enemy distress you, when your frame is fevered and your passions roused, when you say in your heart, What shall I do? Elisha's words shall give you your answer, Fear not, for they that be with us are more than they that be with them. 2 Kings 6:16 He shall pray, Lord, open the eyes of your handmaid that she may see. And then when your eyes have been opened you shall see a fiery chariot like Elijah's waiting to carry you to heaven, and shall joyfully sing: Our soul is escaped as a bird out of the snare of the fowlers: the snare is broken and we are escaped.

4. So long as we are held down by this frail body, so long as we have our treasure in earthen vessels; 2 Corinthians 4:7 so long as the flesh lusts against the spirit and the spirit against the flesh, Galatians 5:17 there can be no sure victory. Our adversary the devil goes about as a roaring lion seeking whom he may devour. 1 Peter 5:8 You make darkness, David says, and it is night: wherein all the beasts of the forest do creep forth. The young lions roar after their prey and seek their meat from God. The devil looks not for unbelievers, for those who are without, whose flesh the Assyrian king roasted in the furnace. Jeremiah 29:22 It is the church of Christ that he makes haste to spoil. According to Habakkuk, His food is of the choicest. A Job is the victim of his machinations, and after devouring Judas he seeks power to sift the [other] apostles. Luke 22:31 The Saviour came not to send peace upon the earth but a sword. Matthew 10:34 Lucifer fell, Lucifer who used to rise at dawn; Isaiah 14:12 and he who was bred up in a paradise of delight

had the well-earned sentence passed upon him, Though thou exalt yourself as the eagle, and though thou set your nest among the stars, thence will I bring you down, says the Lord. Obadiah 4 For he had said in his heart, I will exalt my throne above the stars of God, and I will be like the Most High. Isaiah 14:13-14 Wherefore God says every day to the angels, as they descend the ladder that Jacob saw in his dream, Genesis 28:12 I have said you are Gods and all of you are children of the Most High. But you shall die like men and fall like one of the princes. The devil fell first, and since God stands in the congregation of the Gods and judges among the Gods, the apostle writes to those who are ceasing to be Gods— Whereas there is among you envying and strife, are you not carnal and walk as men? 1 Corinthians 3:3

5. If, then, the apostle, who was a chosen vessel Acts 9:15 separated unto the gospel of Christ, Galatians 1:15 by reason of the pricks of the flesh and the allurements of vice keeps under his body and brings it into subjection, lest when he has preached to others he may himself be a castaway; 1 Corinthians 9:27 and yet, for all that, sees another law in his members warring against the law of his mind, and bringing him into captivity to the law of sin; Romans 7:23 if after nakedness, fasting, hunger, imprisonment, scourging and other torments, he turns back to himself and cries Oh, wretched man that I am, who shall deliver me from the body of this death? Romans 7:24 do you fancy that you ought to lay aside apprehension? See to it that God say not some day of you: The virgin of Israel is fallen and there is none to raise her up. Amos 5:2 I will say it boldly, though God can do all things He cannot raise up a virgin when once she has fallen. He may indeed relieve one who is defiled from the penalty of her sin, but He will not give her a crown. Let us fear lest in us also the prophecy be fulfilled, Good virgins shall faint. Amos 8:13 Notice that it is good virgins who are spoken of, for there are bad ones as well. Whosoever looks on a woman, the Lord says, to lust after her has committed adultery with her already in his heart. Matthew 5:28 So that virginity may be lost even by a thought. Such are evil virgins, virgins in the flesh, not in the spirit; foolish virgins, who, having no oil, are shut out by the Bridegroom.

6. But if even real virgins, when they have other failings, are not saved by their physical virginity, what shall become of those who have prostituted the members of Christ, and have changed the temple of the Holy Ghost into a brothel? Straightway shall they hear the words: Come down and sit in the dust, O virgin daughter of Babylon, sit on the ground; there is no throne, O daughter of the Chaldæans: for you shall no more be called tender and delicate. Take the millstone and grind meal; uncover your locks, make bare the legs, pass over the rivers; your nakedness shall be uncovered, yea, your shame shall be seen. Isaiah 47:1-3 And shall she come to this after the bridal-chamber of God the Son, after the kisses of Him who is to her both kinsman and spouse? Yes, she of whom the prophetic utterance once sang, Upon your right hand stood the queen in a vesture of gold wrought about with various colours, shall be made naked, and her skirts shall be discovered upon her face. Jeremiah 13:26 She shall sit by the waters of loneliness, her pitcher laid aside; and shall open her feet to every one that passes by, and shall be polluted to the crown of her head. Ezekiel 16:25 Better had it been for her to have submitted to the yoke of marriage, to have walked in level places, than thus,

aspiring to loftier heights, to fall into the deep of hell. I pray you, let not Zion the faithful city become a harlot: Isaiah 1:21 let it not be that where the Trinity has been entertained, there demons shall dance and owls make their nests, and jackals build. Let us not loose the belt that binds the breast. When lust tickles the sense and the soft fire of sensual pleasure sheds over us its pleasing glow, let us immediately break forth and cry: The Lord is on my side: I will not fear what the flesh can do unto me. When the inner man shows signs for a time of wavering between vice and virtue, say: Why art you cast down, O my soul, and why are you disquieted within me? Hope thou in God, for I shall yet praise Him who is the health of my countenance and my God. You must never let suggestions of evil grow on you, or a babel of disorder win strength in your breast. Slay the enemy while he is small; and, that you may not have a crop of tares, nip the evil in the bud. Bear in mind the warning words of the Psalmist: Hapless daughter of Babylon, happy shall he be that rewards you as you have served us. Happy shall he be that takes and dashes your little ones against the stones. Because natural heat inevitably kindles in a man sensual passion, he is praised and accounted happy who, when foul suggestions arise in his mind, gives them no quarter, but dashes them instantly against the rock. Now the Rock is Christ. 1 Corinthians 10:4

7. How often, when I was living in the desert, in the vast solitude which gives to hermits a savage dwelling-place, parched by a burning sun, how often did I fancy myself among the pleasures of Rome! I used to sit alone because I was filled with bitterness. Sackcloth disfigured my unshapely limbs and my skin from long neglect had become as black as an Ethiopian's. Tears and groans were every day my portion; and if drowsiness chanced to overcome my struggles against it, my bare bones, which hardly held together, clashed against the ground. Of my food and drink I say nothing: for, even in sickness, the solitaries have nothing but cold water, and to eat one's food cooked is looked upon as self-indulgence. Now, although in my fear of hell I had consigned myself to this prison, where I had no companions but scorpions and wild beasts, I often found myself amid bevies of girls. My face was pale and my frame chilled with fasting; yet my mind was burning with desire, and the fires of lust kept bubbling up before me when my flesh was as good as dead. Helpless, I cast myself at the feet of Jesus, I watered them with my tears, I wiped them with my hair: and then I subdued my rebellious body with weeks of abstinence. I do not blush to avow my abject misery; rather I lament that I am not now what once I was. I remember how I often cried aloud all night till the break of day and ceased not from beating my breast till tranquillity returned at the chiding of the Lord. I used to dread my very cell as though it knew my thoughts; and, stern and angry with myself, I used to make my way alone into the desert. Wherever I saw hollow valleys, craggy mountains, steep cliffs, there I made my oratory, there the house of correction for my unhappy flesh. There, also— the Lord Himself is my witness— when I had shed copious tears and had strained my eyes towards heaven, I sometimes felt myself among angelic hosts, and for joy and gladness sang: because of the savour of your good ointments we will run after you. Song of Songs 1:3-4

8. Now, if such are the temptations of men who, since their bodies are emaciated with fasting, have only evil thoughts to fear, how must it fare with a girl whose

surroundings are those of luxury and ease? Surely, to use the apostle's words, She is dead while she lives. 1 Timothy 5:6 Therefore, if experience gives me a right to advise, or clothes my words with credit, I would begin by urging you and warning you as Christ's spouse to avoid wine as you would avoid poison. For wine is the first weapon used by demons against the young. Greed does not shake, nor pride puff up, nor ambition infatuate so much as this. Other vices we easily escape, but this enemy is shut up within us, and wherever we go we carry him with us. Wine and youth between them kindle the fire of sensual pleasure. Why do we throw oil on the flame— why do we add fresh fuel to a miserable body which is already ablaze. Paul, it is true, says to Timothy drink no longer water, but use a little wine for your stomach's sake, and for your frequent infirmities. 1 Timothy 5:23 But notice the reasons for which the permission is given, to cure an aching stomach and a frequent infirmity. And lest we should indulge ourselves too much on the score of our ailments, he commands that but little shall be taken; advising rather as a physician than as an apostle (though, indeed, an apostle is a spiritual physician). He evidently feared that Timothy might succumb to weakness, and might prove unequal to the constant moving to and fro involved in preaching the Gospel. Besides, he remembered that he had spoken of wine wherein is excess, Ephesians 5:18 and had said, it is good neither to eat flesh nor to drink wine. Romans 14:21 Noah drank wine and became intoxicated; but living as he did in the rude age after the flood, when the vine was first planted, perhaps he did not know its power of inebriation. And to let you see the hidden meaning of Scripture in all its fullness (for the word of God is a pearl and may be pierced on every side) after his drunkenness came the uncovering of his body; self-indulgence culminated in lust. Genesis 9:20-21 First the belly is crammed; then the other members are roused. Similarly, at a later period, The people sat down to eat and to drink and rose up to play. Exodus 32:6 Lot also, God's friend, whom He saved upon the mountain, who was the only one found righteous out of so many thousands, was intoxicated by his daughters. And, although they may have acted as they did more from a desire of offspring than from love of sinful pleasure— for the human race seemed in danger of extinction— yet they were well aware that the righteous man would not abet their design unless intoxicated. In fact he did not know what he was doing, and his sin was not wilful. Still his error was a grave one, for it made him the father of Moab and Ammon, Genesis 19:30-38 Israel's enemies, of whom it is said: Even to the fourteenth generation they shall not enter into the congregation of the Lord forever.

9. When Elijah, in his flight from Jezebel, lay weary and desolate beneath the oak, there came an angel who raised him up and said, Arise and eat. And he looked, and behold there was a cake and a cruse of water at his head. 1 Kings 19:4-6 Had God willed it, might He not have sent His prophet spiced wines and dainty dishes and flesh basted into tenderness? When Elisha invited the sons of the prophets to dinner, he only gave them field-herbs to eat; and when all cried out with one voice: There is death in the pot, the man of God did not storm at the cooks (for he was not used to very sumptuous fare), but caused meal to be brought, and casting it in, sweetened the bitter mess 2 Kings 4:38-41 with spiritual strength as Moses had once sweetened the waters of Mara. Exodus 15:23-25 Again, when men were sent to arrest the prophet, and were smitten with physical and mental blindness,

that he might bring them without their own knowledge to Samaria, notice the food with which Elisha ordered them to be refreshed. Set bread and water, he said, before them, that they may eat and drink and go to their master. 2 Kings 6:18-23 And Daniel, who might have had rich food from the king's table, Daniel 1:8 preferred the mower's breakfast, brought to him by Habakkuk, which must have been but country fare. He was called a man of desires, because he would not eat the bread of desire or drink the wine of concupiscence.

10. There are, in the Scriptures, countless divine answers condemning gluttony and approving simple food. But as fasting is not my present theme and an adequate discussion of it would require a treatise to itself, these few observations must suffice of the many which the subject suggests. By them you will understand why the first man, obeying his belly and not God, was cast down from paradise into this vale of tears; and why Satan used hunger to tempt the Lord Himself in the wilderness; Matthew 4:2-3 and why the apostle cries: Meats for the belly and the belly for meats, but God shall destroy both it and them; 1 Corinthians 6:13 and why he speaks of the self-indulgent as men whose God is their belly. Philippians 3:19 For men invariably worship what they like best. Care must be taken, therefore, that abstinence may bring back to Paradise those whom satiety once drove out.

11. You will tell me, perhaps, that, high-born as you are, reared in luxury and used to lie softly, you cannot do without wine and dainties, and would find a stricter rule of life unendurable. If so, I can only say: Live, then, by your own rule, since God's rule is too hard for you. Not that the Creator and Lord of all takes pleasure in a rumbling and empty stomach, or in fevered lungs; but that these are indispensable as means to the preservation of chastity. Job was dear to God, perfect and upright before Him; Job 2:3 yet hear what he says of the devil: His strength is in the loins, and his force is in the navel.

The terms are chosen for decency's sake, but the reproductive organs of the two sexes are meant. Thus, the descendant of David, who, according to the promise is to sit upon his throne, is said to come from his loins. And the seventy-five souls descended from Jacob who entered Egypt are said to come out of his thigh. Genesis 46:26 So, also, when his thigh shrank after the Lord had wrestled with him, Genesis 32:24-25 he ceased to beget children. The Israelites, again, are told to celebrate the passover with loins girded and mortified. Exodus 12:11 God says to Job: Gird up your loins as a man. Job 38:3 John wears a leathern girdle. Matthew 3:4 The apostles must gird their loins to carry the lamps of the Gospel. Luke 12:35 When Ezekiel tells us how Jerusalem is found in the plain of wandering, covered with blood, he uses the words: Your navel has not been cut. Ezekiel 16:4-6 In his assaults on men, therefore, the devil's strength is in the loins; in his attacks on women his force is in the navel.

12. Do you wish for proof of my assertions? Take examples. Sampson was braver than a lion and tougher than a rock; alone and unprotected he pursued a thousand armed men; and yet, in Delilah's embrace, his resolution melted away. David was a man after God's own heart, and his lips had often sung of the Holy One, the future Christ; and yet as he walked upon his housetop he was fascinated by

Bathsheba's nudity, and added murder to adultery. 2 Samuel xi Notice here how, even in his own house, a man cannot use his eyes without danger. Then repenting, he says to the Lord: Against you, you only, have I sinned and done this evil in Your sight. Being a king he feared no one else. So, too, with Solomon. Wisdom used him to sing her praise, and he treated of all plants from the cedar tree that is in Lebanon even unto the hyssop that springs out of the wall; 1 Kings 4:33 and yet he went back from God because he was a lover of women. 1 Kings 11:1-4 And, as if to show that near relationship is no safeguard, Amnon burned with illicit passion for his sister Tamar. 2 Samuel xiii

13. I cannot bring myself to speak of the many virgins who daily fall and are lost to the bosom of the church, their mother: stars over which the proud foe sets up his throne, Isaiah 14:13 and rocks hollowed by the serpent that he may dwell in their fissures. You may see many women widows before wedded, who try to conceal their miserable fall by a lying garb. Unless they are betrayed by swelling wombs or by the crying of their infants, they walk abroad with tripping feet and heads in the air. Some go so far as to take potions, that they may insure barrenness, and thus murder human beings almost before their conception. Some, when they find themselves with child through their sin, use drugs to procure abortion, and when (as often happens) they die with their offspring, they enter the lower world laden with the guilt not only of adultery against Christ but also of suicide and child murder. Yet it is these who say: 'Unto the pure all things are pure;' Titus 1:15 my conscience is sufficient guide for me. A pure heart is what God looks for. Why should I abstain from meats which God has created to be received with thanksgiving? 1 Timothy 4:3 And when they wish to appear agreeable and entertaining they first drench themselves with wine, and then joining the grossest profanity to intoxication, they say Far be it from me to abstain from the blood of Christ. And when they see another pale or sad they call her wretch or Manichæan; quite logically, indeed, for on their principles fasting involves heresy. When they go out they do their best to attract notice, and with nods and winks encourage troops of young fellows to follow them. Of each and all of these the prophet's words are true: You have a whore's forehead; you refuse to be ashamed. Jeremiah 3:3 Their robes have but a narrow purple stripe, it is true; and their head-dress is somewhat loose, so as to leave the hair free. From their shoulders flutters the lilac mantle which they call ma-forte; they have their feet in cheap slippers and their arms tucked up tight-fitting sleeves. Add to these marks of their profession an easy gait, and you have all the virginity that they possess. Such may have eulogizers of their own, and may fetch a higher price in the market of perdition, merely because they are called virgins. But to such virgins as these I prefer to be displeasing.

14. I blush to speak of it, it is so shocking; yet though sad, it is true. How comes this plague of the agapetæ to be in the church? Whence come these unwedded wives, these novel concubines, these harlots, so I will call them, though they cling to a single partner? One house holds them and one chamber. They often occupy the same bed, and yet they call us suspicious if we fancy anything amiss. A brother leaves his virgin sister; a virgin, slighting her unmarried brother, seeks a brother in a stranger. Both alike profess to have but one object, to find spiritual consolation

from those not of their kin; but their real aim is to indulge in sexual intercourse. It is on such that Solomon in the book of proverbs heaps his scorn. Can a man take fire in his bosom, he says, and his clothes not be burned? Can one go upon hot coals and his feet not be burned? Proverbs 6:27-28

15. We cast out, then, and banish from our sight those who only wish to seem and not to be virgins. Henceforward I may bring all my speech to bear upon you who, as it is your lot to be the first virgin of noble birth in Rome, have to labor the more diligently not to lose good things to come, as well as those that are present. You have at least learned from a case in your own family the troubles of wedded life and the uncertainties of marriage. Your sister, Blæsilla, before you in age but behind you in declining the vow of virginity, has become a widow but seven months after she has taken a husband. Hapless plight of us mortals who know not what is before us! She has lost, at once, the crown of virginity and the pleasures of wedlock. And, although, as a widow, the second degree of chastity is hers, still can you not imagine the continual crosses which she has to bear, daily seeing in her sister what she has lost herself; and, while she finds it hard to go without the pleasures of wedlock, having a less reward for her present continence? Still she, too, may take heart and rejoice. The fruit which is an hundredfold and that which is sixtyfold both spring from one seed, and that seed is chastity. Matthew 13:8

16. Do not court the company of married ladies or visit the houses of the high-born. Do not look too often on the life which you despised to become a virgin. Women of the world, you know, plume themselves because their husbands are on the bench or in other high positions. And the wife of the emperor always has an eager throng of visitors at her door. Why do you, then, wrong your husband? Why do you, God's bride, hasten to visit the wife of a mere man? Learn in this respect a holy pride; know that you are better than they. And not only must you avoid intercourse with those who are puffed up by their husbands' honors, who are hedged in with troops of eunuchs, and who wear robes inwrought with threads of gold. You must also shun those who are widows from necessity and not from choice. Not that they ought to have desired the death of their husbands; but that they have not welcomed the opportunity of continence when it has come. As it is, they only change their garb; their old self-seeking remains unchanged. To see them in their capacious litters, with red cloaks and plump bodies, a row of eunuchs walking in front of them, you would fancy them not to have lost husbands but to be seeking them. Their houses are filled with flatterers and with guests. The very clergy, who ought to inspire them with respect by their teaching and authority, kiss these ladies on the forehead, and putting forth their hands (so that, if you knew no better, you might suppose them in the act of blessing), take wages for their visits. They, meanwhile, seeing that priests cannot do without them, are lifted up into pride; and as, having had experience of both, they prefer the license of widowhood to the restraints of marriage, they call themselves chaste livers and nuns. After an immoderate supper they retire to rest to dream of the apostles.

17. Let your companions be women pale and thin with fasting, and approved by their years and conduct; such as daily sing in their hearts: Tell me where you feed your flock, where you make it to rest at noon, and say, with true earnestness, I have a desire to depart and to be with Christ. Philippians 1:23 Be subject to your

parents, imitating the example of your spouse. Luke 2:51 Rarely go abroad, and if you wish to seek the aid of the martyrs seek it in your own chamber. For you will never need a pretext for going out if you always go out when there is need. Take food in moderation, and never overload your stomach. For many women, while temperate as regards wine, are intemperate in the use of food. When you rise at night to pray, let your breath be that of an empty and not that of an overfull stomach. Read often, learn all that you can. Let sleep overcome you, the roll still in your hands; when your head falls, let it be on the sacred page. Let your fasts be of daily occurrence and your refreshment such as avoids satiety. It is idle to carry an empty stomach if, in two or three days' time, the fast is to be made up for by repletion. When cloyed the mind immediately grows sluggish, and when the ground is watered it puts forth the thorns of lust. If ever you feel the outward man sighing for the flower of youth, and if, as you lie on your couch after a meal, you are excited by the alluring train of sensual desires; then seize the shield of faith, for it alone can quench the fiery darts of the devil. Ephesians 6:16 They are all adulterers, says the prophet; they have made ready their heart like an oven. But do you keep close to the footsteps of Christ, and, intent upon His words, say: Did not our heart burn within us by the way while Jesus opened to us the Scriptures? Luke 24:32 and again: Your word is tried to the uttermost, and your servant loves it. It is hard for the human soul to avoid loving something, and our mind must of necessity give way to affection of one kind or another. The love of the flesh is overcome by the love of the spirit. Desire is quenched by desire. What is taken from the one increases the other. Therefore, as you lie on your couch, say again and again: By night have I sought Him whom my soul loves. Song of Songs 3:1 Mortify, therefore, says the apostle, your members which are upon the earth. Colossians 3:5 Because he himself did so, he could afterwards say with confidence: I live, yet not I, but Christ, lives in me. Galatians 2:20 He who mortifies his members, and feels that he is walking in a vain show, is not afraid to say: I have become like a bottle in the frost. Whatever there was in me of the moisture of lust has been dried out of me. And again: My knees are weak through fasting; I forget to eat my bread. By reason of the voice of my groaning my bones cleave to my skin.

18. Be like the grasshopper and make night musical. Nightly wash your bed and water your couch with your tears. Watch and be like the sparrow alone upon the housetop. Sing with the spirit, but sing with the understanding also.
1 Corinthians 14:15 And let your song be that of the psalmist: Bless the Lord, O my soul; and forget not all his benefits; who forgives all your iniquities; who heals all your diseases; who redeems your life from destruction. Can we, any of us, honestly make his words our own: I have eaten ashes like bread and mingled my drink with weeping? Yet, should we not weep and groan when the serpent invites us, as he invited our first parents, to eat forbidden fruit, and when after expelling us from the paradise of virginity he desires to clothe us with mantles of skins such as that which Elijah, on his return to paradise, left behind him on earth?
2 Kings 2:13 Say to yourself: What have I to do with the pleasures of sense that so soon come to an end? What have I to do with the song of the sirens so sweet and so fatal to those who hear it? I would not have you subject to that sentence whereby condemnation has been passed upon mankind. When God says to Eve, In

pain and in sorrow you shall bring forth children, say to yourself, That is a law for a married woman, not for me. And when He continues, Your desire shall be to your husband, Genesis 3:16 say again: Let her desire be to her husband who has not Christ for her spouse. And when, last of all, He says, You shall surely die, Genesis 2:17 once more, say, Marriage indeed must end in death; but the life on which I have resolved is independent of sex. Let those who are wives keep the place and the time that properly belong to them. For me, virginity is consecrated in the persons of Mary and of Christ.

19. Some one may say, Do you dare detract from wedlock, which is a state blessed by God? I do not detract from wedlock when I set virginity before it. No one compares a bad thing with a good. Wedded women may congratulate themselves that they come next to virgins. Be fruitful, God says, and multiply, and replenish the earth. Genesis 1:28 He who desires to replenish the earth may increase and multiply if he will. But the train to which you belong is not on earth, but in heaven. The command to increase and multiply first finds fulfilment after the expulsion from paradise, after the nakedness and the fig-leaves which speak of sexual passion. Let them marry and be given in marriage who eat their bread in the sweat of their brow; whose land brings forth to them thorns and thistles, Genesis 3:18-19 and whose crops are choked with briars. My seed produces fruit a hundredfold. All men cannot receive God's saying, but they to whom it is given.

Some people may be eunuchs from necessity; I am one of free will. Matthew 19:11-12 There is a time to embrace and a time to refrain from embracing. There is a time to cast away stones, and a time to gather stones together. Ecclesiastes 3:5 Now that out of the hard stones of the Gentiles God has raised up children unto Abraham, Matthew 3:9 they begin to be holy stones rolling upon the earth. They pass through the whirlwinds of the world, and roll on in God's chariot on rapid wheels. Let those stitch coats to themselves who have lost the coat woven from the top throughout; John 19:23 who delight in the cries of infants which, as soon as they see the light, lament that they are born. In paradise Eve was a virgin, and it was only after the coats of skins that she began her married life. Now paradise is your home too. Keep therefore your birthright and say: Return unto your rest, O my soul. To show that virginity is natural while wedlock only follows guilt, what is born of wedlock is virgin flesh, and it gives back in fruit what in root it has lost. There shall come forth a rod out of the stem of Jesse, and a flower shall grow out of his roots. The rod is the mother of the Lord— simple, pure, unsullied; drawing no germ of life from without but fruitful in singleness like God Himself. The flower of the rod is Christ, who says of Himself: I am the rose of Sharon and the lily of the valleys. Song of Songs 2:1 In another place He is foretold to be a stone cut out of the mountain without hands, Daniel 2:45 a figure by which the prophet signifies that He is to be born a virgin of a virgin. For the hands are here a figure of wedlock as in the passage: His left hand is under my head and his right hand does embrace me. Song of Songs 2:6 It agrees, also, with this interpretation that the unclean animals are led into Noah's ark in pairs, while of the clean an uneven number is taken. Genesis 7:2 Similarly, when Moses and Joshua were bidden to remove their shoes because the ground on which they stood was holy, the command had a mystical meaning. So, too, when the disciples were appointed to preach the gospel they were told to take with them neither shoe nor shoe-latchet; and when the soldiers came to cast lots for the garments of Jesus John 19:23-24 they found no boots that they could take away. For the Lord could not Himself possess what He had forbidden to His servants.

20. I praise wedlock, I praise marriage, but it is because they give me virgins. I gather the rose from the thorns, the gold from the earth, the pearl from the shell. Does the plowman plow all day to sow? Isaiah 28:24 Shall he not also enjoy the fruit of his labor? Wedlock is the more honored, the more what is born of it is loved. Why, mother, do you grudge your daughter her virginity? She has been reared on your milk, she has come from your womb, she has grown up in your bosom. Your watchful affection has kept her a virgin. Are you angry with her because she chooses to be a king's wife and not a soldier's? She has conferred on you a high privilege; you are now the mother-in-law of God. Concerning virgins, says the apostle, I have no commandment of the Lord. 1 Corinthians 7:25 Why was this? Because his own virginity was due, not to a command, but to his free choice. For they are not to be heard who feign him to have had a wife; for, when he is discussing continence and commending perpetual chastity, he uses the words, I would that all men were even as I myself. And farther on, I say, therefore, to the unmarried and widows, it is good for them if they abide even as I.
1 Corinthians 7:7-8 And in another place, have we not power to lead about wives even as the rest of the apostles? 1 Corinthians 9:5 Why then has he no commandment from the Lord concerning virginity? Because what is freely offered is worth more than what is extorted by force, and to command virginity would have been to abrogate wedlock. It would have been a hard enactment to compel opposition to nature and to extort from men the angelic life; and not only so, it would have been to condemn what is a divine ordinance.

21. The old law had a different ideal of blessedness, for therein it is said: Blessed is he who has seed in Zion and a family in Jerusalem: and Cursed is the barren who bears not: and Your children shall be like olive-plants round about your table. Riches too are promised to the faithful and we are told that there was not one feeble person among their tribes. But now even to eunuchs it is said, Say not, behold I am a dry tree, Isaiah 56:3 for instead of sons and daughters you have a place forever in heaven. Now the poor are blessed, now Lazarus is set before Dives in his purple. Now he who is weak is counted strong. But in those days the world was still unpeopled: accordingly, to pass over instances of childlessness meant only to serve as types, those only were considered happy who could boast of children. It was for this reason that Abraham in his old age married Keturah; Genesis 25:1 that Leah hired Jacob with her son's mandrakes, Genesis 30:14-16 and that fair Rachel— a type of the church— complained of the closing of her womb. Genesis 30:1-2 But gradually the crop grew up and then the reaper was sent forth with his sickle. Elijah lived a virgin life, so also did Elisha and many of the sons of the prophets. To Jeremiah the command came: You shall not take you a wife. Jeremiah 16:2 He had been sanctified in his mother's womb, Jeremiah 1:5 and now he was forbidden to take a wife because the captivity was near. The apostle gives the same counsel in different words. I think, therefore, that this is good by reason of the present distress, namely that it is good for a man to be as he

is. What is this distress which does away with the joys of wedlock? The apostle tells us, in a later verse: The time is short: it remains that those who have wives be as though they had none. 1 Corinthians 7:29 Nebuchadnezzar is hard at hand. The lion is bestirring himself from his lair. What good will marriage be to me if it is to end in slavery to the haughtiest of kings? What good will little ones be to me if their lot is to be that which the prophet sadly describes: The tongue of the sucking child cleaves to the roof of his mouth for thirst; the young children ask for bread and no man breaks it unto them? Lamentations 4:4 In those days, as I have said, the virtue of continence was found only in men: Eve still continued to travail with children. But now that a virgin has conceived Isaiah 7:14 in the womb and has borne to us a child of which the prophet says that Government shall be upon his shoulder, and his name shall be called the mighty God, the everlasting Father, Isaiah 9:6 now the chain of the curse is broken. Death came through Eve, but life has come through Mary. And thus the gift of virginity has been bestowed most richly upon women, seeing that it has had its beginning from a woman. As soon as the Son of God set foot upon the earth, He formed for Himself a new household there; that, as He was adored by angels in heaven, angels might serve Him also on earth. Then chaste Judith once more cut off the head of Holofernes. Judith xiii Then Haman— whose name means iniquity— was once more burned in fire of his own kindling. Esther 7:10 Then James and John forsook father and net and ship and followed the Saviour: neither kinship nor the world's ties, nor the care of their home could hold them back. Then were the words heard: Whosoever will come after me, let him deny himself and take up his cross and follow me. Mark 8:34 For no soldier goes with a wife to battle. Even when a disciple would have buried his father, the Lord forbade him, and said: Foxes have holes and the birds of the air have nests, but the Son of Man has not where to lay His head. Matthew 8:20-22 So you must not complain if you have but scanty house-room. In the same strain, the apostle writes: He that is unmarried cares for the things that belong to the Lord, how he may please the Lord: but he that is married cares for the things that are of the world how he may please his wife. There is difference also between a wife and a virgin. The unmarried woman cares for the things of the Lord that she may be holy both in body and in spirit. But she that is married cares for the things of the world how she may please her husband. 1 Corinthians 7:32-34

22. How great inconveniences are involved in wedlock and how many anxieties encompass it I have, I think, described shortly in my treatise— published against Helvidius — on the perpetual virginity of the blessed Mary. It would be tedious to go over the same ground now; and any one who pleases may draw from that fountain. But lest I should seem wholly to have passed over the matter, I will just say now that the apostle bids us pray without ceasing, 1 Thessalonians 5:17 and that he who in the married state renders his wife her due cannot so pray. Either we pray always and are virgins, or we cease to pray that we may fulfil the claims of marriage. Still he says: If a virgin marry she has not sinned. Nevertheless such shall have trouble in the flesh. 1 Corinthians 7:28 At the outset I promised that I should say little or nothing of the embarrassments of wedlock, and now I give you notice to the same effect. If you want to know from how many vexations a virgin is free and by how many a wife is fettered you should read Tertullian to a philosophic friend, and his other treatises on virginity, the blessed Cyprian's noble

volume, the writings of Pope Damasus in prose and verse, and the treatises recently written for his sister by our own Ambrose. In these he has poured forth his soul with such a flood of eloquence that he has sought out, set forth, and put in order all that bears on the praise of virgins.

23. We must proceed by a different path, for our purpose is not the praise of virginity but its preservation. To know that it is a good thing is not enough: when we have chosen it we must guard it with jealous care. The first only requires judgment, and we share it with many; the second calls for toil, and few compete with us in it. He that shall endure unto the end, the Lord says, the same shall be saved, Matthew 24:13 and many are called but few are chosen. Therefore I conjure you before God and Jesus Christ and His elect angels to guard that which you have received, not readily exposing to the public gaze the vessels of the Lord's temple (which only the priests are by right allowed to see), that no profane person may look upon God's sanctuary. Uzzah, when he touched the ark which it was not lawful to touch, was struck down suddenly by death. 2 Samuel 6:6-7 And assuredly no gold or silver vessel was ever so dear to God as is the temple of a virgin's body. The shadow went before, but now the reality has come. You indeed may speak in all simplicity, and from motives of amiability may treat with courtesy the veriest strangers, but unchaste eyes see nothing aright. They fail to appreciate the beauty of the soul, and only value that of the body. Hezekiah showed God's treasure to the Assyrians, 2 Kings 20:12-13 who ought never to have seen what they were sure to covet. The consequence was that Judæa was torn by continual wars, and that the very first things carried away to Babylon were these vessels of the Lord. We find Belshazzar at his feast and among his concubines (vice always glories in defiling what is noble) drinking out of these sacred cups. Daniel 5:1-3

24. Never incline your ear to words of mischief. For men often say an improper word to make trial of a virgin's steadfastness, to see if she hears it with pleasure, and if she is ready to unbend at every silly jest. Such persons applaud whatever you affirm and deny whatever you deny; they speak of you as not only holy but accomplished, and say that in you there is no guile. Behold, say they, a true hand-maid of Christ; behold entire singleness of heart. How different from that rough, unsightly, countrified fright, who most likely never married because she could never find a husband. Our natural weakness induces us readily to listen to such flatterers; but, though we may blush and reply that such praise is more than our due, the soul within us rejoices to hear itself praised.

Like the ark of the covenant Christ's spouse should be overlaid with gold within and without; Exodus 25:11 she should be the guardian of the law of the Lord. Just as the ark contained nothing but the tables of the covenant, 1 Kings 8:9 so in you there should be no thought of anything that is outside. For it pleases the Lord to sit in your mind as He once sat on the mercy-seat and the cherubims. Exodus 25:22 As He sent His disciples to loose Him the foal of an ass that he might ride on it, so He sends them to release you from the cares of the world, that leaving the bricks and straw of Egypt, you may follow Him, the true Moses, through the wilderness and may enter the land of promise. Let no one dare to forbid you, neither mother nor sister nor kinswoman nor brother: The Lord has need of you. Matthew 21:1-3

Should they seek to hinder you, let them fear the scourges that fell on Pharaoh, who, because he would not let God's people go that they might serve Him, Exodus 7:16 suffered the plagues described in Scripture. Jesus entering into the temple cast out those things which belonged not to the temple. For God is jealous and will not allow the father's house to be made a den of robbers. Where money is counted, where doves are sold, where simplicity is stifled where, that is, a virgin's breast glows with cares of this world; straightway the veil of the temple is rent, Matthew 27:51 the bridegroom rises in anger, he says: Your house is left unto you desolate. Matthew 23:38 Read the gospel and see how Mary sitting at the feet of the Lord is set before the zealous Martha. In her anxiety to be hospitable Martha was preparing a meal for the Lord and His disciples; yet Jesus said to her: Martha, Martha, you are careful and troubled about many things. But few things are needful or one. And Mary has chosen that good part which shall not be taken away from her. Luke 10:41-42 Be then like Mary; prefer the food of the soul to that of the body. Leave it to your sisters to run to and fro and to seek how they may fitly welcome Christ. But do you, having once for all cast away the burden of the world, sit at the Lord's feet and say: I have found him whom my soul loves; I will hold him, I will not let him go. Song of Songs 3:4 And He will answer: My dove, my undefiled is but one; she is the only one of her mother, she is the choice one of her that bare her. Song of Songs 6:9 Now the mother of whom this is said is the heavenly Jerusalem. Galatians 4:26

25. Ever let the privacy of your chamber guard you; ever let the Bridegroom sport with you within. Genesis 26:8 Do you pray? You speak to the Bridegroom. Do you read? He speaks to you. When sleep overtakes you He will come behind and put His hand through the hole of the door, and your heart shall be moved for Him; and you will awake and rise up and say: I am sick of love. Then He will reply: A garden inclosed is my sister, my spouse; a spring shut up, a fountain sealed. Song of Songs 4:12

Go not from home nor visit the daughters of a strange land, though you have patriarchs for brothers and Israel for a father. Dinah went out and was seduced. Genesis xxxiv Do not seek the Bridegroom in the streets; do not go round the corners of the city. For though you may say: I will rise now and go about the city: in the streets and in the broad ways I will seek Him whom my soul loves, and though you may ask the watchmen: Saw ye Him whom my soul loves? Song of Songs 3:2-3 no one will deign to answer you. The Bridegroom cannot be found in the streets: Strait and narrow is the way which leads unto life. Matthew 7:14 So the Song goes on: I sought him but I could not find him: I called him but he gave me no answer. And would that failure to find Him were all. You will be wounded and stripped, you will lament and say: The watchmen that went about the city found me: they smote me, they wounded me, they took away my veil from me. Song of Songs 5:7 Now if one who could say: I sleep but my heart wakes, Song of Songs 5:2 and A bundle of myrrh is my well beloved unto me; he shall lie all night between my breasts; Song of Songs 1:13 if one who could speak thus suffered so much because she went abroad, what shall become of us who are but young girls; of us who, when the bride goes in with the Bridegroom, still remain without? Jesus is jealous. He does not choose that your face should be seen of others. You may excuse yourself and say: I have drawn close my veil, I have covered my face and I have sought You there and have said: 'Tell me, O Thou whom my soul loves, where You feed Your flock, where You make it to rest at noon. For why should I be as one that is veiled beside the flocks of Your companions?' Yet in spite of your excuses He will be angry, He will swell with anger and say: If you know not yourself, O you fairest among women, go your way forth by the footsteps of the flock and feed your goats beside the shepherd's tents. You may be fair, and of all faces yours may be the dearest to the Bridegroom; yet, unless you know yourself, and keep your heart with all diligence, Proverbs 4:23 unless also you avoid the eyes of the young men, you will be turned out of My bride-chamber to feed the goats, which shall be set on the left hand. Matthew 25:33

26. These things being so, my Eustochium, daughter, lady, fellow-servant, sister— these names refer the first to your age, the second to your rank, the third to your religious vocation, the last to the place which you hold in my affection— hear the words of Isaiah: Come, my people, enter thou into your chambers, and shut your doors about you: hide yourself as it were for a little moment, until the indignation of the Lord be overpast. Isaiah 26:20 Let foolish virgins stray abroad, but for your part stay at home with the Bridegroom; for if you shut your door, and, according to the precept of the Gospel, Matthew 6:6 pray to your Father in secret, He will come and knock, saying: Behold, I stand at the door and knock; if any man...open the door, I will come in to him, and will sup with him, and he with me. Revelation 3:20 Then straightway you will eagerly reply: It is the voice of my beloved that knocks, saying, Open to me, my sister, my love, my dove, my undefiled. It is impossible that you should refuse, and say: I have put off my coat; how shall I put it on? I have washed my feet; how shall I defile them? Song of Songs 5:2-3 Arise immediately and open. Otherwise while you linger He may pass on and you may have mournfully to say: I opened to my beloved, but my beloved had gone. Song of Songs 5:6 Why need the doors of your heart be closed to the Bridegroom? Let them be open to Christ but closed to the devil according to the saying: If the spirit of him who has power rise up against you, leave not your place. Daniel, in that upper story to which he withdrew when he could no longer continue below, had his windows open toward Jerusalem. Do you too keep your windows open, but only on the side where light may enter and whence you may see the eye of the Lord. Open not those other windows of which the prophet says: Death has come up into our windows. Jeremiah 9:21

27. You must also be careful to avoid the snare of a passion for vainglory. How, Jesus says, can you believe which receive glory one from another? What an evil that must be the victim of which cannot believe! Let us rather say: You are my glorying, Jeremiah 9:24 and He that glories, let him glory in the Lord, 1 Corinthians 1:31 and If I yet pleased men I should not be the servant of Christ, Galatians 1:10 and Far be it from me to glory save in the cross of our Lord Jesus Christ, through whom the world has been crucified unto me and I unto the world; and once more: In God we boast all the day long; my soul shall make her boast in the Lord. When you do alms, let God alone see you. When you fast, be of a cheerful countenance. Let your dress be neither too neat nor too slovenly; neither

let it be so remarkable as to draw the attention of passers-by, and to make men point their fingers at you. Is a brother dead? Has the body of a sister to be carried to its burial? Take care lest in too often performing such offices you die yourself. Do not wish to seem very devout nor more humble than need be, lest you seek glory by shunning it. For many, who screen from all men's sight their poverty, charity, and fasting, desire to excite admiration by their very disdain of it, and strangely seek for praise while they profess to keep out of its way. From the other disturbing influences which make men rejoice, despond, hope, and fear I find many free; but this is a defect which few are without, and he is best whose character, like a fair skin, is disfigured by the fewest blemishes. I do not think it necessary to warn you against boasting of your riches, or against priding yourself on your birth, or against setting yourself up as superior to others. I know your humility; I know that you can say with sincerity: Lord, my heart is not haughty nor my eyes lofty; I know that in your breast as in that of your mother the pride through which the devil fell has no place. It would be time wasted to write to you about it; for there is no greater folly than to teach a pupil what he knows already. But now that you have despised the boastfulness of the world, do not let the fact inspire you with new boastfulness. Harbor not the secret thought that having ceased to court attention in garments of gold you may begin to do so in mean attire. And when you come into a room full of brothers and sisters, do not sit in too low a place or plead that you are unworthy of a footstool. Do not deliberately lower your voice as though worn out with fasting; nor, leaning on the shoulder of another, mimic the tottering gait of one who is faint. Some women, it is true, disfigure their faces, that they may appear unto men to fast. Matthew 6:16 As soon as they catch sight of any one they groan, they look down; they cover up their faces, all but one eye, which they keep free to see with. Their dress is sombre, their girdles are of sackcloth, their hands and feet are dirty; only their stomachs— which cannot be seen— are hot with food. Of these the psalm is sung daily: The Lord will scatter the bones of them that please themselves. Others change their garb and assume the mien of men, being ashamed of being what they were born to be— women. They cut off their hair and are not ashamed to look like eunuchs. Some clothe themselves in goat's hair, and, putting on hoods, think to become children again by making themselves look like so many owls.

28. But I will not speak only of women. Avoid men, also, when you see them loaded with chains and wearing their hair long like women, contrary to the apostle's precept, 1 Corinthians 11:14 not to speak of beards like those of goats, black cloaks, and bare feet braving the cold. All these things are tokens of the devil. Such an one Rome groaned over some time back in Antimus; and Sophronius is a still more recent instance. Such persons, when they have once gained admission to the houses of the high-born, and have deceived silly women laden with sins, ever learning and never able to come to the knowledge of the truth, 2 Timothy 3:6-7 feign a sad mien and pretend to make long fasts while at night they feast in secret. Shame forbids me to say more, for my language might appear more like invective than admonition. There are others— I speak of those of my own order— who seek the presbyterate and the diaconate simply that they may be able to see women with less restraint. Such men think of nothing but their dress; they use perfumes freely, and see that there are no creases in their leather

shoes. Their curling hair shows traces of the tongs; their fingers glisten with rings; they walk on tiptoe across a damp road, not to splash their feet. When you see men acting in this way, think of them rather as bridegrooms than as clergymen. Certain persons have devoted the whole of their energies and life to the single object of knowing the names, houses, and characters of married ladies. I will here briefly describe the head of the profession, that from the master's likeness you may recognize the disciples. He rises and goes forth with the sun; he has the order of his visits duly arranged; he takes the shortest road; and, troublesome old man that he is, forces his way almost into the bedchambers of ladies yet asleep. If he sees a pillow that takes his fancy or an elegant table-cover— or indeed any article of household furniture— he praises it, looks admiringly at it, takes it into his hand, and, complaining that he has nothing of the kind, begs or rather extorts it from the owner. All the women, in fact, fear to cross the news-carrier of the town. Chastity and fasting are alike distasteful to him. What he likes is a savory breakfast— say off a plump young crane such as is commonly called a cheeper. In speech he is rude and forward, and is always ready to bandy reproaches. Wherever you turn he is the first man that you see before you. Whatever news is noised abroad he is either the originator of the rumor or its magnifier. He changes his horses every hour; and they are so sleek and spirited that you would take him for a brother of the Thracian king.

29. Many are the stratagems which the wily enemy employs against us. The serpent, we are told, was more subtle than any beast of the field which the Lord God had made. Genesis 3:1 And the apostle says: We are not ignorant of his devices. 2 Corinthians 2:11 Neither an affected shabbiness nor a stylish smartness becomes a Christian. If there is anything of which you are ignorant, if you have any doubt about Scripture, ask one whose life commends him, whose age puts him above suspicion, whose reputation does not belie him; one who may be able to say: I have espoused you to one husband that I may present you as a chaste virgin to Christ. Or if there should be none such able to explain, it is better to avoid danger at the price of ignorance than to court it for the sake of learning. Remember that you walk in the midst of snares, and that many veteran virgins, of a chastity never called in question, have, on the very threshold of death, let their crowns fall from their hands.

If any of your handmaids share your vocation, do not lift up yourself against them or pride yourself because you are their mistress. You have all chosen one Bridegroom; you all sing the same psalms; together you receive the Body of Christ. Why then should your thoughts be different? You must try to win others, and that you may attract the more readily you must treat the virgins in your train with the greatest respect. If you find one of them weak in the faith, be attentive to her, comfort her, caress her, and make her chastity your treasure. But if a girl pretends to have a vocation simply because she desires to escape from service, read aloud to her the words of the apostle: It is better to marry than to burn. 1 Corinthians 7:9

Idle persons and busybodies, whether virgins or widows; such as go from house to house calling on married women and displaying an unblushing effrontery greater than that of a stage parasite, cast from you as you would the plague. For evil communications corrupt good manners, 1 Corinthians 15:33 and women like these care for nothing but their lowest appetites. They will often urge you, saying, My dear creature, make the best of your advantages, and live while life is yours, and Surely you are not laying up money for your children. Given to wine and wantonness, they instill all manner of mischief into people's minds, and induce even the most austere to indulge in enervating pleasures. And when they have begun to wax wanton against Christ they will marry, having condemnation because they have rejected their first faith. 1 Timothy 5:11-12

Do not seek to appear over-eloquent, nor trifle with verse, nor make yourself gay with lyric songs. And do not, out of affectation, follow the sickly taste of married ladies who, now pressing their teeth together, now keeping their lips wide apart, speak with a lisp, and purposely clip their words, because they fancy that to pronounce them naturally is a mark of country breeding. Accordingly they find pleasure in what I may call an adultery of the tongue. For what communion has light with darkness? And what concord has Christ with Belial? 2 Corinthians 6:14-15 How can Horace go with the psalter, Virgil with the gospels, Cicero with the apostle? Is not a brother made to stumble if he sees you sitting at meat in an idol's temple? 1 Corinthians 8:10 Although unto the pure all things are pure, Titus 1:15 and nothing is to be refused if it be received with thanksgiving, 1 Timothy 4:4 still we ought not to drink the cup of Christ, and, at the same time, the cup of devils. 1 Corinthians 10:21 Let me relate to you the story of my own miserable experience.

30. Many years ago, when for the kingdom of heaven's sake I had cut myself off from home, parents, sister, relations, and— harder still— from the dainty food to which I had been accustomed; and when I was on my way to Jerusalem to wage my warfare, I still could not bring myself to forego the library which I had formed for myself at Rome with great care and toil. And so, miserable man that I was, I would fast only that I might afterwards read Cicero. After many nights spent in vigil, after floods of tears called from my inmost heart, after the recollection of my past sins, I would once more take up Plautus. And when at times I returned to my right mind, and began to read the prophets, their style seemed rude and repellent. I failed to see the light with my blinded eyes; but I attributed the fault not to them, but to the sun. While the old serpent was thus making me his plaything, about the middle of Lent a deep-seated fever fell upon my weakened body, and while it destroyed my rest completely— the story seems hardly credible— it so wasted my unhappy frame that scarcely anything was left of me but skin and bone. Meantime preparations for my funeral went on; my body grew gradually colder, and the warmth of life lingered only in my throbbing breast. Suddenly I was caught up in the spirit and dragged before the judgment seat of the Judge; and here the light was so bright, and those who stood around were so radiant, that I cast myself upon the ground and did not dare to look up. Asked who and what I was I replied: I am a Christian. But He who presided said: Thou liest, you are a follower of Cicero and not of Christ. For 'where your treasure is, there will your heart be also.' Matthew 6:21 Instantly I became dumb, and amid the strokes of the lash— for He had ordered me to be scourged— I was tortured more severely still by the fire of conscience, considering with myself that verse, In the grave who shall give you

thanks? Yet for all that I began to cry and to bewail myself, saying: Have mercy upon me, O Lord: have mercy upon me. Amid the sound of the scourges this cry still made itself heard. At last the bystanders, falling down before the knees of Him who presided, prayed that He would have pity on my youth, and that He would give me space to repent of my error. He might still, they urged, inflict torture on me, should I ever again read the works of the Gentiles. Under the stress of that awful moment I should have been ready to make even still larger promises than these. Accordingly I made oath and called upon His name, saying: Lord, if ever again I possess worldly books, or if ever again I read such, I have denied You. Dismissed, then, on taking this oath, I returned to the upper world, and, to the surprise of all, I opened upon them eyes so drenched with tears that my distress served to convince even the incredulous. And that this was no sleep nor idle dream, such as those by which we are often mocked, I call to witness the tribunal before which I lay, and the terrible judgment which I feared. May it never, hereafter, be my lot to fall under such an inquisition! I profess that my shoulders were black and blue, that I felt the bruises long after I awoke from my sleep, and that thenceforth I read the books of God with a zeal greater than I had previously given to the books of men.

31. You must also avoid the sin of covetousness, and this not merely by refusing to seize upon what belongs to others, for that is punished by the laws of the state, but also by not keeping your own property, which has now become no longer yours. If have not been faithful, the Lord says, in that which is another man's, who shall give you that which is your own? Luke 16:12 That which is another man's is a quantity of gold or of silver, while that which is our own is the spiritual heritage of which it is elsewhere said: The ransom of a man's life is his riches. No man can serve two masters, for either he will hate the one and love the other; or else he will hold to the one and despise the other. You cannot serve God and Mammon. Matthew 6:24 Riches, that is; for in the heathen tongue of the Syrians riches are called mammon. The thorns which choke our faith Matthew 13:7, 22 are the taking thought for our life. Matthew 6:25 Care for the things which the Gentiles seek after Matthew 6:32 is the root of covetousness.

But you will say: I am a girl delicately reared, and I cannot labor with my hands. Suppose that I live to old age and then fall sick, who will take pity on me? Hear Jesus speaking to the apostles: Take no thought what you shall eat; nor yet for your body what you shall put on. Is not the life more than meat, and the body than raiment? Behold the fowls of the air: for they sow not, neither do they reap nor gather into barns; yet your heavenly Father feeds them. Matthew 6:25-26 Should clothing fail you, set the lilies before your eyes. Should hunger seize you, think of the words in which the poor and hungry are blessed. Should pain afflict you, read Therefore I take pleasure in infirmities, and There was given to me a thorn in the flesh, the messenger of Satan to buffet me, lest I should be exalted above measure. Rejoice in all God's judgments; for does not the psalmist say: The daughters of Judah rejoiced because of your judgments, O Lord? Let the words be ever on your lips: Naked came I out of my mother's womb, and naked shall I return there; Job 1:21 and We brought nothing into this world, and it is certain we can carry nothing out. 1 Timothy 6:7

32. Today you may see women cramming their wardrobes with dresses, changing their gowns from day to day, and for all that unable to vanquish the moths. Now and then one more scrupulous wears out a single dress; yet, while she appears in rags, her boxes are full. Parchments are dyed purple, gold is melted into lettering, manuscripts are decked with jewels, while Christ lies at the door naked and dying. When they hold out a hand to the needy they sound a trumpet; Matthew 6:2 when they invite to a love-feast they engage a crier. I lately saw the noblest lady in Rome— I suppress her name, for I am no satirist— with a band of eunuchs before her in the basilica of the blessed Peter. She was giving money to the poor, a coin apiece; and this with her own hand, that she might be accounted more religious. Hereupon a by no means uncommon incident occurred. An old woman, full of years and rags, ran forward to get a second coin, but when her turn came she received not a penny but a blow hard enough to draw blood from her guilty veins.

The love of money is the root of all evil, 1 Timothy 6:10 and the apostle speaks of covetousness as being idolatry. Colossians 3:5 Seek ye first the kingdom of God and all these things shall be added unto you. Matthew 6:33 The Lord will never allow a righteous soul to perish of hunger. I have been young, the psalmist says, and now am old, yet have I not seen the righteous forsaken nor his seed begging bread. Elijah is fed by ministering ravens. 1 Kings 17:4, 6 The widow of Zarephath, who with her sons expected to die the same night, went without food herself that she might feed the prophet. He who had come to be fed then turned feeder, for, by a miracle, he filled the empty barrel. 1 Kings 17:9-16 The apostle Peter says: Silver and gold have I none, but such as I have give I you. In the name of Jesus Christ rise up and walk. Acts 3:6 But now many, while they do not say it in words, by their deeds declare: Faith and pity have I none; but such as I have, silver and gold, these I will not give you. Having food and raiment let us be therewith content. 1 Timothy 6:8 Hear the prayer of Jacob: If God will be with me and will keep me in this way that I go, and will give me bread to eat and raiment to put on, then shall the Lord be my God. Genesis 28:20-21 He prayed only for things necessary; yet, twenty years afterwards, he returned to the land of Canaan rich in substance and richer still in children. Genesis 32:5, 10 Numberless are the instances in Scripture which teach men to Beware of covetousness. Luke 12:15

33. As I have been led to touch to the subject— it shall have a treatise to itself if Christ permit— I will relate what took place not very many years ago at Nitria. A brother, more thrifty than covetous, and ignorant that the Lord had been sold for thirty pieces of silver, Matthew 26:15 left behind him at his death a hundred pieces of money which he had earned by weaving linen. As there were about five thousand monks in the neighborhood, living in as many separate cells, a council was held as to what should be done. Some said that the coins should be distributed among the poor; others that they should be given to the church, while others were for sending them back to the relatives of the deceased. However, Macarius, Pambo, Isidore and the rest of those called fathers, speaking by the Spirit, decided that they should be interred with their owner, with the words: Your money perish with you. Acts 8:20 Nor was this too harsh a decision; for so great fear has fallen upon all throughout Egypt, that it is now a crime to leave after one a single shilling.

34. As I have mentioned the monks, and know that you like to hear about holy things, lend an ear to me for a few moments. There are in Egypt three classes of monks. First, there are the cœnobites, called in their Gentile language Sauses, or, as we should say, men living in a community. Secondly, there are the anchorites, who live in the desert, each man by himself, and are so called because they have withdrawn from human society. Thirdly, there is the class called Remoboth, a very inferior and little regarded type, peculiar to my own province, or, at least, originating there. These live together in twos and threes, but seldom in larger numbers, and are bound by no rule; but do exactly as they choose. A portion of their earnings they contribute to a common fund, out of which food is provided for all. In most cases they reside in cities and strongholds; and, as though it were their workmanship which is holy, and not their life, all that they sell is extremely dear. They often quarrel because they are unwilling, while supplying their own food, to be subordinate to others. It is true that they compete with each other in fasting; they make what should be a private concern an occasion for a triumph. In everything they study effect: their sleeves are loose, their boots bulge, their garb is of the coarsest. They are always sighing, or visiting virgins, or sneering at the clergy; yet when a holiday comes, they make themselves sick— they eat so much.

35. Having then rid ourselves of these as of so many plagues, let us come to that more numerous class who live together, and who are, as we have said, called Cœnobites. Among these the first principle of union is to obey superiors and to do whatever they command. They are divided into bodies of ten and of a hundred, so that each tenth man has authority over nine others, while the hundredth has ten of these officers under him. They live apart from each other, in separate cells. According to their rule, no monk may visit another before the ninth hour; except the deans above mentioned, whose office is to comfort, with soothing words, those whose thoughts disquiet them. After the ninth hour they meet together to sing psalms and read the Scriptures according to usage. Then when the prayers have ended and all have sat down, one called the father stands up among them and begins to expound the portion of the day. While he is speaking the silence is profound; no man ventures to look at his neighbor or to clear his throat. The speaker's praise is in the weeping of his hearers. Silent tears roll down their cheeks, but not a sob escapes from their lips. Yet when he begins to speak of Christ's kingdom, and of future bliss, and of the glory which is to come, every one may be noticed saying to himself, with a gentle sigh and uplifted eyes: Oh, that I had wings like a dove! For then would I fly away and be at rest. After this the meeting breaks up and each company of ten goes with its father to its own table. This they take in turns to serve each for a week at a time. No noise is made over the food; no one talks while eating. Bread, pulse and greens form their fare, and the only seasoning that they use is salt. Wine is given only to the old, who with the children often have a special meal prepared for them to repair the ravages of age and to save the young from premature decay. When the meal is over they all rise together, and, after singing a hymn, return to their dwellings. There each one talks till evening with his comrade thus: Have you noticed so-and-so? What grace he has! How silent he is! How soberly he walks! If any one is weak they comfort him; or if he is fervent in love to God, they encourage him to fresh earnestness. And because at night, besides the public prayers, each man keeps vigil in his own

chamber, they go round all the cells one by one, and putting their ears to the doors, carefully ascertain what their occupants are doing. If they find a monk slothful, they do not scold him; but, dissembling what they know, they visit him more frequently, and at first exhort rather than compel him to pray more. Each day has its allotted task, and this being given in to the dean, is by him brought to the steward. This latter, once a month, gives a scrupulous account to their common father. He also tastes the dishes when they are cooked, and, as no one is allowed to say, I am without a tunic or a cloak or a couch of rushes, he so arranges that no one need ask for or go without what he wants. In case a monk falls ill, he is moved to a more spacious chamber, and there so attentively nursed by the old men, that he misses neither the luxury of cities nor a mother's kindness. Every Lord's day they spend their whole time in prayer and reading; indeed, when they have finished their tasks, these are their usual occupations. Every day they learn by heart a portion of Scripture. They keep the same fasts all the year round, but in Lent they are allowed to live more strictly. After Whitsuntide they exchange their evening meal for a midday one; both to satisfy the tradition of the church and to avoid overloading their stomachs with a double supply of food.

A similar description is given of the Essenes by Philo, Plato's imitator; also by Josephus, the Greek Livy, in his narrative of the Jewish captivity.

36. As my present subject is virgins, I have said rather too much about monks. I will pass on, therefore, to the third class, called anchorites, who go from the monasteries into the deserts, with nothing but bread and salt. Paul introduced this way of life; Antony made it famous, and— to go farther back still— John the Baptist set the first example of it. The prophet Jeremiah describes one such in the words: It is good for a man that he bear the yoke in his youth. He sits alone and keeps silence, because he has borne it upon him. He gives his cheek to him that smites him, he is filled full with reproach. For the Lord will not cast off forever. The struggle of the anchorites and their life— in the flesh, yet not of the flesh— I will, if you wish, explain to you at some other time. I must now return to the subject of covetousness, which I left to speak of the monks. With them before your eyes you will despise, not only gold and silver in general, but earth itself and heaven. United to Christ, you will sing, The Lord is my portion.

37. Farther, although the apostle bids us to pray without ceasing, 1 Thessalonians 5:17 and although to the saints their very sleep is a supplication, we ought to have fixed hours of prayer, that if we are detained by work, the time may remind us of our duty. Prayers, as every one knows, ought to be said at the third, sixth and ninth hours, at dawn and at evening. No meal should be begun without prayer, and before leaving table thanks should be returned to the Creator. We should rise two or three times in the night, and go over the parts of Scripture which we know by heart. When we leave the roof which shelters us, prayer should be our armor; and when we return from the street we should pray before we sit down, and not give the frail body rest until the soul is fed. In every act we do, in every step we take, let our hand trace the Lord's cross. Speak against nobody, and do not slander your mother's son. Who are you that judgest the servant of another? To his own lord he stands or falls; yea, he shall be made to stand, for the Lord has power to make him stand. If you have fasted two or three days, do not think

yourself better than others who do not fast. You fast and are angry; another eats and wears a smiling face. You work off your irritation and hunger in quarrels. He uses food in moderation and gives God thanks. Daily Isaiah cries: Is it such a fast that I have chosen, says the Lord? Isaiah 58:5 and again: In the day of your fast ye find your own pleasure, and oppress all your laborers. Behold ye fast for strife and contention, and to smite with the fist of wickedness. How fast ye unto me? What kind of fast can his be whose wrath is such that not only does the night go down upon it, but that even the moon's changes leave it unchanged?

38. Look to yourself and glory in your own success and not in others' failure. Some women care for the flesh and reckon up their income and daily expenditure: such are no fit models for you. Judas was a traitor, but the eleven apostles did not waver. Phygellus and Alexander made shipwreck; but the rest continued to run the race of faith. Say not: So-and-so enjoys her own property, she is honored of men, her brothers and sisters come to see her. Has she then ceased to be a virgin? In the first place, it is doubtful if she is a virgin. For the Lord sees not as man sees; for man looks upon the outward appearance, but the Lord looks on the heart. 1 Samuel 16:7 Again, she may be a virgin in body and not in spirit. According to the apostle, a true virgin is holy both in body and in spirit. 1 Corinthians 7:34 Lastly, let her glory in her own way. Let her override Paul's opinion and live in the enjoyment of her good things. But you and I must follow better examples.

Set before you the blessed Mary, whose surpassing purity made her meet to be the mother of the Lord. When the angel Gabriel came down to her, in the form of a man, and said: Hail, you that are highly favored; the Lord is with you, Luke 1:28 she was terror-stricken and unable to reply, for she had never been saluted by a man before. But, on learning who he was, she spoke, and one who had been afraid of a man conversed fearlessly with an angel. Now you, too, may be the Lord's mother. Take you a great roll and write in it with a man's pen Maher-shalal-hash-baz. And when you have gone to the prophetess, and have conceived in the womb, and have brought forth a son, say: Lord, we have been with child by your fear, we have been in pain, we have brought forth the spirit of your salvation, which we have wrought upon the earth. Then shall your Son reply: Behold my mother and my brethren. Matthew 12:49 And He whose name you have so recently inscribed upon the table of your heart, and have written with a pen upon its renewed surface — He, after He has recovered the spoil from the enemy, and has spoiled principalities and powers, nailing them to His cross Colossians 2:14-15 — having been miraculously conceived, grows up to manhood; and, as He becomes older, regards you no longer as His mother, but as His bride. To be as the martyrs, or as the apostles, or as Christ, involves a hard struggle, but brings with it a great reward.

All such efforts are only of use when they are made within the church's pale; we must celebrate the passover in the one house, Exodus 12:46 we must enter the ark with Noah, 1 Peter 3:20-21 we must take refuge from the fall of Jericho with the justified harlot, Rahab. James 2:25 Such virgins as there are said to be among the heretics and among the followers of the infamous Manes must be considered, not virgins, but prostitutes. For if— as they allege— the devil is the author of the body, how can they honor that which is fashioned by their foe? No; it is because they know that the name virgin brings glory with it, that they go about as wolves in sheep's clothing. Matthew 7:15 As antichrist pretends to be Christ, such virgins assume an honorable name, that they may the better cloak a discreditable life. Rejoice, my sister; rejoice, my daughter; rejoice, my virgin; for you have resolved to be, in reality, that which others insincerely feign.

39. The things that I have here set forth will seem hard to her who loves not Christ. But one who has come to regard all the splendor of the world as off-scourings, and to hold all things under the sun as vain, that he may win Christ; Philippians 3:8 one who has died with his Lord and risen again, and has crucified the flesh with its affections and lusts; he will boldly cry out: Who shall separate us from the love of Christ? Shall tribulation, or distress, or persecution, or famine, or nakedness, or peril, or sword? and again: I am persuaded that neither death nor life, nor angels, nor principalities nor powers, nor things present, nor things to come, nor height, nor depth, nor any other creature shall be able to separate us from the love of God which is in Christ Jesus, our Lord.

For our salvation the Son of God is made the Son of Man. Nine months He awaits His birth in the womb, undergoes the most revolting conditions, and comes forth covered with blood, to be swathed in rags and covered with caresses. He who shuts up the world in His fist is contained in the narrow limits of a manger. I say nothing of the thirty years during which he lives in obscurity, satisfied with the poverty of his parents. Luke 2:51-52 When He is scourged He holds His peace; when He is crucified, He prays for His crucifiers. What shall I render unto the Lord for all His benefits towards me? I will take the cup of salvation and call upon the name of the Lord. Precious in the sight of the Lord is the death of His saints. The only fitting return that we can make to Him is to give blood for blood; and, as we are redeemed by the blood of Christ, gladly to lay down our lives for our Redeemer. What saint has ever won his crown without first contending for it? Righteous Abel is murdered. Abraham is in danger of losing his wife. And, as I must not enlarge my book unduly, seek for yourself: you will find that all holy men have suffered adversity. Solomon alone lived in luxury and perhaps it was for this reason that he fell. For whom the Lord loves, He chastens, and scourges every son whom He receives. Hebrews 12:6 Which is best— for a short time to do battle, to carry stakes for the palisades, to bear arms, to faint under heavy bucklers, that ever afterwards we may rejoice as victors? Or to become slaves forever, just because we cannot endure for a single hour?

40. Love finds nothing hard; no task is difficult to the eager. Think of all that Jacob bore for Rachel, the wife who had been promised to him. Jacob, the Scripture says, served seven years for Rachel. And they seemed unto him but a few days for the love he had to her. Genesis 29:20 Afterwards he himself tells us what he had to undergo. In the day the drought consumed me and the frost by night. Genesis 31:40 So we must love Christ and always seek His embraces. Then everything difficult will seem easy; all things long we shall account short; and smitten with His arrows, we shall say every moment: Woe is me that I have prolonged my pilgrimage. For the sufferings of this present time are not worthy to be compared with the glory which shall be revealed in us. Romans 8:18 For tribulation works patience, and patience experience, and experience hope; and

hope makes not ashamed. Romans 5:3-5 When your lot seems hard to bear read Paul's second epistle to the Corinthians: In labors more abundant; in stripes above measure; in prisons more frequent; in deaths oft. Of the Jews five times received I forty stripes save one; thrice was I beaten with rods; once was I stoned; thrice I suffered shipwreck; a night and a day I have been in the deep; in journeyings often, in perils of waters, in perils of robbers, in perils by my own countrymen, in perils by the heathen, in perils in the city, in perils in the wilderness, in perils in the sea, in perils among false brethren, in weariness and painfulness, in watchings often, in hunger and thirst, in fastings often, in cold and nakedness. 2 Corinthians 11:23-27 Which of us can claim the veriest fraction of the virtues here enumerated? Yet it was these which afterwards made him bold to say: I have finished my course, I have kept the faith. Henceforth there is laid up for me a crown of righteousness which the Lord, the righteous Judge, shall give me at that day. 2 Timothy 4:7-8

But we, if our food is less appetizing than usual, get sullen, and fancy that we do God a favor by drinking watered wine. And if the water brought to us is a trifle too warm, we break the cup and overturn the table and scourge the servant in fault until blood comes. The kingdom of heaven suffers violence and the violent take it by force. Matthew 11:12 Still, unless you use force you will never seize the kingdom of heaven. Unless you knock importunately you will never receive the sacramental bread. Luke 11:5-8 Is it not truly violence, think you, when the flesh desires to be as God and ascends to the place whence angels have fallen Isaiah 14:12-13 to judge angels?

41. Emerge, I pray you, for a while from your prison-house, and paint before your eyes the reward of your present toil, a reward which eye has not seen, nor ear heard, neither has it entered into the heart of man. 1 Corinthians 2:9 What will be the glory of that day when Mary, the mother of the Lord, shall come to meet you, accompanied by her virgin choirs! When, the Red Sea past and Pharaoh drowned with his host, Miriam, Aaron's sister, her timbrel in her hand, shall chant to the answering women: Sing ye unto the Lord, for he has triumphed gloriously; the horse and his rider has he thrown into the sea. Exodus 15:20-21 Then shall Thecla fly with joy to embrace you. Then shall your Spouse himself come forward and say: Rise up, my love, my fair one, and come away, for lo! The winter is past, the rain is over and gone. Song of Songs 2:10-11 Then shall the angels say with wonder: Who is she that looks forth as the morning, fair as the moon, clear as the sun? Song of Songs 6:10 The daughters shall see you and bless you; yea, the queens shall proclaim and the concubines shall praise you. Song of Songs 6:9 And, after these, yet another company of chaste women will meet you. Sarah will come with the wedded; Anna, the daughter of Phanuel, with the widows. In the one band you will find your natural mother and in the other your spiritual. The one will rejoice in having borne, the other will exult in having taught you. Then truly will the Lord ride upon his ass, and thus enter the heavenly Jerusalem. Then the little ones (of whom, in Isaiah, the Saviour says: Behold, I and the children whom the Lord has given me Isaiah 8:18) shall lift up palms of victory and shall sing with one voice: Hosanna in the highest, blessed is he that comes in the name of the Lord, hosanna in the highest. Matthew 21:9 Then shall the hundred and forty and

four thousand hold their harps before the throne and before the elders and shall sing the new song. And no man shall have power to learn that song save those for whom it is appointed. These are they which were not defiled with women; for they are virgins. These are they which follow the Lamb wherever he goes. Revelation 14:1-4 As often as this life's idle show tries to charm you; as often as you see in the world some vain pomp, transport yourself in mind to Paradise, essay to be now what you will be hereafter, and you will hear your Spouse say: Set me as a sunshade in your heart and as a seal upon your arm. And then, strengthened in body as well as in mind, you, too, will cry aloud and say: Many waters cannot quench love, neither can the floods drown it. Song of Songs 8:7

LETTER XXIII

To Marcella

Jerome writes to Marcella to console her for the loss of a friend who, like herself, was the head of a religious society at Rome. The news of Lea's death had first reached Marcella when she was engaged with Jerome in the study of the 73d psalm. Later in the day he writes this letter in which, after extolling Lea, he contrasts her end with that of the consul-elect, Vettius Agorius Prætextatus, a man of great ability and integrity, whom he declares to be now in Tartarus. Written at Rome in 384 A.D.

1. Today, about the third hour, just as I was beginning to read with you the seventy-second psalm — the first, that is, of the third book— and to explain that its title belonged partly to the second book and partly to the third— the previous book, I mean, concluding with the words the prayers of David the son of Jesse are ended, and the next commencing with the words a psalm of Asaph — and just as I had come on the passage in which the righteous man declares: If I say, I will speak thus; behold I should offend against the generation of your children, a verse which is differently rendered in our Latin version: — suddenly the news came that our most saintly friend Lea had departed from the body. As was only natural, you turned deadly pale; for there are few persons, if any, who do not burst into tears when the earthen vessel breaks. 2 Corinthians 4:7 But if you wept it was not from doubt as to her future lot, but only because you had not rendered to her the last sad offices which are due to the dead. Finally, as we were still conversing together, a second message informed us that her remains had been already conveyed to Ostia.

2. You may ask what is the use of repeating all this. I will reply in the apostle's words, much every way. Romans 3:2 First, it shows that all must hail with joy the release of a soul which has trampled Satan under foot, and won for itself, at last, a crown of tranquillity. Secondly, it gives me an opportunity of briefly describing her life. Thirdly, it enables me to assure you that the consul-elect, that detractor of his age, is now in Tartarus.

Who can sufficiently eulogize our dear Lea's mode of living? So complete was her conversion to the Lord that, becoming the head of a monastery, she showed herself a true mother to the virgins in it, wore coarse sackcloth instead of soft raiment, passed sleepless nights in prayer, and instructed her companions even more by example than by precept. So great was her humility that she, who had once been the mistress of many, was accounted the servant of all; and certainly, the less she was reckoned an earthly mistress the more she became a servant of Christ. She was careless of her dress, neglected her hair, and ate only the coarsest food. Still, in all that she did, she avoided ostentation that she might not have her reward in this world. Matthew 6:2

3. Now, therefore, in return for her short toil, Lea enjoys everlasting felicity; she is welcomed into the choirs of the angels; she is comforted in Abraham's bosom. And, as once the beggar Lazarus saw the rich man, for all his purple, lying in

torment, so does Lea see the consul, not now in his triumphal robe but clothed in mourning, and asking for a drop of water from her little finger. Luke 16:19-24 How great a change have we here! A few days ago the highest dignitaries of the city walked before him as he ascended the ramparts of the capitol like a general celebrating a triumph; the Roman people leapt up to welcome and applaud him, and at the news of his death the whole city was moved. Now he is desolate and naked, a prisoner in the foulest darkness, and not, as his unhappy wife falsely asserts, set in the royal abode of the milky way. On the other hand Lea, who was always shut up in her one closet, who seemed poor and of little worth, and whose life was accounted madness, Wisdom 5:4 now follows Christ and sings, Like as we have heard, so have we seen in the city of our God.

4. And now for the moral of all this, which, with tears and groans, I conjure you to remember. While we run the way of this world, we must not clothe ourselves with two coats, that is, with a twofold faith, or burden ourselves with leathern shoes, that is, with dead works; we must not allow scrips filled with money to weigh us down, or lean upon the staff of worldly power. Matthew 10:10 We must not seek to possess both Christ and the world. No; things eternal must take the place of things transitory; 2 Corinthians 4:18 and since, physically speaking, we daily anticipate death, if we wish for immortality we must realize that we are but mortal.

LETTER XXIV

To Marcella

Concerning the virgin Asella. Dedicated to God before her birth, Marcella's sister had been made a church-virgin at the age of ten. From that time she had lived a life of the severest asceticism, first as a member and then as the head of Marcella's community upon the Aventine. Jerome, who subsequently wrote her a letter (XLV) on his departure from Rome, now holds her up as a model to be admired and imitated. Written at Rome A.D. 384.

1. Let no one blame my letters for the eulogies and censures which are contained in them. To arraign sinners is to admonish those in like case, and to praise the virtuous is to quicken the zeal of those who wish to do right. The day before yesterday I spoke to you concerning Lea of blessed memory, and I had hardly done so, when I was pricked in my conscience. It would be wrong for me, I thought, to ignore a virgin after speaking of one who, as a widow, held a lower place. Accordingly, in my present letter, I mean to give you a brief sketch of the life of our dear Asella. Please do not read it to her; for she is sure to be displeased with eulogies of which she is herself the object. Show it rather to the young girls of your acquaintance, that they may guide themselves by her example, and may take her behavior as the pattern of a perfect life.

2. I pass over the facts that, before her birth, she was blessed while still in her mother's womb, and that, virgin-like, she was delivered to her father in a dream in a bowl of shining glass brighter than a mirror. And I say nothing of her consecration to the blessed life of virginity, a ceremony which took place when she was hardly more than ten years old, a mere babe still wrapped in swaddling clothes. For all that comes before works should be counted of grace; Romans 11:6 although, doubtless, God foreknew the future when He sanctified Jeremiah as yet unborn, Jeremiah 1:5 when He made John to leap in his mother's womb, Luke 1:41 and when, before the foundation of the world, He set apart Paul to preach the gospel of His son. Ephesians 1:4

3. I come now to the life which after her twelfth year she, by her own exertion, chose, laid hold of, held fast to, entered upon, and fulfilled. Shut up in her narrow cell she roamed through paradise. Fasting was her recreation and hunger her refreshment. If she took food it was not from love of eating, but because of bodily exhaustion; and the bread and salt and cold water to which she restricted herself sharpened her appetite more than they appeased it.

But I have almost forgotten to mention that of which I should have spoken first. When her resolution was still fresh she took her gold necklace made in the lamprey pattern (so called because bars of metal are linked together so as to form a flexible chain), and sold it without her parents' knowledge. Then putting on a dark dress such as her mother had never been willing that she should wear, she concluded her pious enterprise by consecrating herself immediately to the Lord.

She thus showed her relatives that they need hope to wring no farther concessions from one who, by her very dress, had condemned the world.

4. To go on with my story, her ways were quiet and she lived in great privacy. In fact, she rarely went abroad or spoke to a man. More wonderful still, much as she loved her virgin sister, she did not care to see her. She worked with her own hands, for she knew that it was written: If any will not work neither shall he eat. 2 Thessalonians 3:10 To the Bridegroom she spoke constantly in prayer and psalmody. She hurried to the martyrs' shrines unnoticed. Such visits gave her pleasure, and the more so because she was never recognized. All the year round she observed a continual fast, remaining without food for two or three days at a time; but when Lent came she hoisted— if I may so speak— every stitch of canvas and fasted nearly from week's end to week's end with a cheerful countenance. Matthew 6:17 What would perhaps be incredible, were it not that with God all things are possible, Matthew 19:26 is that she lived this life until her fiftieth year without weakening her digestion or bringing on herself the pain of colic. Lying on the dry ground did not affect her limbs, and the rough sackcloth that she wore failed to make her skin either foul or rough. With a sound body and a still sounder soul she sought all her delight in solitude, and found for herself a monkish hermitage in the centre of busy Rome.

5. You are better acquainted with all this than I am, and the few details that I have given I have learned from you. So intimate are you with Asella that you have seen, with your own eyes, her holy knees hardened like those of a camel from the frequency of her prayers. I merely set forth what I can glean from you. She is alike pleasant in her serious moods and serious in her pleasant ones: her manner, while winning, is always grave, and while grave is always winning. Her pale face indicates continence but does not betoken ostentation. Her speech is silent and her silence is speech. Her pace is neither too fast nor too slow. Her demeanor is always the same. She disregards refinement and is careless about her dress. When she does attend to it it is without attending. So entirely consistent has her life been that here in Rome, the centre of vain shows, wanton license, and idle pleasure, where to be humble is to be held spiritless, the good praise her conduct and the bad do not venture to impugn it. Let widows and virgins imitate her, let wedded wives make much of her, let sinful women fear her, and let bishops look up to her.

LETTER XXV

To Marcella

An explanation of the ten names given to God in the Hebrew Scriptures. The ten names are El, Elohim, Sabaôth, Eliôn, Asher yeheyeh Exodus 3:14, Adonai, Jah, the tetragram JHVH, and Shaddai. Written at Rome 384 A.D.

LETTER XXVI

To Marcella

An explanation of certain Hebrew words which have been left untranslated in the versions. The words are Alleluia, Amen, Maran atha. Written at Rome 384 A.D.

LETTER XXVII

To Marcella

In this letter Jerome defends himself against the charge of having altered the text of Scripture, and shows that he has merely brought the Latin Version of the N.T. into agreement with the Greek original. Written at Rome 384 A.D.

1. After I had written my former letter, containing a few remarks on some Hebrew words, a report suddenly reached me that certain contemptible creatures were deliberately assailing me with the charge that I had endeavored to correct passages in the gospels, against the authority of the ancients and the opinion of the whole world. Now, though I might — as far as strict right goes — treat these persons with contempt (it is idle to play the lyre for an ass), yet, lest they should follow their usual habit and reproach me with superciliousness, let them take my answer as follows: I am not so dull-wilted nor so coarsely ignorant (qualities which they take for holiness, calling themselves the disciples of fishermen as if men were made holy by knowing nothing)— I am not, I repeat, so ignorant as to suppose that any of the Lord's words is either in need of correction or is not divinely inspired; but the Latin manuscripts of the Scriptures are proved to be faulty by the variations which all of them exhibit, and my object has been to restore them to the form of the Greek original, from which my detractors do not deny that they have been translated. If they dislike water drawn from the clear spring, let them drink of the muddy streamlet, and when they come to read the Scriptures, let them lay aside the keen eye which they turn on woods frequented by game-birds and waters abounding in shellfish. Easily satisfied in this instance alone, let them, if they will, regard the words of Christ as rude sayings, albeit that over these so many great intellects have labored for so many ages rather to divine than to expound the meaning of each single word. Let them charge the great apostle with want of literary skill, although it is said of him that much learning made him mad. Acts 26:24

2. I know that as you read these words you will knit your brows, and fear that my freedom of speech is sowing the seeds of fresh quarrels; and that, if you could, you would gladly put your finger on my mouth to prevent me from even speaking of things which others do not blush to do. But, I ask you, wherein have I used too great license? Have I ever embellished my dinner plates with engravings of idols? Have I ever, at a Christian banquet, set before the eyes of virgins the polluting spectacle of Satyrs embracing bacchanals? Or have I ever assailed any one in too bitter terms? Have I ever complained of beggars turned millionaires? Have I ever censured heirs for the funerals which they have given to their benefactors? The one thing that I have unfortunately said has been that virgins ought to live more in the company of women than of men, and by this I have made the whole city look scandalized and caused every one to point at me the finger of scorn. They that hate

me without a cause are more than the hairs of mine head, and I have become a proverb to them. Do you suppose after this that I will now say anything rash?

3. But when I set the wheel rolling I began to form a wine flagon; how comes it that a waterpot is the result? Lest Horace laugh at me I come back to my two-legged asses, and din into their ears, not the music of the lute, but the blare of the trumpet. They may say if they will, rejoicing in hope; serving *the time*, but we will say rejoicing in hope; serving *the Lord*. They may see fit to receive an accusation against a presbyter unconditionally; but we will say in the words of Scripture, Against an elder receive not an accusation, *but before two or three witnesses.* Them that sin rebuke before all. 1 Timothy 5:19-20 They may choose to read, It is *a man's* saying, and worthy of all acceptation; we are content to err with the Greeks, that is to say with the apostle himself, who spoke Greek. Our version, therefore, is, it is a *faithful* saying, and worthy of all acceptation. 1 Timothy 1:15 Lastly, let them take as much pleasure as they please in their Gallican geldings; we will be satisfied with the simple ass of Zechariah, loosed from its halter and made ready for the Saviour's service, which received the Lord on its back, and so fulfilled Isaiah's prediction: Blessed is he that sows beside all waters, where the ox and the ass tread under foot.

LETTER XXVIII

To Marcella

An explanation of the Hebrew word Selah. This word, rendered by the LXX. διάψαλμα and by Aquila ὰ εί, was as much a crux in Jerome's day as it is in ours. Some, he writes, make it a 'change of metre,' others 'a pause for breath,' others 'the beginning of a new subject.' According to yet others it has something to do with rhythm or marks a burst of instrumental music. Jerome himself inclines to follow Aquila and Origen, who make the word mean forever, and suggests that it betokens completion, like the explicit or feliciter in contemporary Latin manuscripts. Written at Rome A.D. 384.

Letter XXIX.

To Marcella.

An explanation of the Hebrew words Ephod bad 1 Samuel 2:18 and Teraphim Judges 17:5. Written at Rome to Marcella, also at Rome A.D. 384.

LETTER XXX

To Paula

Some account of the so-called alphabetical psalms (XXXVII., CXI., CXII., CXIX., CXLV.). After explaining the mystical meaning of the alphabet, Jerome goes on thus: What honey is sweeter than to know the wisdom of God? Others, if they will, may possess riches, drink from a jewelled cup, shine in silks, and try in vain to exhaust their wealth in the most varied pleasures. Our riches are to meditate in the law of the Lord day and night, to knock at the closed door, Matthew 7:7 to receive the 'three loaves' of the Trinity, Luke 11:5-8 and, when the Lord goes before us, to walk upon the water of the world. Matthew 14:25-33 Written at Rome A.D. 384.

LETTER XXXI

To Eustochium

Jerome writes to thank Eustochium for some presents sent to him by her on the festival of St. Peter. He also moralizes on the mystical meaning of the articles sent. The letter should be compared with Letter XLIV., of which the theme is similar. Written at Rome in 384 A.D. (on St. Peter's Day).

1. Doves, bracelets, and a letter are outwardly but small gifts to receive from a virgin, but the action which has prompted them enhances their value. And since honey may not be offered in sacrifice to God, Leviticus 2:11 you have shown skill in taking off their overmuch sweetness and making them pungent — if I may so say — with a dash of pepper. For nothing that is simply pleasurable or merely sweet can please God. Everything must have in it a sharp seasoning of truth. Christ's passover must be eaten with bitter herbs. Exodus 12:8

2. It is true that a festival such as the birthday of Saint Peter should be seasoned with more gladness than usual; still our merriment must not forget the limit set by Scripture, and we must not stray too far from the boundary of our wrestling-ground. Your presents, indeed, remind me of the sacred volume, for in it Ezekiel decks Jerusalem with bracelets, Ezekiel 16:11 Baruch receives letters from Jeremiah, and the Holy Spirit descends in the form of a dove at the baptism of Christ. Matthew 3:16 But to give you, too, a sprinkling of pepper and to remind you of my former letter, I send you today this three-fold warning. Cease not to adorn yourself with good works — the true bracelets of a Christian woman. 1 Timothy 2:10 Rend not the letter written on your heart 2 Corinthians 3:2 as the profane king cut with his penknife that delivered to him by Baruch. Jeremiah 36:23 Let not Hosea say to you as to Ephraim, You are like a silly dove. Hosea 7:11

My words are too harsh, you will say, and hardly suitable to a festival like the present. If so, you have provoked me to it by the nature of your own gifts. So long as you put bitter with sweet, you must expect the same from me, sharp words that is, as well as praise.

3. However, I do not wish to make light of your gifts, least of all the basket of fine cherries, blushing with such a virgin modesty that I can fancy them freshly gathered by Lucullus himself. For it was he who first introduced the fruit at Rome after his conquest of Pontus and Armenia; and the cherry tree is so called because he brought it from Cerasus. Now as the Scriptures do not mention cherries, but do speak of a basket of figs, Jeremiah 24:1-3 I will use these instead to point my moral. May you be made of fruits such as those which grow before God's temple and of which He says, Behold they are good, very good. Jeremiah 24:3 The

Saviour likes nothing that is half and half, and, while he welcomes the hot and does not shun the cold, he tells us in the Apocalypse that he will spew the lukewarm out of his mouth. Revelation 3:15-16 Wherefore we must be careful to celebrate our holy day not so much with abundance of food as with exultation of spirit. For it is altogether unreasonable to wish to honor a martyr by excess who himself, as you know, pleased God by fasting. When you take food always recollect that eating should be followed by reading, and also by prayer. And if, by taking this course, you displease some, repeat to yourself the words of the Apostle: If I yet pleased men I should not be the servant of Christ Galatians 1:10

LETTER XXXII

To Marcella

Jerome writes that he is busy collating Aquila's Greek version of the Old Testament with the Hebrew, inquires after Marcella's mother, and forwards the two preceding letters (XXX., XXXI.). Written at Rome in 384 A.D.

1. There are two reasons for the shortness of this letter, one that its bearer is impatient to start, and the other that I am too busy to waste time on trifles. You ask what business can be so urgent as to stop me from a chat on paper. Let me tell you, then, that for some time past I have been comparing Aquila's version of the Old Testament with the scrolls of the Hebrew, to see if from hatred to Christ the synagogue has changed the text; and — to speak frankly to a friend — I have found several variations which confirm our faith. After having exactly revised the prophets, Solomon, the psalter, and the books of Kings, I am now engaged on Exodus (called by the Jews, from its opening words, Eleh shemôth), and when I have finished this I shall go on to Leviticus. Now you see why I can let no claim for a letter withdraw me from my work. However, as I do not wish my friend Currentius to run altogether in vain, I have tacked on to this little talk two letters which I am sending to your sister Paula, and to her dear child Eustochium. Read these, and if you find them instructive or pleasant, take what I have said to them as meant for you also.

2. I hope that Albina, your mother and mine, is well. In bodily health, I mean, for I doubt not of her spiritual welfare. Pray salute her for me, and cherish her with double affection, both as a Christian and as a mother.

LETTER XXXIII

To Paula

A fragment of a letter in which Jerome institutes a comparison between the industry as writers of M. T. Varro and Origen. It is noteworthy as passing an unqualified eulogium upon Origen, which contrasts strongly with the tone adopted by the writer in subsequent years (see, e.g., Letter LXXXIV.). Its date is probably 384 A.D.

1. Antiquity marvels at Marcus Terentius Varro, because of the countless books which he wrote for Latin readers; and Greek writers are extravagant in their praise of their man of brass, because he has written more works than one of us could so much as copy. But since Latin ears would find a list of Greek writings tiresome, I shall confine myself to the Latin Varro. I shall try to show that we of today are sleeping the sleep of Epimenides, and devoting to the amassing of riches the energy which our predecessors gave to sound, if secular, learning.

2. Varro's writings include forty-five books of antiquities, four concerning the life of the Roman people.

3. But why, you ask me, have I thus mentioned Varro and the man of brass? Simply to bring to your notice our Christian man of brass, or, rather, man of adamant — Origen, I mean — whose zeal for the study of Scripture has fairly earned for him this latter name. Would you learn what monuments of his genius he has left us? The following list exhibits them. His writings comprise thirteen books on Genesis, two books of Mystical Homilies, notes on Exodus, notes on Leviticus, * * * * also single books, four books on First Principles, two books on the Resurrection, two dialogues on the same subject.

* * * * * * * * * * *

With the second phrase he deals at greater length. After showing that Hilary of Poitiers's view (viz. that the persons meant are the apostles, who were told to shake the dust off their feet, Matthew 10:14) is untenable and would require shakers off to be substituted for shaken off, Jerome reverts to the Hebrew as before and declares that the true rendering is that of Symmachus and Theodotion, viz. children of youth. He points out that the LXX. (by whom the Latin translators had been misled) fall into the same mistake at Neh. iv. 16. Finally he corrects a slip of Hilary as to Ps. cxxviii. 2, where, through a misunderstanding of the LXX., the latter had substituted the labors of your fruits for the labors of your hands. He speaks throughout with high respect of Hilary, and says that it was not the bishop's fault that he was ignorant of Hebrew. The date of the letter is probably A.D. 384.

4. So, you see, the labors of this one man have surpassed those of all previous writers, Greek and Latin. Who has ever managed to read all that he has written? Yet what reward have his exertions brought him? He stands condemned by his

bishop, Demetrius, only the bishops of Palestine, Arabia, Phenicia, and Achaia dissenting. Imperial Rome consents to his condemnation, and even convenes a senate to censure him, not — as the rabid hounds who now pursue him cry — because of the novelty or heterodoxy of his doctrines, but because men could not tolerate the incomparable eloquence and knowledge which, when once he opened his lips, made others seem dumb.

5. I have written the above quickly and incautiously, by the light of a poor lantern. You will see why, if you think of those who today represent Epicurus and Aristippus.

LETTER XXXIV

To Marcella.

In reply to a request from Marcella for information concerning two phrases in Ps. cxxvii. (bread of sorrow, Psalm 126:2, and children of the shaken off, A.V. of the youth, Psalm 126:4). Jerome, after lamenting that Origen's notes on the psalm are no longer extant, gives the following explanations:

The Hebrew phrase bread of sorrow is rendered by the LXX. bread of idols; by Aquila, bread of troubles; by Symmachus, bread of misery. Theodotion follows the LXX. So does Origen's Fifth Version. The Sixth renders bread of error. In support of the LXX. the word used here is in Ps. cxv. 4, translated idols. Either the troubles of life are meant or else the tenets of heresy.

LETTER XXXV

From Pope Damasus

Damasus addresses five questions to Jerome with a request for information concerning them. They are:

1. What is the meaning of the words Whosoever slays Cain vengeance shall be taken on him sevenfold? Genesis 4:5

2. If God has made all things good, how comes it that He gives charge to Noah concerning unclean animals, and says to Peter, What God has cleansed that call not thou common? Acts 10:15

3. How is Gen. xv. 16, in the fourth generation they shall come hither again, to be reconciled with Ex. xiii. 18, LXX, in the fifth generation the children of Israel went up out of the land of Egypt?

4. Why did Abraham receive circumcision as a seal of his faith? Romans 4:11

5. Why was Isaac, a righteous man and dear to God, allowed by God to become the dupe of Jacob? Genesis 27 Written at Rome 384 A.D.

LETTER XXXVI

To Pope Damasus

Jerome's reply to the foregoing. For the second and fourth questions he refers Damasus to the writings of Tertullian, Novatian, and Origen. The remaining three he deals with in detail.

Gen. iv. 15, he understands to mean the slayer of Cain shall complete the sevenfold vengeance which is to be wreaked upon him.

Exodus xiii. 18, he proposes to reconcile with Gen. xv. 16, by supposing that in the one place the tribe of Levi is referred to, in the other the tribe of Judah. He suggests, however, that the words rendered by the LXX. in the fifth generation more probably mean harnessed (so A.V.) or laden. In reply to the question about Isaac he says: No man save Him who for our salvation has deigned to put on flesh has full knowledge and a complete grasp of the truth. Paul, Samuel, David, Elisha, all make mistakes, and holy men only know what God reveals to them. He then goes on to give a mystical interpretation of the passage suggested by the martyr Hippolytus. Written the day after the previous letter.

LETTER XXXVII

To Marcella

Marcella had asked Jerome to lend her a copy of a commentary by Rhetitius, bishop of Augustodunum (Autun), on the Song of Songs. He now refuses to do so on the ground that the work abounds with errors, of which the two following are samples: (1) Rhetitius identifies Tharshish with Tarsus, and (2) he supposes that Uphaz (in the phrase gold of Uphaz) is the same as Cephas. Written at Rome A.D. 384.

LETTER XXXVIII

To Marcella

Blæsilla, the daughter of Paula and sister of Eustochium, had lost her husband seven months after her marriage. A dangerous illness had then led to her conversion, and she was now famous throughout Rome for the length to which she carried her austerities. Many censured her for what they deemed her fanaticism, and Jerome, as her spiritual adviser, came in for some of the blame. In the present letter he defends her conduct, and declares that persons who cavil at lives like hers have no claim to be considered Christians. Written at Rome in 385 A.D.

1. When Abraham is tempted to slay his son the trial only serves to strengthen his faith. Genesis xxii When Joseph is sold into Egypt, his sojourn there enables him to support his father and his brothers. When Hezekiah is panic-stricken at the near approach of death, his tears and prayers obtain for him a respite of fifteen years. If the faith of the apostle, Peter, is shaken by his Lord's passion, it is that, weeping bitterly, he may hear the soothing words: Feed my sheep. If Paul, that ravening wolf, Genesis 49:27 that little Benjamin, is blinded in a trance, it is that he may receive his sight, and may be led, by the sudden horror of surrounding darkness, to call Him Lord Whom before he persecuted as man. Acts 9:3-18

2. So is it now, my dear Marcella, with our beloved Blæsilla. The burning fever from which we have seen her suffering unceasingly for nearly thirty days has been sent to teach her to renounce her over-great attention to that body which the worms must shortly devour. The Lord Jesus has come to her in her sickness, and has taken her by the hand, and behold, she arises and ministers unto Him. Mark 1:30-31 Formerly her life savored somewhat of carelessness; and, fast bound in the bands of wealth, she lay as one dead in the tomb of the world. But Jesus was moved with indignation, and was troubled in spirit, and cried aloud and said, Blæsilla, come forth. John 11:38-44 She, at His call, has arisen and has come forth, and sits at meat with the Lord. John 12:2 The Jews, if they will, may threaten her in their wrath; they may seek to slay her, because Christ has raised her up. John 12:10 It is enough that the apostles give God the glory. Blæsilla knows that her life is due to Him who has given it back to her. She knows that now she can clasp the feet of Him whom but a little while ago she dreaded as her judge. Luke 7:38 Then life had all but forsaken her body, and the approach of death made her gasp and shiver. What succour did she obtain in that hour from her kinsfolk? What comfort was there in their words lighter than smoke? She owes no debt to you, you unkindly kindred, now that she is dead to the world and alive unto Christ. Romans 6:11 The Christian must rejoice that it is so, and he that is vexed must admit that he has no claim to be called a Christian.

3. A widow who is loosed from the law of her husband Romans 7:2 has, for her one duty, to continue a widow. But, you will say, a sombre dress vexes the world. In that case, John the Baptist would vex it, too; and yet, among those that are born of women, there has not been a greater than he. Luke 7:28 He was called an angel;

he baptized the Lord Himself, and yet he was clothed in raiment of camel's hair, and girded with a leathern girdle. Matthew 3:4 Is the world displeased because a widow's food is coarse? Nothing can be coarser than locusts, and yet these were the food of John. The women who ought to scandalize Christians are those who paint their eyes and lips with rouge and cosmetics; whose chalked faces, unnaturally white, are like those of idols; upon whose cheeks every chance tear leaves a furrow; who fail to realize that years make them old; who heap their heads with hair not their own; who smooth their faces, and rub out the wrinkles of age; and who, in the presence of their grandsons, behave like trembling school-girls. A Christian woman should blush to do violence to nature, or to stimulate desire by bestowing care upon the flesh. They that are in the flesh, the apostle tells us, cannot please God. Romans 8:8

4. In days gone by our dear widow was extremely fastidious in her dress, and spent whole days before her mirror to correct its deficiencies. Now she boldly says: We all with unveiled face, beholding as in a glass the glory of the Lord, are changed into the same image, from glory to glory, even as by the spirit of the Lord. In those days maids arranged her hair, and her head, which had done no harm, was forced into a waving head-dress. Now she leaves her hair alone, and her only head-dress is a veil. In those days the softest feather-bed seemed hard to her, and she could scarcely find rest on a pile of mattresses. Now she rises eager for prayer, her shrill voice cries Alleluia before every other, she is the first to praise her Lord. She kneels upon the bare ground, and with frequent tears cleanses a face once defiled with white lead. After prayer comes the singing of psalms, and it is only when her neck aches and her knees totter, and her eyes begin to close with weariness, that she gives them leave reluctantly to rest. As her dress is dark, lying on the ground does not soil it. Cheap shoes permit her to give to the poor the price of gilded ones. No gold and jewels adorn her girdle; it is made of wool, plain and scrupulously clean. It is intended to keep her clothes right, and not to cut her waist in two. Therefore, if the scorpion looks askance upon her purpose, and with alluring words tempts her once more to eat of the forbidden tree, she must crush him beneath her feet with a curse, and say, as he lies dying in his allotted dust: Genesis 3:14 Get behind me, Satan. Matthew 16:23 Satan means adversary, 1 Peter 5:8 and one who dislikes Christ's commandments, is more than Christ's adversary; he is anti-christ.

5. But what, I ask you, have we ever done that men should be offended at us? Have we ever imitated the apostles? We are told of the first disciples that they forsook their boat and their nets, and even their aged father. Matthew 4:18-22 The publican stood up from the receipt of custom and followed the Saviour once for all. Matthew 9:9 And when a disciple wished to return home, that he might take leave of his kinsfolk, the Master's voice refused consent. Luke 9:61-62 A son was even forbidden to bury his father, Matthew 8:21 as if to show that it is sometimes a religious duty to be undutiful for the Lord's sake. Luke 14:26 With us it is different. We are held to be monks if we refuse to dress in silk. We are called sour and severe if we keep sober and refrain from excessive laughter. The mob salutes us as Greeks and impostors if our tunics are fresh and clean. They may deal in still severer witticisms if they please; they may parade every fat paunch they can lay

hold of, to turn us into ridicule. Our Blæsilla will laugh at their efforts, and will bear with patience the taunts of all such croaking frogs, for she will remember that men called her Lord, Beelzebub. Matthew 10:25

LETTER XXXIX

To Paula

Blæsilla died within three months of her conversion, and Jerome now writes to Paula to offer her his sympathy and, if possible, to moderate her grief. He asks her to remember that Blæsilla is now in paradise, and so far to control herself as to prevent enemies of the faith from cavilling at her conduct. Then he concludes with the prophecy (since more than fulfilled) that in his writings Blæsilla's name shall never die. Written at Rome in 389 A.D.

1. Oh that my head were waters and my eyes a fountain of tears: that I might weep, not as Jeremiah says, For the slain of my people, Jeremiah 9:1 nor as Jesus, for the miserable fate of Jerusalem, Luke 19:41 but for holiness, mercy, innocence, chastity, and all the virtues, for all are gone now that Blæsilla is dead. For her sake I do not grieve, but for myself I must; my loss is too great to be borne with resignation. Who can recall with dry eyes the glowing faith which induced a girl of twenty to raise the standard of the Cross, and to mourn the loss of her virginity more than the death of her husband? Who can recall without a sigh the earnestness of her prayers, the brilliancy of her conversation, the tenacity of her memory, and the quickness of her intellect? Had you heard her speak Greek you would have deemed her ignorant of Latin; yet when she used the tongue of Rome her words were free from a foreign accent. She even rivalled the great Origen in those acquirements which won for him the admiration of Greece. For in a few months, or rather days, she so completely mastered the difficulties of Hebrew as to emulate her mother's zeal in learning and singing the psalms. Her attire was plain, but this plainness was not, as it often is, a mark of pride. Indeed, her self-abasement was so perfect that she dressed no better than her maids, and was only distinguished from them by the greater ease of her walk. Her steps tottered with weakness, her face was pale and quivering, her slender neck scarcely upheld her head. Still she always had in her hand a prophet or a gospel. As I think of her my eyes fill with tears, sobs impede my voice, and such is my emotion that my tongue cleaves to the roof of my mouth. As she lay there dying, her poor frame parched with burning fever, and her relatives gathered round her bed, her last words were: Pray to the Lord Jesus, that He may pardon me, because what I would have done I have not been able to do. Be at peace, dear Blæsilla, in full assurance that your garments are always white. Ecclesiastes 9:8 For yours is the purity of an everlasting virginity. I feel confident that my words are true: conversion can never be too late. The words to the dying robber are a pledge of this: Verily I say unto you, today shall you be with me in paradise. Luke 23:43 When at last her spirit was delivered from the burden of the flesh, and had returned to Him who gave it; Ecclesiastes 12:7 when, too, after her long pilgrimage, she had ascended up into her ancient heritage, her obsequies were celebrated with customary splendor. People of rank headed the procession, a pall made of cloth of gold covered her bier. But I seemed to hear a voice from heaven, saying: I do not recognize these trappings; such is not the garb I used to wear; this magnificence is strange to me.

2. But what is this? I wish to check a mother's weeping, and I groan myself. I make no secret of my feelings; this entire letter is written in tears. Even Jesus wept for Lazarus because He loved him. John 11:35-36 But he is a poor comforter who is overcome by his own sighs, and from whose afflicted heart tears are wrung as well as words. Dear Paula, my agony is as great as yours. Jesus knows it, whom Blæsilla now follows; the holy angels know it, whose company she now enjoys. I was her father in the spirit, her foster-father in affection. Sometimes I say: Let the day perish wherein I was born, and again, Woe is me, my mother, that you have borne me a man of strife and a man of contention to the whole earth. Jeremiah 15:10 I cry: Righteous are you, O Lord...yet let me talk with you of your judgments. Wherefore does the way of the wicked prosper? Jeremiah 12:1 and as for me, my feet were almost gone, my steps had nearly slipped. For I was envious at the foolish when I saw the prosperity of the wicked, and I said: How does God know? And is there knowledge in the most high? Behold these are the ungodly who prosper in the world; they increase in riches. But again I recall other words, If I say I will speak thus, behold I should offend against the generation of your children. Do not great waves of doubt surge up over my soul as over yours? How comes it, I ask, that godless men live to old age in the enjoyment of this world's riches? How comes it that untutored youth and innocent childhood are cut down while still in the bud? Why is it that children three years old or two, and even unweaned infants, are possessed with devils, covered with leprosy, and eaten up with jaundice, while godless men and profane, adulterers and murderers, have health and strength to blaspheme God? Are we not told that the unrighteousness of the father does not fall upon the son, Ezekiel 18:20 and that the soul that sins it shall die? Ezekiel 18:4 Or if the old doctrine holds good that the sins of the fathers must be visited upon the children, Exodus 20:5 an old man's countless sins cannot fairly be avenged upon a harmless infant. And I have said: Verily, I have cleansed my heart in vain, and washed my hands in innocency. For all the day long have I been plagued. Yet when I have thought of these things, like the prophet I have learned to say: When I thought to know this, it was too painful for me; until I went into the sanctuary of God; then understood I their end. Truly the judgments of the Lord are a great deep. O the depth of the riches both of the wisdom and knowledge of God! How unsearchable are His judgments, and His ways past finding out! Romans 11:33 God is good, and all that He does must be good also. Does He decree that I must lose my husband? I mourn my loss, but because it is His will I bear it with resignation. Is an only son snatched from me? The blow is hard, yet it can be borne, for He who has taken away is He who gave. Job 1:21 If I become blind a friend's reading will console me. If I become deaf I shall escape from sinful words, and my thoughts shall be of God alone. And if, besides such trials as these, poverty, cold, sickness, and nakedness oppress me, I shall wait for death, and regard them as passing evils, soon to give way to a better issue. Let us reflect on the words of the sapiential psalm: Righteous are you, O Lord, and upright are your judgments. Only he can speak thus who in all his troubles magnifies the Lord, and, putting down his sufferings to his sins, thanks God for his clemency.

The daughters of Judah, we are told, rejoiced, because of all the judgments of the Lord. Therefore, since Judah means confession, and since every believing soul confesses its faith, Romans 10:10 he who claims to believe in Christ must rejoice in all Christ's judgments. Am I in health? I thank my Creator. Am I sick? In this case, too, I praise God's will. For when I am weak, then am I strong; and the strength of the spirit is made perfect in the weakness of the flesh. Even an apostle must bear what he dislikes, that ailment for the removal of which he besought the Lord thrice. God's reply was: My grace is sufficient for you; for my strength is made perfect in weakness. Lest he should be unduly elated by his revelations, a reminder of his human weakness was given to him, just as in the triumphal car of the victorious general there was always a slave to whisper constantly, amid the cheerings of the multitude, Remember that you are but man.

3. But why should that be hard to bear which we must one day ourselves endure? And why do we grieve for the dead? We are not born to live forever. Abraham, Moses, and Isaiah, Peter, James, and John, Paul, the chosen vessel, Acts 9:15 and even the Son of God Himself have all died; and are we vexed when a soul leaves its earthly tenement? Perhaps he is taken away, lest that wickedness should alter his understanding...for his soul pleased the Lord: therefore hasted he to take him away from the people — lest in life's long journey he should lose his way in some trackless maze. We should indeed mourn for the dead, but only for him whom Gehenna receives, whom Tartarus devours, and for whose punishment the eternal fire burns. But we who, in departing, are accompanied by an escort of angels, and met by Christ Himself, should rather grieve that we have to tarry yet longer in this tabernacle of death. 2 Corinthians 5:4 For while we are at home in the body, we are absent from the Lord. 2 Corinthians 5:6 Our one longing should be that expressed by the psalmist: Woe is me that my pilgrimage is prolonged, that I have dwelt with them that dwell in Kedar, that my soul has made a far pilgrimage. Kedar means darkness, and darkness stands for this present world (for, we are told, the light shines in darkness; and the darkness comprehends it not John 1:5). Therefore we should congratulate our dear Blæsilla that she has passed from darkness to light, Ephesians 5:8 and has in the first flush of her dawning faith received the crown of her completed work. Had she been cut off (as I pray that none may be) while her thoughts were full of worldly desires and passing pleasures, then mourning would indeed have been her due, and no tears shed for her would have been too many. As it is, by the mercy of Christ she, four months ago, renewed her baptism in her vow of widowhood, and for the rest of her days spurned the world, and thought only of the religious life. Have you no fear, then, lest the Saviour may say to you: Are you angry, Paula, that your daughter has become my daughter? Are you vexed at my decree, and do you, with rebellious tears, grudge me the possession of Blæsilla? You ought to know what my purpose is both for you and for yours. You deny yourself food, not to fast but to gratify your grief; and such abstinence is displeasing to me. Such fasts are my enemies. I receive no soul which forsakes the body against my will. A foolish philosophy may boast of martyrs of this kind; it may boast of a Zeno a Cleombrotus, or a Cato. My spirit rests only upon him that is poor and of a contrite spirit, and that trembles at my word. Isaiah 66:2 Is this the meaning of your vow to me that you would lead a religious life? Is it for this that you dress yourself differently from other matrons, and array yourself in the garb of a nun? Mourning is for those who wear silk dresses. In the midst of your tears the call will come, and you, too, must die; yet you flee from me as from a cruel judge, and fancy that you can avoid

falling into my hands. Jonah, that headstrong prophet, once fled from me, yet in the depths of the sea he was still mine. Jonah 2:2-7 If you really believed your daughter to be alive, you would not grieve that she had passed to a better world. This is the commandment that I have given you through my apostle, that you sorrow not for them that sleep, even as the Gentiles, which have no hope. 1 Thessalonians 4:13 Blush, for you are put to shame by the example of a heathen. The devil's handmaid is better than mine. For, while she imagines that her unbelieving husband has been translated to heaven, you either do not or will not believe that your daughter is at rest with me.

4. Why should I not mourn, you say? Jacob put on sackcloth for Joseph, and when all his family gathered round him, refused to be comforted. I will go down, he said, into the grave unto my son mourning. Genesis 37:35 David also mourned for Absalom, covering his face, and crying: O my son, Absalom...my son, Absalom! Would God I had died for you, O Absalom, my son! 2 Samuel 18:33 Moses, Deuteronomy 34:8 too, and Aaron, Numbers 20:29 and the rest of the saints were mourned for with a solemn mourning. The answer to your reasoning is simple. Jacob, it is true, mourned for Joseph, whom he fancied slain, and thought to meet only in the grave (his words were: I will go down into the grave unto my son mourning), but he only did so because Christ had not yet broken open the door of paradise, nor quenched with his blood the flaming sword and the whirling of the guardian cherubim. (Hence in the story of Dives and Lazarus, Abraham and the beggar, though really in a place of refreshment, are described as being in hell.) And David, who, after interceding in vain for the life of his infant child, refused to weep for it, knowing that it had not sinned, did well to weep for a son who had been a parricide — in will, if not in deed. 2 Samuel 17:1-4 And when we read that, for Moses and Aaron, lamentation was made after ancient custom, this ought not to surprise us, for even in the Acts of the Apostles, in the full blaze of the gospel, we see that the brethren at Jerusalem made great lamentation for Stephen. Acts 8:2 This great lamentation, however, refers not to the mourners, but to the funeral procession and to the crowds which accompanied it. This is what the Scripture says of Jacob: Joseph went up to bury his father: and with him went up all the servants of Pharaoh, the elders of his house, and all the elders of the land of Egypt, and all the house of Joseph and his brethren; and a few lines farther on: And there went up with him both chariots and horsemen: and it was a great company. Finally, they mourned with a great and very sore lamentation. This solemn lamentation does not impose prolonged weeping upon the Egyptians, but simply describes the funeral ceremony. In like manner, when we read of weeping made for Moses and Aaron, this is all that is meant.

I cannot adequately extol the mysteries of Scripture, nor sufficiently admire the spiritual meaning conveyed in its most simple words. We are told, for instance, that lamentation was made for Moses; yet when the funeral of Joshua is described Joshua 24:30 no mention at all is made of weeping. The reason, of course, is that under Moses— that is under the old Law — all men were bound by the sentence passed on Adam's sin, and when they descended into hell were rightly accompanied with tears. For, as the apostle says, death reigned from Adam to Moses, even over them that had not sinned. Romans 5:14 But under Jesus, that is, under the Gospel of Christ, who has unlocked for us the gate of paradise, death is accompanied, not with sorrow, but with joy. The Jews go on weeping to this day; they make bare their feet, they crouch in sackcloth, they roll in ashes. And to make their superstition complete, they follow a foolish custom of the Pharisees, and eat lentils, to show, it would seem, for what poor fare they have lost their birthright. Genesis 25:34 Of course they are right to weep, for as they do not believe in the Lord's resurrection they are being made ready for the advent of antichrist. But we who have put on Christ Galatians 3:27 and according to the apostle are a royal and priestly race, 1 Peter 2:9 we ought not to grieve for the dead. Moses, the Scripture tells us, said to Aaron and unto Eleazar, and unto Ithamar, his sons that were left: Uncover not your heads, neither rend your clothes; lest ye die, and lest wrath come upon all the people. Leviticus 10:6, 12 Rend not your clothes, he says, neither mourn as pagans, lest you die. For, for us sin is death. In this same book, Leviticus, there is a provision which may perhaps strike some as cruel, yet is necessary to faith: the high priest is forbidden to approach the dead bodies of his father and mother, of his brothers and of his children; Leviticus 21:10-12 to the end, that no grief may distract a soul engaged in offering sacrifice to God, and wholly devoted to the Divine mysteries. Are we not taught the same lesson in the Gospel in other words? Is not the disciple forbidden to say farewell to his home or to bury his dead father? Luke 9:59-62 Of the high priest, again, it is said: He shall not go out of the sanctuary, and the sanctification of his God shall not be contaminated, for the anointing oil of his God is upon him. Certainly, now that we have believed in Christ, and bear Him within us, by reason of the oil of His anointing which we have received, 1 John 2:27 we ought not to depart from His temple — that is, from our Christian profession — we ought not to go forth to mingle with the unbelieving Gentiles, but always to remain within, as servants obedient to the will of the Lord.

5. I have spoken plainly, lest you might ignorantly suppose that Scripture sanctions your grief; and that, if you err, you have reason on your side. And, so far, my words have been addressed to the average Christian woman. But now it will not be so. For in your case, as I well know, renunciation of the world has been complete; you have rejected and trampled on the delights of life, and you give yourself daily to fasting, to reading, and to prayer. Like Abraham, Genesis 12:1-4 you desire to leave your country and kindred, to forsake Mesopotamia and the Chaldæans, to enter into the promised land. Dead to the world before your death, you have spent all your mere worldly substance upon the poor, or have bestowed it upon your children. I am the more surprised, therefore, that you should act in a manner which in others would justly call for reprehension. You call to mind Blæsilla's companionship, her conversation, and her endearing ways; and you cannot endure the thought that you have lost them all. I pardon you the tears of a mother, but I ask you to restrain your grief. When I think of the parent I cannot blame you for weeping: but when I think of the Christian and the recluse, the mother disappears from my view. Your wound is still fresh, and any touch of mine, however gentle, is more likely to inflame than to heal it. Yet why do you not try to overcome by reason a grief which time must inevitably assuage? Naomi, fleeing because of famine to the land of Moab, there lost her husband and her sons. Yet when she was thus deprived of her natural protectors, Ruth, a stranger, never

left her side. Ruth i And see what a great thing it is to comfort a lonely woman! Ruth, for her reward, is made an ancestress of Christ. Matthew 1:5 Consider the great trials which Job endured, and you will see that you are over-delicate. Amid the ruins of his house, the pains of his sores, his countless bereavements, and, last of all, the snares laid for him by his wife, he still lifted up his eyes to heaven, and maintained his patience unbroken. I know what you are going to say: All this befell him as a righteous man, to try his righteousness. Well, choose which alternative you please. Either you are holy, in which case God is putting your holiness to the proof; or else you are a sinner, in which case you have no right to complain. For if so, you endure far less than your deserts.

Why should I repeat old stories? Listen to a modern instance. The holy Melanium, eminent among Christians for her true nobility (may the Lord grant that you and I may have part with her in His day!), while the dead body of her husband was still unburied, still warm, had the misfortune to lose at one stroke two of her sons. The sequel seems incredible, but Christ is my witness that my words are true. Would you not suppose that in her frenzy she would have unbound her hair, and rent her clothes, and torn her breast? Yet not a tear fell from her eyes. Motionless she stood there; then casting herself at the feet of Christ, she smiled, as though she held Him with her hands. Henceforth, Lord, she said, I will serve You more readily, for You have freed me from a great burden. But perhaps her remaining children overcame her determination. No, indeed; she set so little store by them that she gave up all that she had to her only son, and then, in spite of the approaching winter, took ship for Jerusalem.

6. Spare yourself, I beseech you, spare Blæsilla, who now reigns with Christ; at least spare Eustochium, whose tender years and inexperience depend on you for guidance and instruction. Now does the devil rage and complain that he is set at naught, because he sees one of your children exalted in triumph. The victory which he failed to win over her that is gone he hopes to obtain over her who still remains. Too great affection towards one's children is disaffection towards God. Abraham gladly prepares to slay his only son, and do you complain if one child out of several has received her crown? I cannot say what I am going to say without a groan. When you were carried fainting out of the funeral procession, whispers such as these were audible in the crowd. Is not this what we have often said. She weeps for her daughter, killed with fasting. She wanted her to marry again, that she might have grandchildren. How long must we refrain from driving these detestable monks out of Rome? Why do we not stone them or hurl them into the Tiber? They have misled this unhappy lady; that she is not a nun from choice is clear. No heathen mother ever wept for her children as she does for Blæsilla. What sorrow, think you, must not Christ have endured when He listened to such words as these! And how triumphantly must Satan have exulted, eager as he is to snatch your soul! Luring you with the claims of a grief which seems natural and right, and always keeping before you the image of Blæsilla, his aim is to slay the mother of the victress, and then to fall upon her forsaken sister. I do not speak thus to terrify you. The Lord is my witness that I address you now as though I were standing at His judgment seat. Tears which have no meaning are an object of abhorrence. Yours are detestable tears, sacrilegious tears, unbelieving tears; for

they know no limits, and bring you to the verge of death. You shriek and cry out as though on fire within, and do your best to put an end to yourself. But to you and others like you Jesus comes in His mercy and says: Why do you weep? The damsel is not dead but sleeps. Mark 5:39 The bystanders may laugh him to scorn; such unbelief is worthy of the Jews. If you prostrate yourself in grief at your daughter's tomb you too will hear the chiding of the angel, Why do you seek the living among the dead? Luke 24:5 It was because Mary Magdalene had done this that when she recognized the Lord's voice calling her and fell at His feet, He said to her: Touch me not, for I am not yet ascended to my Father; John 20:17 that is to say, you are not worthy to touch, as risen, one whom you suppose still in the tomb.

7. What crosses and tortures, think you, must not our Blæsilla endure to see Christ angry with you, though it be but a little! At this moment she cries to you as you weep: If ever you loved me, mother, if I was nourished at your breast, if I was taught by your precepts, do not grudge me my exaltation, do not so act that we shall be separated forever. Do you fancy that I am alone? In place of you I now have Mary the mother of the Lord. Here I see many whom before I have not known. My companions are infinitely better than any that I had on earth. Here I have the company of Anna, the prophetess of the Gospel; Luke 2:36-37 and — what should kindle in you more fervent joy— I have gained in three short months what cost her the labor of many years to win. Both of us widows indeed, we have been both rewarded with the palm of chastity. Do you pity me because I have left the world behind me? It is I who should, and do, pity you who, still immured in its prison, daily fight with anger, with covetousness, with lust, with this or that temptation leading the soul to ruin. If you wish to be indeed my mother, you must please Christ. She is not my mother who displeases my Lord. Many other things does she say which here I pass over; she prays also to God for you. For me, too, I feel sure, she makes intercession and asks God to pardon my sins in return for the warnings and advice that I bestowed on her, when to secure her salvation I braved the ill will of her family.

8. Therefore, so long as breath animates my body, so long as I continue in the enjoyment of life, I engage, declare, and promise that Blæsilla's name shall be forever on my tongue, that my labors shall be dedicated to her honor, and that my talents shall be devoted to her praise. No page will I write in which Blæsilla's name shall not occur. Wherever the records of my utterance shall find their way, there she, too, will travel with my poor writings. Virgins, widows, monks and priests, as they read, will see how deeply her image is impressed upon my mind. Everlasting remembrance will make up for the shortness of her life. Living as she does with Christ in heaven, she will live also on the lips of men. The present will soon pass away and give place to the future, and that future will judge her without partiality and without prejudice. As a childless widow she will occupy a middle place between Paula, the mother of children, and Eustochium the virgin. In my writings she will never die. She will hear me conversing of her always, either with her sister or with her mother.

THE LETTERS OF ST. JEROME

LETTER XL

To Marcella

Onasus, of Segesta, the subject of this letter, was among Jerome's Roman opponents. He is here held up to ridicule in a manner which reflects little credit on the writer's urbanity. The date of the letter is 385 A.D.

1. The medical men called surgeons pass for being cruel, but really deserve pity. For is it not pitiful to cut away the dead flesh of another man with merciless knives without being moved by his pangs? Is it not pitiful that the man who is curing the patient is callous to his sufferings, and has to appear as his enemy? Yet such is the order of nature. While truth is always bitter, pleasantness waits upon evil-doing. Isaiah goes naked without blushing as a type of captivity to come. Isaiah 20:2 Jeremiah is sent from Jerusalem to the Euphrates (a river in Mesopotamia), and leaves his girdle to be marred in the Chaldæan camp, among the Assyrians hostile to his people. Jeremiah 13:6-7 Ezekiel is told to eat bread made of mingled seeds and sprinkled with the dung of men and cattle. Ezekiel 4:9-16 He has to see his wife die without shedding a tear. Ezekiel 24:15-18 Amos is driven from Samaria. Amos 7:12-13 Why is he driven from it? Surely in this case as in the others, because he was a spiritual surgeon, who cut away the parts diseased by sin and urged men to repentance. The apostle Paul says: Am I therefore become your enemy because I tell you the truth? Galatians 4:16 And so the Saviour Himself found it, from whom many of the disciples went back because His sayings seemed hard. John 6:60, 66

2. It is not surprising, then, that by exposing their faults I have offended many. I have arranged to operate on a cancerous nose; let him who suffers from wens tremble. I wish to rebuke a chattering daw; let the crow realize that she is offensive. Yet, after all, is there but one person in Rome

Whose nostrils are disfigured by a scar?

Is Onasus of Segesta alone in puffing out his cheeks like bladders and balancing hollow phrases on his tongue?

I say that certain persons have, by crime, perjury, and false pretences, attained to this or that high position. How does it hurt you who know that the charge does not touch you? I laugh at a pleader who has no clients, and sneer at a penny-a-liner's eloquence. What does it matter to you who are such a refined speaker? It is my whim to inveigh against mercenary priests. You are rich already, why should you be angry? I wish to shut up Vulcan and burn him in his own flames. Are you his or his neighbor that you try to save an idol's shrine from the fire? I choose to make merry over ghosts and owls and monsters of the Nile; and whatever I say, you take it as aimed at you. At whatever fault I point my pen, you cry out that you are meant. You collar me and drag me into court and absurdly charge me with writing satires when I only write plain prose!

So you really think yourself a pretty fellow just because you have a lucky name! Why it does not follow at all. A broke is called a broke just because the light does not break through it. The Fates are called sparers, just because they never spare. The Furies are spoken of as gracious, because they show no grace. And in common speech Ethiopians go by the name of silverlings. Still, if the showing up of faults always angers you, I will soothe you now with the words of Persius: May you be a catch for my lord and lady's daughter! May the pretty ladies scramble for you! May the ground you walk on turn to a rose-bed!

3. All the same, I will give you a hint what features to hide if you want to look your best. Show no nose upon your face and keep your mouth shut. You will then stand some chance of being counted both handsome and eloquent.

LETTER XLI

To Marcella

An effort having been made to convert Marcella to Montanism, Jerome here summarizes for her its leading doctrines, which he contrasts with those of the Church. Written at Rome in 385 A.D.

1. As regards the passages brought together from the gospel of John with which a certain votary of Montanus has assailed you, passages in which our Saviour promises that He will go to the Father, and that He will send the Paraclete — as regards these, the Acts of the Apostles inform us both for what time the promises were made, and at what time they were actually fulfilled. Ten days had elapsed, we are told, from the Lord's ascension and fifty from His resurrection, when the Holy Spirit came down, and the tongues of the believers were cloven, so that each spoke every language. Then it was that, when certain persons of those who as yet believed not declared that the disciples were drunk with new wine, Peter standing in the midst of the apostles, and of all the concourse said: You men of Judæa and all you that dwell at Jerusalem, be this known unto you and hearken to my words: for these are not drunken as you suppose, seeing it is but the third hour of the day. But this is that which was spoken of by the prophet Joel. And it shall come to pass in the last days, says God, I will pour out of my spirit upon all flesh: and your sons and daughters shall prophesy, and your young men shall see visions, and your old men shall dream dreams: and on my servants, and on my handmaidens I will pour out...of my spirit. Acts 2:14-18

2. If, then, the apostle Peter, upon whom the Lord has founded the Church, Matthew 16:18 has expressly said that the prophecy and promise of the Lord were then and there fulfilled, how can we claim another fulfilment for ourselves? If the Montanists reply that Philip's four daughters prophesied Acts 21:9 at a later date, and that a prophet is mentioned named Agabus, and that in the partition of the spirit, prophets are spoken of as well as apostles, teachers and others, and that Paul himself prophesied many things concerning heresies still future, and the end of the world; we tell them that we do not so much reject prophecy— for this is attested by the passion of the Lord — as refuse to receive prophets whose utterances fail to accord with the Scriptures old and new.

3. In the first place we differ from the Montanists regarding the rule of faith. We distinguish the Father, the Son, and the Holy Spirit as three persons, but unite them as one substance. They, on the other hand, following the doctrine of Sabellius, force the Trinity into the narrow limits of a single personality. We, while we do not encourage them, yet allow second marriages, since Paul bids the younger widows to marry. 1 Timothy 5:14 They suppose a repetition of marriage a sin so awful that he who has committed it is to be regarded as an adulterer. We, according to the apostolic tradition (in which the whole world is at one with us), fast through one Lent yearly; whereas they keep three in the year as though three

saviours had suffered. I do not mean, of course, that it is unlawful to fast at other times through the year — always excepting Pentecost — only that while in Lent it is a duty of obligation, at other seasons it is a matter of choice. With us, again, the bishops occupy the place of the apostles, but with them a bishop ranks not first but third. For while they put first the patriarchs of Pepusa in Phrygia, and place next to these the ministers called stewards, the bishops are relegated to the third or almost the lowest rank. No doubt their object is to make their religion more pretentious by putting that last which we put first. Again they close the doors of the Church to almost every fault, while we read daily, I desire the repentance of a sinner rather than his death, Ezekiel 18:23 and Shall they fall and not arise, says the Lord, Jeremiah 8:4 and once more Return ye backsliding children and I will heal your backslidings. Jeremiah 3:22 Their strictness does not prevent them from themselves committing grave sins, far from it; but there is this difference between us and them, that, whereas they in their self-righteousness blush to confess their faults, we do penance for ours, and so more readily gain pardon for them.

4. I pass over their sacraments of sin, made up as they are said to be, of sucking children subjected to a triumphant martyrdom. I prefer, I say, not to credit these; accusations of blood-shedding may well be false. But I must confute the open blasphemy of men who say that God first determined in the Old Testament to save the world by Moses and the prophets, but that finding Himself unable to fulfil His purpose He took to Himself a body of the Virgin, and preaching under the form of the Son in Christ, underwent death for our salvation. Moreover that, when by these two steps He was unable to save the world, He last of all descended by the Holy Spirit upon Montanus and those demented women Prisca and Maximilia; and that thus the mutilated and emasculate Montanus possessed a fullness of knowledge such as was never claimed by Paul; for he was content to say, We know in part, and we prophesy in part, and again, Now we see through a glass darkly. 1 Corinthians 13:9, 12

These are statements which require no refutation. To expose the infidelity of the Montanists is to triumph over it. Nor is it necessary that in so short a letter as this I should overthrow the several absurdities which they bring forward. You are well acquainted with the Scriptures; and, as I take it, you have written, not because you have been disturbed by their cavils, but only to learn my opinion about them.

LETTER XLII

To Marcella

At Marcella's request Jerome explains to her what is the sin against the Holy Ghost spoken of by Christ, and shows Novatian's explanation of it to be untenable. Written at Rome in 385 A.D.

1. The question you send is short and the answer is clear. There is this passage in the gospel: Whosoever speaks a word against the Son of Man, it shall be forgiven him; but whosoever speaks against the Holy Ghost, it shall not be forgiven him neither in this world nor in the world to come. Matthew 12:32 Now if Novatian affirms that none but Christian renegades can sin against the Holy Ghost, it is plain that the Jews who blasphemed Christ were not guilty of this sin. Yet they were wicked husbandmen, they had slain the prophets, they were then compassing the death of the Lord; Matthew 21:33 and so utterly lost were they that the Son of God told them that it was they whom he had come to save. Matthew 18:11 It must be proved to Novatian, therefore, that the sin which shall never be forgiven is not the blasphemy of men disembowelled by torture who in their agony deny their Lord, but is the captious clamor of those who, while they see that God's works are the fruit of virtue, ascribe the virtue to a demon and declare the signs wrought to belong not to the divine excellence but to the devil. And this is the whole gist of our Saviour's argument, when He teaches that Satan cannot be cast out by Satan, and that his kingdom is not divided against itself. Matthew 12:25-26 If it is the devil's object to injure God's creation, how can he wish to cure the sick and to expel himself from the bodies possessed by him? Let Novatian prove that of those who have been compelled to sacrifice before a judge's tribunal any has declared of the things written in the gospel that they were wrought not by the Son of God but by Beelzebub, the prince of the devils; Matthew 12:24 and then he will be able to make good his contention that this is the blasphemy against the Holy Ghost which shall never be forgiven.

2. But to put a more searching question still: let Novatian tell us how he distinguishes speaking against the Son of Man from blasphemy against the Holy Ghost. For I maintain that on his principles men who have denied Christ under persecution have only spoken against the Son of Man, and have not blasphemed the Holy Ghost. For when a man is asked if he is a Christian, and declares that he is not; obviously in denying Christ, that is the Son of Man, he does no despite to the Holy Ghost. But if his denial of Christ involves a denial of the Holy Ghost, this heretic can perhaps tell us how the Son of Man can be denied without sinning against the Holy Ghost. If he thinks that we are here intended by the term Holy Ghost to understand the Father, no mention at all of the Father is made by the denier in his denial. When the apostle Peter, taken aback by a maid's question, denied the Lord, did he sin against the Son of Man or against the Holy Ghost? If Novatian absurdly twists Peter's words, I know not the man, Matthew 26:74 to mean a denial not of Christ's Messiahship but of His humanity, he will make the

Saviour a liar, for He foretold that He Himself, that is His divine Sonship, must be denied. Now, when Peter denied the Son of God, he wept bitterly and effaced his threefold denial by a threefold confession. John 21:15-17 His sin, therefore, was not the sin against the Holy Ghost which can never be forgiven. It is obvious, then, that this sin involves blasphemy, calling one Beelzebub for his actions, whose virtues prove him to be God. If Novatian can bring an instance of a renegade who has called Christ Beelzebub, I will at once give up my position and admit that after such a fall the denier can win no forgiveness. To give way under torture and to deny oneself to be a Christian is one thing, to say that Christ is the devil is another. And this you will yourself see if you read the passage attentively.

3. I ought to have discussed the matter more fully, but some friends have visited my humble abode, and I cannot refuse to give myself up to them. Still, as it might seem arrogant not to answer you at once, I have compressed a wide subject into a few words, and have sent you not a letter but an explanatory note.

LETTER XLIII

To Marcella

Jerome draws a contrast between his daily life and that of Origen, and sorrowfully admits his own shortcomings. He then suggests to Marcella the advantages which life in the country offers over life in town, and hints that he is himself disposed to make trial of it. Written at Rome in 385 A.D.

1. Ambrose who supplied Origen, true man of adamant and of brass, with money, materials and amanuenses to bring out his countless books — Ambrose, in a letter to his friend from Athens, states that they never took a meal together without something being read, and never went to bed till some portion of Scripture had been brought home to them by a brother's voice. Night and day, in fact, were so ordered that prayer only gave place to reading and reading to prayer.

2. Have we, brute beasts that we are, ever done the like? Why, we yawn if we read for over an hour; we rub our foreheads and vainly try to suppress our languor. And then, after this great feat, we plunge for relief into worldly business once more.

I say nothing of the meals with which we dull our faculties, and I would rather not estimate the time that we spend in paying and receiving visits. Next we fall into conversation; we waste our words, we attack people behind their backs, we detail their way of living, we carp at them and are carped at by them in turn. Such is the fare that engages our attention at dinner and afterwards. Then, when our guests have retired, we make up our accounts, and these are sure to cause us either anger or anxiety. The first makes us like raging lions, and the second seeks vainly to make provision for years to come. We do not recollect the words of the Gospel: You fool, this night your soul shall be required of you: then whose shall those things be which you have provided? Luke 12:20 The clothing which we buy is designed not merely for use but for display. Where there is a chance of saving money we quicken our pace, speak promptly, and keep our ears open. If we hear of household losses — such as often occur — our looks become dejected and gloomy. The gain of a penny fills us with joy; the loss of a half-penny plunges us into sorrow. One man is of so many minds that the prophet's prayer is: Lord, in your city scatter their image. For created as we are in the image of God and after His likeness, Genesis 1:26 it is our own wickedness which makes us assume masks. Just as on the stage the same actor now figures as a brawny Hercules, now softens into a tender Venus, now shivers in the role of Cybele; so we — who, if we were not of the world, would be hated by the world John 15:19 — for every sin that we commit have a corresponding mask.

3. Wherefore, seeing that we have journeyed for much of our life through a troubled sea, and that our vessel has been in turn shaken by raging blasts and shattered upon treacherous reefs, let us, as soon as may be, make for the haven of rural quietude. There such country dainties as milk and household bread, and greens watered by our own hands, will supply us with coarse but harmless fare. So

living, sleep will not call us away from prayer, nor satiety from reading. In summer the shade of a tree will afford us privacy. In autumn the quality of the air and the leaves strewn under foot will invite us to stop and rest. In springtime the fields will be bright with flowers, and our psalms will sound the sweeter for the twittering of the birds. When winter comes with its frost and snow, I shall not have to buy fuel, and, whether I sleep or keep vigil, shall be warmer than in town. At least, so far as I know, I shall keep off the cold at less expense. Let Rome keep to itself its noise and bustle, let the cruel shows of the arena go on, let the crowd rave at the circus, let the playgoers revel in the theatres and — for I must not altogether pass over our Christian friends — let the House of Ladies hold its daily sittings. It is good for us to cleave to the Lord, and to put our hope in the Lord God, so that when we have exchanged our present poverty for the kingdom of heaven, we may be able to exclaim: Whom have I in heaven but you? And there is none upon earth that I desire beside you. Surely if we can find such blessedness in heaven we may well grieve to have sought after pleasures poor and passing here upon earth. Farewell.

LETTER XLIV

To Marcella

Marcella had sent some small articles as a present (probably to Paula and Eustochium) and Jerome now writes in their name to thank her for them. He notices the appropriateness of the gifts, not only to the ladies, but also to himself. Written at Rome in 385 A.D.

When absent in body we are wont to converse together in spirit. Colossians 2:5 Each of us does what he or she can. You send us gifts, we send you back letters of thanks. And as we are virgins who have taken the veil, it is our duty to show that hidden meanings lurk under your nice presents. Sackcloth, then, is a token of prayer and fasting, the chairs remind us that a virgin should never stir abroad, and the wax tapers that we should look for the bridegroom's coming with our lights burning. Matthew 25:1 The cups also warn us to mortify the flesh and always to be ready for martyrdom. How bright, says the psalmist, is the cup of the Lord, intoxicating them that drink it! Moreover, when you offer to matrons little fly-flaps to brush away mosquitoes, it is a charming way of hinting that they should at once check voluptuous feelings, for dying flies, we are told, spoil sweet ointment. In such presents, then, as these, virgins can find a model, and matrons a pattern. To me, too, your gifts convey a lesson, although one of an opposite kind. For chairs suit idlers, sackcloth does for penitents, and cups are wanted for the thirsty. And I shall be glad to light your tapers, if only to banish the terrors of the night and the fears of an evil conscience.

LETTER XLV

To Asella

After leaving Rome for the East, Jerome writes to Asella to refute the calumnies by which he had been assailed, especially as regards his intimacy with Paula and Eustochium. Written on board ship at Ostia, in August, 385 A.D.

1. Were I to think myself able to requite your kindness I should be foolish. God is able in my stead to reward a soul which is consecrated to Him. So unworthy, indeed, am I of your regard that I have never ventured to estimate its value or even to wish that it might be given me for Christ's sake. Some consider me a wicked man, laden with iniquity; and such language is more than justified by my actual sins. Yet in dealing with the bad you do well to account them good. It is dangerous to judge another man's servant; Romans 14:4 and to speak evil of the righteous is a sin not easily pardoned. The day will surely come when you and I shall mourn for others; for not a few will be in the flames.

2. I am said to be an infamous turncoat, a slippery knave, one who lies and deceives others by Satanic arts. Which is the safer course, I should like to know, to invent or credit these charges against innocent persons, or to refuse to believe them, even of the guilty? Some kissed my hands, yet attacked me with the tongues of vipers; sympathy was on their lips, but malignant joy in their hearts. The Lord saw them and had them in derision, reserving my poor self and them for judgment to come. One would attack my gait or my way of laughing; another would find something amiss in my looks; another would suspect the simplicity of my manner. Such is the company in which I have lived for almost three years.

It often happened that I found myself surrounded with virgins, and to some of these I expounded the divine books as best I could. Our studies brought about constant intercourse, this soon ripened into intimacy, and this, in turn, produced mutual confidence. If they have ever seen anything in my conduct unbecoming a Christian let them say so. Have I taken any one's money? Have I not disdained all gifts, whether small or great? Has the chink of any one's coin been heard in my hand? 1 Samuel 12:3 Has my language been equivocal, or my eye wanton? No; my sex is my one crime, and even on this score I am not assailed, save when there is a talk of Paula going to Jerusalem. Very well, then. They believed my accuser when he lied; why do they not believe him when he retracts? He is the same man now that he was then, and yet he who before declared me guilty now confesses that I am innocent. Surely a man's words under torture are more trustworthy than in moments of gayety, except, indeed, that people are prone to believe falsehoods designed to gratify their ears, or, worse still, stories which, till then uninvented, they have urged others to invent.

3. Before I became acquainted with the family of the saintly Paula, all Rome resounded with my praises. Almost every one concurred in judging me worthy of the episcopate. Damasus, of blessed memory, spoke no words but mine. Men called me holy, humble, eloquent.

Did I ever cross the threshold of a light woman? Was I ever fascinated by silk dresses, or glowing gems, or rouged faces, or display of gold? Of all the ladies in Rome but one had power to subdue me, and that one was Paula. She mourned and fasted, she was squalid with dirt, her eyes were dim from weeping. For whole nights she would pray to the Lord for mercy, and often the rising sun found her still at her prayers. The psalms were her only songs, the Gospel her whole speech, continence her one indulgence, fasting the staple of her life. The only woman who took my fancy was one whom I had not so much as seen at table. But when I began to revere, respect, and venerate her as her conspicuous chastity deserved, all my former virtues forsook me on the spot.

4. Oh! envy, that dost begin by tearing yourself! Oh! cunning malignity of Satan, that dost always persecute things holy! Of all the ladies in Rome, the only ones that caused scandal were Paula and Melanium, who, despising their wealth and deserting their children, uplifted the cross of the Lord as a standard of religion. Had they frequented the baths, or chosen to use perfumes, or taken advantage of their wealth and position as widows to enjoy life and to be independent, they would have been saluted as ladies of high rank and saintliness. As it is, of course, it is in order to appear beautiful that they put on sackcloth and ashes, and they endure fasting and filth merely to go down into the Gehenna of fire! As if they could not perish with the crowd whom the mob applauds! If it were Gentiles or Jews who thus assailed their mode of life, they would at least have the consolation of failing to please only those whom Christ Himself has failed to please. But, shameful to say, it is Christians who thus neglect the care of their own households, and, disregarding the beams in their own eyes, look for motes in those of their neighbors. Matthew 7:3 They pull to pieces every profession of religion, and think that they have found a remedy for their own doom, if they can disprove the holiness of others, if they can detract from every one, if they can show that those who perish are many, and sinners, a great multitude.

5. You bathe daily; another regards such over-niceness as defilement. You surfeit yourself on wild fowl and pride yourself on eating sturgeon; I, on the contrary, fill my belly with beans. You find pleasure in troops of laughing girls; I prefer Paula and Melanium who weep. You covet what belongs to others; they disdain what is their own. You like wines flavored with honey; they drink cold water, more delicious still. You count as lost what you cannot have, eat up, and devour on the moment; they believe in the Scriptures, and look for good things to come. And if they are wrong, and if the resurrection of the body on which they rely is a foolish delusion, what does it matter to you? We, on our side, look with disfavor on such a life as yours. You can fatten yourself on your good things as much as you please; I for my part prefer paleness and emaciation. You suppose that men like me are unhappy; we regard you as more unhappy still. Thus we reciprocate each other's thoughts, and appear to each other mutually insane.

6. I write this in haste, dear Lady Asella, as I go on board, overwhelmed with grief and tears; yet I thank my God that I am counted worthy of the world's hatred. John 15:18 Pray for me that, after Babylon, I may see Jerusalem once more; that Joshua, the son of Josedech, may have dominion over me, Haggai 1:1 and not Nebuchadnezzar, that Ezra, whose name means helper, may come and restore me to my own country. I was a fool in wishing to sing the Lord's song in a strange land, and in leaving Mount Sinai, to seek the help of Egypt. I forgot that the Gospel warns us Luke 10:30-35 that he who goes down from Jerusalem immediately falls among robbers, is spoiled, is wounded, is left for dead. But, although priest and Levite may disregard me, there is still the good Samaritan who, when men said to him, You are a Samaritan and hast a devil, John 8:48 disclaimed having a devil, but did not disclaim being a Samaritan, John 8:49 this being the Hebrew equivalent for our word guardian. Men call me a mischief-maker, and I take the title as a recognition of my faith. For I am but a servant, and the Jews still call my master a magician. The apostle, likewise, is spoken of as a deceiver. There has no temptation taken me but such as is common to man. 1 Corinthians 10:13 How few distresses have I endured, I who am yet a soldier of the cross! Men have laid to my charge a crime of which I am not guilty; but I know that I must enter the kingdom of heaven through evil report as well as through good. 2 Corinthians 6:8

7. Salute Paula and Eustochium, who, whatever the world may think, are always mine in Christ. Salute Albina, your mother, and Marcella, your sister; Marcellina also, and the holy Felicitas; and say to them all: We must all stand before the judgment seat of Christ, Romans 14:10 and there shall be revealed the principle by which each has lived.

And now, illustrious model of chastity and virginity, remember me, I beseech you, in your prayers, and by your intercessions calm the waves of the sea.

LETTER XLVI

Paula and Eustochium to Marcella

Jerome writes to Marcella in the name of Paula and Eustochium, describing the charms of the Holy Land, and urging her to leave Rome and to join her old companions at Bethlehem. Much of the letter is devoted to disposing of the objection that since the Passion of Christ the Holy Land has been under a curse. The date of the letter is A.D. 386. It is written from Bethlehem, which now becomes Jerome's home for the remainder of his life.

1. Love cannot be measured, impatience knows no bounds, and eagerness can brook no delay. Wherefore we, oblivious of our weakness, and relying more on our will than our capacity, desire — pupils though we be — to instruct our mistress. We are like the sow in the proverb, which sets up to teach the goddess of invention. You were the first to set our tinder alight; the first, by precept and example, to urge us to adopt our present life. As a hen gathers her chickens, so did you take us under your wing. And will you now let us fly about at random with no mother near us? Will you leave us to dread the swoop of the hawk and the shadow of each passing bird of prey? Separated from you, we do what we can: we utter our mournful plaint, and more by sobs than by tears we adjure you to give back to us the Marcella whom we love. She is mild, she is suave, she is sweeter than the sweetest honey. She must not, therefore, be stern and morose to us, whom her winning ways have roused to adopt a life like her own.

2. Assuming that what we ask is for the best, our eagerness to obtain it is nothing to be ashamed of. And if all the Scriptures agree with our view, we are not too bold in urging you to a course to which you have yourself often urged us.

What are God's first words to Abraham? Get you out of your country and from your kindred unto a land that I will show you. Genesis 12:1 The patriarch — the first to receive a promise of Christ — is here told to leave the Chaldees, to leave the city of confusion and its *rehoboth* Genesis 10:11 or broad places; to leave also the plain of Shinar, where the tower of pride had been raised to heaven. He has to pass through the waves of this world, and to ford its rivers; those by which the saints sat down and wept when they remembered Zion, and Chebar's flood, whence Ezekiel was carried to Jerusalem by the hair of his head. Ezekiel 8:3 All this Abraham undergoes that he may dwell in a land of promise watered from above, and not like Egypt, from below, Deuteronomy 11:10 no producer of herbs for the weak and ailing, Romans 14:2 but a land that looks for the early and the latter rain from heaven. It is a land of hills and valleys, Deuteronomy 11:11 and stands high above the sea. The attractions of the world it entirely wants, but its spiritual attractions are for this all the greater. Mary, the mother of the Lord, left the lowlands and made her way to the hill country, when, after receiving the angel's message, she realized that she bore within her womb the Son of God. When of old the Philistines had been overcome, when their devilish audacity had

been smitten, when their champion had fallen on his face to the earth,
1 Samuel 17:49 it was from this city that there went forth a procession of jubilant souls, a harmonious choir to sing our David's victory over tens of thousands. Here, too, it was that the angel grasped his sword, and while he laid waste the whole of the ungodly city, marked out the temple of the Lord in the threshing floor of Ornan, king of the Jebusites. Thus early was it made plain that Christ's church would grow up, not in Israel, but among the Gentiles. Turn back to Genesis, Genesis 14:18 and you will find that this was the city over which Melchizedek held sway, that king of Salem who, as a type of Christ, offered to Abraham bread and wine, and even then consecrated the mystery which Christians consecrate in the body and blood of the Saviour.

3. Perhaps you will tacitly reprove us for deserting the order of Scripture, and letting our confused account ramble this way and that, as one thing or another strikes us. If so, we say once more what we said at the outset: love has no logic, and impatience knows no rule. In the Song of Songs the precept is given as a hard one: Regulate your love towards me. And so we plead that, if we err, we do so not from ignorance but from feeling.

Well, then, to bring forward something still more out of place, we must go back to yet remoter times. Tradition has it that in this city, nay, more, on this very spot, Adam lived and died. The place where our Lord was crucified is called Calvary, because the skull of the primitive man was buried there. So it came to pass that the second Adam, that is the blood of Christ, as it dropped from the cross, washed away the sins of the buried protoplast, the first Adam, and thus the words of the apostle were fulfilled: Awake, you that sleep, and arise from the dead, and Christ shall give you light. Ephesians 5:14

It would be tedious to enumerate all the prophets and holy men who have been sent forth from this place. All that is strange and mysterious to us is familiar and natural to this city and country. By its very names, three in number, it proves the doctrine of the trinity. For it is called first Jebus, then Salem, then Jerusalem: names of which the first means down-trodden, the second peace, and the third vision of peace. For it is only by slow stages that we reach our goal; it is only after we have been trodden down that we are lifted up to see the vision of peace. Because of this peace Solomon, the man of peace, was born there, and in peace was his place made. King of kings, and lord of lords, his name and that of the city show him to be a type of Christ. Need we speak of David and his descendants, all of whom reigned here? As Judæa is exalted above all other provinces, so is this city exalted above all Judæa. To speak more tersely, the glory of the province is derived from its capital; and whatever fame the members possess is in every case due to the head.

4. You have long been anxious to break forth into speech; the very letters we have formed perceive it, and our paper already understands the question you are going to put. You will reply to us by saying: it was so of old, when the Lord loved the gates of Zion more than all the dwellings of Jacob, and when her foundations were in the holy mountains. Even these verses, however, are susceptible of a deeper interpretation. But things are changed since then. The risen Lord has proclaimed in

tones of thunder: Your house is left unto you desolate. With tears He has prophesied its downfall: O Jerusalem, Jerusalem, you that killest the prophets, and stone them which are sent unto you; how often would I have gathered your children together even as a hen gathers her chickens under her wings, and you would not. Behold your house is left unto you desolate. Matthew 23:37-38 The veil of the temple has been rent; Matthew 27:51 an army has encompassed Jerusalem, it has been stained by the blood of the Lord. Now, therefore, its guardian angels have forsaken it and the grace of Christ has been withdrawn. Josephus, himself a Jewish writer, asserts that at the Lord's crucifixion there broke from the temple voices of heavenly powers, saying: Let us depart hence. These and other considerations show that where grace abounded there did sin much more abound. Romans 5:20 Again, when the apostles received the command: Go and teach all nations, Matthew 28:19 and when they said themselves: It was necessary that the word of God should first have been spoken to you, but seeing ye put it from you...lo we turn to the Gentiles, Acts 13:46 then all the spiritual importance of Judæa and its old intimacy with God were transferred by the apostles to the nations.

5. The difficulty is strongly stated, and may well puzzle even those proficient in Scripture; but for all that, it admits of an easy solution. The Lord wept for the fall of Jerusalem, Luke 19:41 and He would not have done so if He did not love it. He wept for Lazarus because He loved him. John 11:35-36 The truth is that it was the people who sinned and not the place. The capture of a city is involved in the slaying of its inhabitants. If Jerusalem was destroyed, it was that its people might be punished; if the temple was overthrown, it was that its figurative sacrifices might be abolished. As regards its site, lapse of time has but invested it with fresh grandeur. The Jews of old reverenced the Holy of Holies, because of the things contained in it — the cherubim, the mercy-seat, the Ark of the Covenant, the manna, Aaron's rod, and the golden altar. Hebrews 9:3-5 Does the Lord's sepulchre seem less worthy of veneration? As often as we enter it we see the Saviour in His grave clothes, and if we linger we see again the angel sitting at His feet, and the napkin folded at His head. Long before this sepulchre was hewn out by Joseph, its glory was foretold in Isaiah's prediction, his rest shall be glorious, Isaiah 11:10 meaning that the place of the Lord's burial should be held in universal honor.

6. How, then, you will say, do we read in the apocalypse written by John: The beast that ascends out of the bottomless pit shall...kill them [that is, obviously, the prophets], and their dead bodies shall lie in the street of the great city which spiritually is called Sodom and Egypt, where also their Lord was crucified? If the great city where the Lord was crucified is Jerusalem, and if the place of His crucifixion is spiritually called Sodom and Egypt; then as the Lord was crucified at Jerusalem, Jerusalem must be Sodom and Egypt. Holy Scripture, I reply first of all, cannot contradict itself. One book cannot invalidate the drift of the whole. A single verse cannot annul the meaning of a book. Ten lines earlier in the apocalypse it is written: Rise and measure the temple of God, and the altar, and them that worship therein. But the court which is without the temple leave out and measure it not; for it is given unto the Gentiles; and the holy city shall they tread

under foot forty and two months. Revelation 11:2 The apocalypse was written by John long after the Lord's passion, yet in it he speaks of Jerusalem as the holy city. But if so, how can he spiritually call it Sodom and Egypt? It is no answer to say that the Jerusalem which is called holy is the heavenly one which is to be, while that which is called Sodom is the earthly one tottering to its downfall. For it is the Jerusalem to come that is referred to in the description of the beast, which shall ascend out of the bottomless pit, and shall make war against the two prophets, and shall overcome them and kill them, and their dead bodies shall lie in the street of the great city. Revelation 11:7-8 At the close of the book it is farther described thus: And the city lies four-square, and the length of it and the breadth are the same as the height; and he measured the city with the golden reed twelve thousand furlongs. The length and the breadth and the height of it are equal. And he measured the walls thereof, an hundred and forty and four cubits, according to the measure of a man, that is, of the angel. And the building of the wall of it was of jasper; and the city was pure gold Revelation 21:16-18 — and so on. Now where there is a square there can be neither length nor breadth. And what kind of measurement is that which makes length and breadth equal to height? And how can there be walls of jasper, or a whole city of pure gold; its foundations and its streets of precious stones, and its twelve gates each glowing with pearls?

7. Evidently this description cannot be taken literally (in fact, it is absurd to suppose a city the length, breadth and height of which are all twelve thousand furlongs), and therefore the details of it must be mystically understood. The great city which Cain first built and called after his son Genesis 4:17 must be taken to represent this world, which the devil, that accuser of his brethren, that fratricide who is doomed to perish, has built of vice cemented with crime, and filled with iniquity. Therefore it is spiritually called Sodom and Egypt. Thus it is written, Sodom shall return to her former estate, Ezekiel 16:55 that is to say, the world must be restored as it has been before. For we cannot believe that Sodom and Gomorrha, Admah and Zeboim Deuteronomy 29:23 are to be built again: they must be left to lie in ashes forever. We never read of Egypt as put for Jerusalem: it always stands for this world. To collect from Scripture the countless proofs of this would be tedious: I shall adduce but one passage, a passage in which this world is most clearly called Egypt. The apostle Jude, the brother of James, writes thus in his catholic epistle: I will, therefore, put you in remembrance, though ye once knew this how that Jesus, having saved the people out of the land of Egypt, afterward destroyed them that believed not. Jude 5 And, lest you should fancy Joshua the Son of Nun to be meant, the passage goes on thus: And the angels which kept not their first estate, but left their own habitation, he has reserved in everlasting chains, under darkness, unto the judgment of the great day. Jude 6 Moreover, to convince you that in every place where Egypt, Sodom and Gomorrha are named together it is not these spots, but the present world, which is meant, he mentions them immediately in this sense. Even as Sodom and Gomorrha, he writes, and the cities about them, in like manner giving themselves over to fornication and going after strange flesh, are set forth for an example, suffering the vengeance of eternal fire. Jude 7 But what need is there to collect more proofs when, after the passion and the resurrection of the Lord, the evangelist Matthew tells us: The rocks rent, and the graves were opened; and many bodies of the saints

which slept arose and came out of the graves after his resurrection, and went into the holy city and appeared unto many? Matthew 27:51, 53 We must not interpret this passage straight off, as many people absurdly do, of the heavenly Jerusalem: the apparition there of the bodies of the saints could be no sign to men of the Lord's rising. Since, therefore, the evangelists and all the Scriptures speak of Jerusalem as the holy city, and since the psalmist commands us to worship the Lord at his footstool; allow no one to call it Sodom and Egypt, for by it the Lord forbids men to swear because it is the city of the great king. Matthew 5:35

8. The land is accursed, you say, because it has drunk in the blood of the Lord. On what grounds, then, do men regard as blessed those spots where Peter and Paul, the leaders of the Christian host, have shed their blood for Christ? If the confession of men and servants is glorious, must there not be glory likewise in the confession of their Lord and God? Everywhere we venerate the tombs of the martyrs; we apply their holy ashes to our eyes; we even touch them, if we may, with our lips. And yet some think that we should neglect the tomb in which the Lord Himself is buried. If we refuse to believe human testimony, let us at least credit the devil and his angels. Matthew 25:41 For when in front of the Holy Sepulchre they are driven out of those bodies which they have possessed, they moan and tremble as if they stood before Christ's judgment-seat, and grieve, too late that they have crucified Him in whose presence they now cower. If — as a wicked theory maintains — this holy place has, since the Lord's passion, become an abomination, why was Paul in such haste to reach Jerusalem to keep Pentecost in it? Acts 20:16 Yet to those who held him back he said: What mean ye to weep and to break my heart? For I am ready not to be bound only, but also to die at Jerusalem, for the name of the Lord Jesus. Acts 21:13 Need I speak of those other holy and illustrious men who, after the preaching of Christ, brought their votive gifts and offerings to the brethren who were at Jerusalem?

9. Time forbids me to survey the period which has passed since the Lord's ascension, or to recount the bishops, the martyrs, the divines, who have come to Jerusalem from a feeling that their devotion and knowledge would be incomplete and their virtue without the finishing touch, unless they adored Christ in the very spot where the gospel first flashed from the gibbet. If a famous orator blames a man for having learned Greek at Lilybæum instead of at Athens, and Latin in Sicily instead of at Rome (on the ground, obviously, that each province has its own characteristics), can we suppose a Christian's education complete who has not visited the Christian Athens?

10. In speaking thus we do not mean to deny that the kingdom of God is within us, Luke 17:21 or to say that there are no holy men elsewhere; we merely assert in the strongest manner that those who stand first throughout the world are here gathered side by side. We ourselves are among the last, not the first; yet we have come hither to see the first of all nations. Of all the ornaments of the Church our company of monks and virgins is one of the finest; it is like a fair flower or a priceless gem. Every man of note in Gaul hastens hither. The Briton, sundered from our world, no sooner makes progress in religion than he leaves the setting sun in quest of a spot of which he knows only through Scripture and common report. Need we recall the Armenians, the Persians, the peoples of India and

Arabia? Or those of our neighbor, Egypt, so rich in monks; of Pontus and Cappadocia; of Cæle-Syria and Mesopotamia and the teeming east? In fulfilment of the Saviour's words, Wherever the body is, there will the eagles be gathered together, Luke 17:37 they all assemble here and exhibit in this one city the most varied virtues. Differing in speech, they are one in religion, and almost every nation has a choir of its own. Yet amid this great concourse there is no arrogance, no disdain of self-restraint; all strive after humility, that greatest of Christian virtues. Whosoever is last is here regarded as first. Matthew 19:30 Their dress neither provokes remark nor calls for admiration. In whatever guise a man shows himself he is neither censured nor flattered. Long fasts help no one here. Starvation wins no deference, and the taking of food in moderation is not condemned. To his own master each one stands or falls. Romans 14:4 No man judges another lest he be judged of the Lord. Matthew 7:1 Backbiting, so common in other parts, is wholly unknown here. Sensuality and excess are far removed from us. And in the city there are so many places of prayer that a day would not be sufficient to go round them all.

11. But, as every one praises most what is within his reach, let us pass now to the cottage-inn which sheltered Christ and Mary. Luke 2:7 With what expressions and what language can we set before you the cave of the Saviour? The stall where he cried as a babe can be best honored by silence; for words are inadequate to speak its praise. Where are the spacious porticoes? Where are the gilded ceilings? Where are the mansions furnished by the miserable toil of doomed wretches? Where are the costly halls raised by untitled opulence for man's vile body to walk in? Where are the roofs that intercept the sky, as if anything could be finer than the expanse of heaven? Behold, in this poor crevice of the earth the Creator of the heavens was born; here He was wrapped in swaddling clothes; here He was seen by the shepherds; here He was pointed out by the star; here He was adored by the wise men. This spot is holier, me-thinks, than that Tarpeian rock which has shown itself displeasing to God by the frequency with which it has been struck by lightning.

12. Read the apocalypse of John, and consider what is sung therein of the woman arrayed in purple, and of the blasphemy written upon her brow, of the seven mountains, of the many waters, and of the end of Babylon. Come out of her, my people, so the Lord says, that you be not partakers of her sins, and that you receive not of her plagues. Revelation 18:4 Turn back also to Jeremiah and pay heed to what he has written of like import: Flee out of the midst of Babylon, and deliver every man his soul. Jeremiah 51:6 For Babylon the great is fallen, is fallen, and has become the habitation of devils, and the hold of every foul spirit. Revelation 18:2 It is true that Rome has a holy church, trophies of apostles and martyrs, a true confession of Christ. The faith has been preached there by an apostle, heathenism has been trodden down, the name of Christian is daily exalted higher and higher. But the display, power, and size of the city, the seeing and the being seen, the paying and the receiving of visits, the alternate flattery and detraction, talking and listening, as well as the necessity of facing so great a throng even when one is least in the mood to do so — all these things are alike foreign to the principles and fatal to the repose of the monastic life. For when people come in our way we either see them coming and are compelled to speak, or we do not see

them and lay ourselves open to the charge of haughtiness. Sometimes, also, in returning visits we are obliged to pass through proud portals and gilded doors and to face the clamor of carping lackeys. But, as we have said above, in the cottage of Christ all is simple and rustic: and except for the chanting of psalms there is complete silence. Wherever one turns the laborer at his plough sings alleluia, the toiling mower cheers himself with psalms, and the vine-dresser while he prunes his vine sings one of the lays of David. These are the songs of the country; these, in popular phrase, its love ditties: these the shepherd whistles; these the tiller uses to aid his toil.

13. But what are we doing? Forgetting what is required of us, we are taken up with what we wish. Will the time never come when a breathless messenger shall bring the news that our dear Marcella has reached the shores of Palestine, and when every band of monks and every troop of virgins shall unite in a song of welcome? In our excitement we are already hurrying to meet you: without waiting for a vehicle, we hasten off at once on foot. We shall clasp you by the hand, we shall look upon your face; and when, after long waiting, we at last embrace you, we shall find it hard to tear ourselves away. Will the day never come when we shall together enter the Saviour's cave, and together weep in the sepulchre of the Lord with His sister and with His mother? John 19:25 Then shall we touch with our lips the wood of the cross, and rise in prayer and resolve upon the Mount of Olives with the ascending Lord. Acts 1:9, 12 We shall see Lazarus come forth bound with grave clothes, John 11:43-44 we shall look upon the waters of Jordan purified for the washing of the Lord. Matthew 3:13 Thence we shall pass to the folds of the shepherds, Luke 2:8 we shall pray together in the mausoleum of David.
1 Kings 2:10 We shall see the prophet, Amos, upon his crag blowing his shepherd's horn. We shall hasten, if not to the tents, to the monuments of Abraham, Isaac and Jacob, and of their three illustrious wives. We shall see the fountain in which the eunuch was immersed by Philip. Acts 8:36 We shall make a pilgrimage to Samaria, and side by side venerate the ashes of John the Baptist, of Elisha, 2 Kings 13:21 and of Obadiah. We shall enter the very caves where in the time of persecution and famine the companies of the prophets were fed.
1 Kings 18:3-4 If only you will come, we shall go to see Nazareth, as its name denotes, the flower of Galilee. Not far off Cana will be visible, where the water was turned into wine. John 2:1-11 We shall make our way to Tabor,
Matthew 17:1-9 and see the tabernacles there which the Saviour shares, not, as Peter once wished, with Moses and Elijah, but with the Father and with the Holy Ghost. Thence we shall come to the Sea of Gennesaret, and when there we shall see the spots where the five thousand were filled with five loaves, and the four thousand with seven. The town of Nain will meet our eyes, at the gate of which the widow's son was raised to life. Hermon too will be visible, and the torrent of Endor, at which Sisera was vanquished. Our eyes will look also on Capernaum, the scene of so many of our Lord's signs — yes, and on all Galilee besides. And when, accompanied by Christ, we shall have made our way back to our cave through Shiloh and Bethel, and those other places where churches are set up like standards to commemorate the Lord's victories, then we shall sing heartily, we shall weep copiously, we shall pray unceasingly. Wounded with the Saviour's

shaft, we shall say one to another: I have found Him whom my soul loves; I will hold Him and will not let Him go.

LETTER XLVII

To Desiderius

Jerome invites two of his old friends at Rome, Desiderius and his sister (or wife) Serenilla, to join him at Bethlehem. It is possible but not probable that this Desiderius is the same with Desiderius of Aquitaine, who afterwards induced Jerome to write against Vigilantius.

An interval of seven years separates this letter (of which the date is 393 A.D.) from the preceding, and all the letters written during this period have wholly perished.

1. Surprised as I have been, my excellent friend, to read the language which your kindness has prompted you to hold concerning me, I have rejoiced that I possess the testimony of one both eloquent and sincere; but when I turn from you to myself I feel vexed that, owing to my unworthiness, your words of praise and eulogy rather weigh me down than lift me up. You know, of course, that I make it a principle to raise the standard of humility, and to prepare for scaling the heights by walking for the present in the lowest places. For what am I or what is my significance that I should have the voice of learning raised to bear witness of me, or that the palm of eloquence should be laid at my feet by one whose style is so charming that it has almost deterred me from writing a letter at all? I must, however, make the attempt in order that charity which seeks not her own 1 Corinthians 13:5 but always her neighbor's good, may at least return a compliment, since it cannot convey a lesson.

2. I offer my congratulations to you and to your holy and revered sister, Serenilla, who, true to her name, has trodden down the troubled waves of the world, and has passed to Christ's calm haven: a happiness which — if we may trust the augury of your name — is in store for you also. For we read that the holy Daniel was called a man of desires, and the friend of God, because he desired to know His mysteries. Therefore, I do with pleasure what the revered Paula has asked of me. I urge and implore you both by the charity of the Lord that you will give your presence to us, and that a visit to the holy places may induce you to enrich us with this great gift. Even supposing that you do not care for our society, it is still your duty as believers to worship on the spot where the Lord's feet once stood and to see for yourselves the still fresh traces of His birth, His cross, and His passion.

3. Several of my little pieces have flown away out of their nest, and have rashly sought for themselves the honor of publication. I have not sent you any lest I should send works which you already have. But if you care to borrow copies of them, you can do so either from our holy sister, Marcella, who has her abode upon the Aventine, or from that holy man, Domnio, who is the Lot of our times. 2 Peter 2:7-8 Meantime, I look for your arrival, and will give you all I have when you once come; or, if any hindrances prevent you from joining us, I will gladly send you such treatises as you shall desire. Following the example of Tranquillus and of Apollonius the Greek, I have written a book concerning illustrious men

from the apostles' time to our own; and after enumerating a great number I have put myself down on the last page as one born out of due time, and the least of all Christians. 1 Corinthians 15:8-9 Here I have found it necessary to give a short account of my writings down to the fourteenth year of the Emperor Theodosius. If you find, on procuring this treatise from the persons mentioned above, that there are any pieces mentioned which you have not already got, I will have them copied for you by degrees, if you wish it.

LETTER LXVIII

To Pammachius

An apology for the two books against Jovinian which Jerome had written a short time previously, and of which he had sent copies to Rome. These Pammachius and his other friends had withheld from publication, thinking that Jerome had unduly exalted virginity at the expense of marriage. He now writes to make good his position, and to do this makes copious extracts from the obnoxious treatise. The date of the letter is 393 or 394 A.D.

1. Your own silence is my reason for not having written hitherto. For I feared that, if I were to write to you without first hearing from you, you would consider me not so much a conscientious as a troublesome correspondent. But, now that I have been challenged by your most delightful letter, a letter which calls upon me to defend my views by an appeal to first principles, I receive my old fellow-learner, companion, and friend with open arms, as the saying goes; and I look forward to having in you a champion of my poor writings; if, that is to say, I can first conciliate your judgment to give sentence in my favor, and can instruct my advocate in all those points on which I am assailed. For both your favorite, Cicero, and before him — in his one short treatise — Antonius, write to this effect, that the chief requisite for victory is to acquaint one's self carefully with the case which one has to plead.

2. Certain persons find fault with me because in the books which I have written against Jovinian I have been excessive (so they say) in praise of virginity and in depreciation of marriage; and they affirm that to preach up chastity till no comparison is left between a wife and a virgin is equivalent to a condemnation of matrimony. If I remember aright the point of the dispute, the question at issue between myself and Jovinian is that he puts marriage on a level with virginity, while I make it inferior; he declares that there is little or no difference between the two states, I assert that there is a great deal. Finally — a result due under God to your agency — he has been condemned because he has dared to set matrimony on an equality with perpetual chastity. Or, if a virgin and a wife are to be looked on as the same, how comes it that Rome has refused to listen to this impious doctrine? A virgin owes her being to a man, but a man does not owe his to a virgin. There can be no middle course. Either my view of the matter must be embraced, or else that of Jovinian. If I am blamed for putting wedlock below virginity, he must be praised for putting the two states on a level. If, on the other hand, he is condemned for supposing them equal, his condemnation must be taken as testimony in favor of my treatise. If men of the world chafe under the notion that they occupy a position inferior to that of virgins, I wonder that clergymen and monks— who both live celibate lives — refrain from praising what they consistently practise. They cut themselves off from their wives to imitate the chastity of virgins, and yet they will have it that married women are as good as these. They should either be joined again to their wives whom they have renounced, or, if they persist in living apart from them, they will have to confess — by their lives if not by their words

— that, in preferring virginity to marriage, they have chosen the better course. Am I then a mere novice in the Scriptures, reading the sacred volumes for the first time? And is the line there drawn between virginity and marriage so fine that I have been unable to observe it? I could know nothing, forsooth, of the saying, Be not righteous overmuch! Thus, while I try to protect myself on one side, I am wounded on the other; to speak more plainly still, while I close with Jovinian in hand-to-hand combat, Manichæus stabs me in the back. Have I not, I would ask, in the very forefront of my work set the following preface: We are no disciples of Marcion or of Manichæus, to detract from marriage. Nor are we deceived by the error of Tatian, the chief of the Encratites, into supposing all cohabitation unclean. For he condemns and reprobates not marriage only, but foods also which God has created for us to enjoy. 1 Timothy 4:3 We know that in a large house there are vessels not only of silver and of gold, but of wood also and of earth.
2 Timothy 2:20 We know, too, that on the foundation of Christ which Paul the master builder has laid, some build up gold, silver, and precious stones; others, on the contrary, hay, wood, and stubble. 1 Corinthians 3:10-12 We are not ignorant that 'marriage is honorable...and the bed undefiled.' Hebrews 13:4 We have read the first decree of God: 'Be fruitful and multiply and replenish the earth.' Genesis 1:28 But while we allow marriage, we prefer the virginity which springs from it. Gold is more precious than silver, but is silver on that account the less silver? Is it an insult to a tree to prefer its apples to its roots or its leaves? Is it an injury to grain to put the ear before the stalk and the blade? As apples come from the tree and grain from the straw, so virginity comes from wedlock. Yields of one hundredfold, of sixtyfold, and of thirtyfold Matthew 13:8 may all come from one soil and from one sowing, yet they will differ widely in quantity. The yield thirtyfold signifies wedlock, for the joining together of the fingers to express that number, suggestive as it is of a loving gentle kiss or embracing, aptly represents the relation of husband and wife. The yield sixtyfold refers to widows who are placed in a position of distress and tribulation. Accordingly, they are typified by that finger which is placed under the other to express the number sixty; for, as it is extremely trying when one has once tasted pleasure to abstain from its enticements, so the reward of doing this is proportionately great. Moreover, a hundred — I ask the reader to give me his best attention — necessitates a change from the left hand to the right; but while the hand is different the fingers are the same as those which on the left hand signify married women and widows; only in this instance the circle formed by them indicates the crown of virginity.

3. Does a man who speaks thus, I would ask you, condemn marriage? If I have called virginity gold, I have spoken of marriage as silver. I have set forth that the yields an hundredfold, sixtyfold, and thirtyfold — all spring from one soil and from one sowing, although in amount they differ widely. Will any of my readers be so unfair as to judge me, not by my words, but by his own opinion? At any rate, I have dealt much more gently with marriage than most Latin and Greek writers; who, by referring the hundredfold yield to martyrs, the sixtyfold to virgins, and the thirtyfold to widows, show that in their opinion married persons are excluded from the good ground and from the seed of the great Father. But, lest it might be supposed that, though cautious at the outset, I was imprudent in the remainder of my work, have I not, after marking out the divisions of it, on coming to the actual

questions immediately introduced the following: I ask all of you of both sexes, at once those who are virgins and continent and those who are married or twice married, to aid my efforts with your prayers. Jovinian is the foe of all indiscriminately, but can I condemn as Manichæan heretics persons whose prayers I need and whose assistance I entreat to help me in my work?

4. As the brief compass of a letter does not suffer us to delay too long on a single point, let us now pass to those which remain. In explaining the testimony of the apostle, The wife has not power of her own body, but the husband; and likewise, also, the husband has not power of his own body, but the wife, 1 Corinthians 7:4 we have subjoined the following: The entire question relates to those who are living in wedlock, whether it is lawful for them to put away their wives, a thing which the Lord also has forbidden in the Gospel. Matthew 19:9 Hence, also, the apostle says: 'It is good for a man not to touch' a wife or 'a woman,' 1 Corinthians 7:1 as if there were danger in the contact which he who should so touch one could not escape. Accordingly, when the Egyptian woman desired to touch Joseph he flung away his cloak and fled from her hands. Genesis 39:12-13 But as he who has once married a wife cannot, except by consent, abstain from intercourse with her or repudiate her, so long as she does not sin, he must render unto his wife her due, because he has of his own free will bound himself to render it under compulsion. Can one who declares that it is a precept of the Lord that wives should not be put away, and that what God has joined together man must not, without consent, put asunder Matthew 19:6 — can such an one be said to condemn marriage? Again, in the verses which follow, the apostle says: But every man has his proper gift of God, one after this manner, and another after that. 1 Corinthians 7:7 In explanation of this saying we made the following remarks: What I myself would wish, he says, is clear. But since there are diversities of gifts in the church, 1 Corinthians 12:4 I allow marriage as well, that I may not appear to condemn nature. Reflect, too, that the gift of virginity is one thing, that of marriage another. For had there been one reward for married women and for virgins he would never, after giving the counsel of continence, have gone on to say: 'But every man has his proper gift of God, one after this manner and another after that.' Where each class has its proper gift, there must be some distinction between the classes. I allow that marriage, as well as virginity, is the gift of God, but there is a great difference between gift and gift. Finally, the apostle himself says of one who had lived in incest and afterwards repented: 'Contrariwise ye ought rather to forgive him and comfort him,' 2 Corinthians 2:7 and 'To whom you forgive anything, I forgive also.' 2 Corinthians 2:10 And, lest we might suppose a man's gift to be but a small thing, he has added: 'For if I forgave anything, to whom I forgave it, for your sakes forgave I it in the sight of Christ.' 2 Corinthians 2:10 The gifts of Christ are different. Hence Joseph as a type of Him had a coat of many colors. Genesis 37:23 So in the forty-fourth psalm we read of the Church: 'Upon your right hand stood the queen in a vesture of gold, wrought about with various colors.' The apostle Peter, too, speaks (of husbands and wives) 'as being heirs together of the manifold grace of God.' In Greek the expression is still more striking, the word used being ποικίλη, that is, 'many-colored.'

5. I ask, then, what is the meaning of men's obstinate determination to shut their eyes and to refuse to look on what is as clear as day? I have said that there are diversities of gifts in the Church, and that virginity is one gift and wedlock another. And shortly after I have used the words: I allow marriage also to be a gift of God, but there is a great difference between gift and gift. Can it be said that I condemn that which in the clearest terms I declare to be the gift of God? Moreover, if Joseph is taken as a type of the Lord, his coat of many colors is a type of virgins and widows, celibates and wedded. Can any one who has any part in Christ's tunic be regarded as an alien? Have we not spoken of the very queen herself — that is, the Church of the Saviour — as wearing a vesture of gold wrought about with various colors? Moreover, when I came to discuss marriage in connection with the following verses, 1 Corinthians 7:8-10 I still adhered to the same view. This passage, I said, has indeed no relation to the present controversy; for, following the decision of the Lord, the apostle teaches that a wife must not be put away saving for fornication, and that, if she has been put away, she cannot during the lifetime of her husband marry another man, or, at any rate, that she ought, if possible, to be reconciled to her husband. In another verse he speaks to the same effect: 'The wife is bound...as long as her husband lives; but if her husband be dead, she is loosed from the law of her husband; Romans 7:2 she is at liberty to be married to whom she will; only in the Lord,' 1 Corinthians 7:39 that is to a Christian. Thus the apostle, while he allows a second or a third marriage in the Lord, forbids even a first with a heathen.

6. I ask my detractors to open their ears and to realize the fact that I have allowed second and third marriages in the Lord. If, then, I have not condemned second and third marriages, how can I have proscribed a first? Moreover, in the passage where I interpret the words of the apostle, Is any man called being circumcised? Let him not become uncircumcised. Is any called in uncircumcision? Let him not be circumcised 1 Corinthians 7:18 (a passage, it is true, which some most careful interpreters of Scripture refer to the circumcision and slavery of the Law), do I not in the clearest terms stand up for the marriage-tie? My words are these: 'If any man is called in uncircumcision, let him not be circumcised.' You had a wife, the apostle says, when you believed. Do not fancy your faith in Christ to be a reason for parting from her. For 'God has called us in peace.' 'Circumcision is nothing and uncircumcision is nothing but the keeping of the commandments of God.' 1 Corinthians 7:19 Neither celibacy nor wedlock is of the slightest use without works, since even faith, the distinguishing mark of Christians, if it have not works, is said to be dead, James 2:17 and on such terms as these the virgins of Vesta or of Juno, who was constant to one husband, might claim to be numbered among the saints. And a little further on he says: 'Are you called being a servant, care not for it; but, if you may be made free, use it rather;' 1 Corinthians 7:21 that is to say, if you have a wife, and are bound to her, and render her her due, and have not power of your own body — or, to speak yet more plainly — if you are the slave of a wife, do not allow this to cause you sorrow, do not sigh over the loss of your virginity. Even if you can find pretexts for parting from her to enjoy the freedom of chastity, do not seek your own welfare at the price of another's ruin. Keep your wife for a little, and do not try too hastily to overcome her reluctance. Wait till she follows

your example. If you only have patience, your wife will some day become your sister.

7. In another passage we have discussed the reasons which led Paul to say: Now concerning virgins, I have no commandment of the Lord: yet I give my judgment, as one that has obtained mercy of the Lord to be faithful. 1 Corinthians 7:25 Here also, while we have extolled virginity, we have been careful to give marriage its due. Had the Lord commanded virginity, we said, He would have seemed to condemn marriage and to do away with that seed-plot of humanity from which virginity itself springs. Had He cut away the root how could He have looked for fruit? Unless He had first laid the foundations, how could He have built the edifice or crowned it with a roof made to cover its whole extent? If we have spoken of marriage as the root whose fruit is virginity, and if we have made wedlock the foundation on which the building or the roof of perpetual chastity is raised, which of my detractors can be so captious or so blind as to ignore the foundation on which the fabric and its roof are built, while he has before his eyes both the fabric and the roof themselves? Once more, in another place, we have brought forward the testimony of the apostle to this effect: Are you bound unto a wife? Seek not to be loosed. Are you loosed from a wife? Seek not a wife. 1 Corinthians 7:21 To this we have appended the following remarks: Each of us has his own sphere allotted to him. Let me have mine, and do you keep yours. If you are bound to a wife, do not put her away. If I am loosed from a wife, let me not seek a wife. Just as I do not loose marriage-ties when they are once made, so do you refrain from binding together what at present is loosed from such ties. Yet another passage bears unmistakable testimony to the view which we have taken of virginity and of wedlock: The apostle casts no snare upon us, 1 Corinthians 7:35 nor does he compel us to be what we do not wish. He only urges us to what is honorable and seemly, inciting us earnestly to serve the Lord, to be anxious always to please Him, and to look for His will which He has prepared for us to do. We are to be like alert and armed soldiers, who immediately execute the orders given to them and perform them without that travail of mind which, according to the preacher, is given to the men of this world 'to be exercised therewith.' At the end, also, of our comparison of virgins and married women we have summed up the discussion thus: When one thing is good and another thing is better; when that which is good has a different reward from that which is better; and when there are more rewards than one, then, obviously, there exists a diversity of gifts. The difference between marriage and virginity is as great as that between not doing evil and doing good — or, to speak more favorably still, as that between what is good and what is still better.

8. In the sequel we go on to speak thus: The apostle, in concluding his discussion of marriage and of virginity, is careful to observe a mean course in discriminating between them, and, turning neither to the right hand nor to the left, he keeps to the King's highway, Numbers 20:17 and thus fulfils the injunction, 'Be not righteous overmuch.' Ecclesiastes 7:16 Moreover, when he goes on to compare monogamy with digamy, he puts digamy after monogamy, just as before he subordinated marriage to virginity. Do we not clearly show by this language what is typified in the Holy Scriptures by the terms right and left, and also what we take to be the

meaning of the words Be not righteous overmuch? We turn to the left if, following the lust of Jews and Gentiles, we burn for sexual intercourse; we turn to the right if, following the error of the Manichæans, we under a pretence of chastity entangle ourselves in the meshes of unchastity. But we keep to the King's highway if we aspire to virginity yet refrain from condemning marriage. Can any one, moreover, be so unfair in his criticism of my poor treatise as to allege that I condemn first marriages, when he reads my opinion on second ones as follows: The apostle, it is true, allows second marriages, but only to such women as are bent upon them, to such as cannot contain, 1 Corinthians 7:9 lest 'when they have begun to wax wanton against Christ they marry, having condemnation because they have rejected their first faith,' and he makes this concession because many 'are turned aside after Satan.' 1 Timothy 5:15 But they will be happier if they abide as widows. To this he immediately adds his apostolic authority, 'after my judgment.' Moreover, lest any should consider that authority, being human, to be of small weight, he goes on to say, 'and I think also that I have the spirit of God.' 1 Corinthians 7:40 Thus, where he urges men to continence he appeals not to human authority, but to the Spirit of God; but when he gives them permission to marry he does not mention the Spirit of God, but allows prudential considerations to turn the balance, relaxing the strictness of his code in favor of individuals according to their several needs. Having thus brought forward proofs that second marriages are allowed by the apostle, we at once added the remarks which follow: As marriage is permitted to virgins by reason of the danger of fornication, and as what in itself is not desirable is thus made excusable, so by reason of the same danger widows are permitted to marry a second time. For it is better that a woman should know one man (though he should be a second husband or a third) than that she should know several. In other words, it is preferable that she should prostitute herself to one rather than to many. Calumny may do its worst. We have spoken here not of a first marriage, but of a second, of a third, or (if you like) of a fourth. But lest any one should apply my words (that it is better for a woman to prostitute herself to one man than to several) to a first marriage when my whole argument dealt with digamy and trigamy, I marked my own view of these practices with the words: 'All things are lawful, but all things are not expedient.' 1 Corinthians 6:12 I do not condemn digamists nor yet trigamists, nor even, to put an extreme, case, octogamists. I will make a still greater concession: I am ready to receive even a whore-monger, if penitent. In every case where fairness is possible, fair consideration must be shown.

9. My calumniator should blush at his assertion that I condemn first marriages when he reads my words just now quoted: I do not condemn digamists or trigamists, or even, to put an extreme case, octogamists. Not to condemn is one thing, to commend is another. I may concede a practice as allowable and yet not praise it as meritorious. But if I seem severe in saying, In every case where fairness is possible, fair consideration must be shown, no one, I fancy, will judge me either cruel or stern who reads that the places prepared for virgins and for wedded persons are different from those prepared for trigamists, octogamists, and penitents. That Christ Himself, although in the flesh a virgin, was in the spirit a monogamist, having one wife, even the Church, Ephesians 5:23-24 I have shown in the latter part of my argument. And yet I am supposed to condemn marriage! I

am said to condemn it, although I use such words as these: It is an undoubted fact that the levitical priests were descended from the stock of Aaron, Eleazar, and Phinehas; and, as all these were married men, we might well be confronted with them if, led away by the error of the Encratites, we were to contend that marriage is in itself deserving of condemnation. Here I blame Tatian, the chief of the Encratites, for his rejection of marriage, and yet I myself am said to condemn it! Once more, when I contrast virgins with widows, my own words show what my view is concerning wedlock, and set forth the threefold gradation which I propose of virgins, widows— whether in practice or in fact — and wedded wives. I do not deny — these are my words — the blessedness of widows who continue such after their baptism, nor do I undervalue the merit of wives who live in chastity with their husbands; but, just as widows receive a greater reward from God than wives obedient to their husbands, they, too, must be content to see virgins preferred before themselves.

10. Again, when explaining the witness of the apostle to the Galatians, By the works of the law shall no flesh be justified, I have spoken to the following effect: Marriages also are works of the law. And for this reason there is a curse upon such as do not produce offspring. They are permitted, it is true, even under the Gospel; but it is one thing to concede an indulgence to what is a weakness and quite another to promise a reward to what is a virtue. See my express declaration that marriage is allowed in the Gospel, yet that those who are married cannot receive the rewards of chastity so long as they render their due one to another. If married men feel indignant at this statement, let them vent their anger not on me but on the Holy Scriptures; nay, more, upon all bishops, presbyters, and deacons, and the whole company of priests and levites, who know that they cannot offer sacrifices if they fulfil the obligations of marriage. Again, when I adduce evidence from the Apocalypse, is it not clear what view I take concerning virgins, widows, and wives? These are they who sing a new song Revelation 14:3 which no man can sing except he be a virgin. These are 'the first fruits unto God and unto the Lamb,' Revelation 14:4 and they are without spot. If virgins are the first fruits unto God, then widows and wives who live in continence must come after the first fruits — that is to say, in the second place and in the third. We place widows, then, and wives in the second place and in the third, and for this we are charged by the frenzy of a heretic with condemning marriage altogether.

11. Throughout the book I have made many remarks in a tone of great moderation on virginity, widowhood, and marriage. But for the sake of brevity, I will here adduce but one passage, and that of such a kind that no one, I think, will be found to gainsay it save some one who wishes to prove himself malicious or mad. In describing our Lord's visit to the marriage at Cana in Galilee, John 2:1-2 after some other remarks I have added these: He who went but once to a marriage has taught us that a woman should marry but once; and this fact might tell against virginity if we failed to give marriage its due place — after virginity that is, and chaste widowhood. But, as it is only heretics who condemn marriage and tread under foot the ordinance of God, we listen with gladness to every word said by our Lord in praise of marriage. For the Church does not condemn marriage, but only subordinates it. It does not reject it altogether, but regulates it, knowing (as I have

said above) that 'in a great house there are not only vessels of gold and of silver, but also of wood and of earth; and some to honor and some to dishonor. If a man, therefore, purge himself...he shall be a vessel unto honor meet...and prepared unto every good work.' 2 Timothy 2:20-21 I listen with gladness, I say here, to every word said by the apostle in praise of marriage. Do I listen with gladness to the praise of marriage, and do I yet condemn marriage? The Church, I say, does not condemn wedlock, but subordinates it. Whether you like it or not, marriage is subordinated to virginity and widowhood. Even when marriage continues to fulfil its function, the Church does not condemn it, but only subordinates it; it does not reject it, but only regulates it. It is in your power, if you will, to mount the second step of chastity. Why are you angry if, standing on the third and lowest step, you will not make haste to go up higher?

12. Since, then, I have so often reminded my reader of my views; and since I have picked my way like a prudent traveller over every inch of the road, stating repeatedly that, while I receive marriage as a thing in itself admissible, I yet prefer continence, widowhood, and virginity, the wise and generous reader ought to have judged what seemed hard sayings by my general drift, and not to have charged me with putting forward inconsistent opinions in one and the same book. For who is so dull or so inexperienced in writing as to praise and to condemn one and the same object, as to destroy what he has built up, and to build up what he has destroyed; and when he has vanquished his opponent, to turn his sword, last of all against himself? Were my detractors country bred or unacquainted with the arts of rhetoric or of logic, I should pardon their want of insight; nor should I censure them for accusing me if I saw that their ignorance was in fault and not their will. As it is men of intellect who have enjoyed a liberal education make it their object less to understand me than to wound me, and for such I have this short answer, that they should correct my faults and not merely censure me for them. The lists are open, I cry; your enemy has marshalled his forces, his position is plain, and (if I may quote Virgil)—

The foeman calls you: meet him face to face.

Such men should answer their opponent. They ought to keep within the limits of debate, and not to wield the schoolmaster's rod. Their books should aim at showing in what my statements have fallen short of the truth, and in what they have exceeded it. For, although I will not listen to fault-finders, I will follow the advice of teachers. To direct the fighter how to fight when you yourself occupy a post of vantage on the wall is a kind of teaching that does not commend itself; and when you are yourself bathed in perfumes, it is unworthy to charge a bleeding soldier with cowardice. Nor in saying this do I lay myself open to a charge of boasting that while others have slept I only have entered the lists. My meaning simply is that men who have seen me wounded in this warfare may possibly be a little too cautious in their methods of fighting. I would not have you engage in an encounter in which you will have nothing to do but to protect yourself, your right hand remaining motionless while your left manages your shield. You must either strike or fall. I cannot account you a victor unless I see your opponent put to the sword.

13. You are, no doubt, men of vast acquirements; but we too have studied in the schools, and, like you, we have learned from the precepts of Aristotle — or, rather, from those which he has derived from Gorgias — that there are different ways of speaking; and we know, among other things, that he who writes for display uses one style, and he who writes to convince, another. In the former case the debate is desultory; to confute the opposer, now this argument is adduced and now that. One argues as one pleases, saying one thing while one means another. To quote the proverb, With one hand one offers bread, in the other one holds a stone. In the latter case a certain frankness and openness of countenance are necessary. For it is one thing to start a problem and another to expound what is already proved. The first calls for a disputant, the second for a teacher. I stand in the thick of the fray, my life in constant danger: you who profess to teach me are a man of books. Do not, you say, attack unexpectedly or wound by a side-thrust. Strike straight at your opponent. You should be ashamed to resort to feints instead of force. As if it were not the perfection of fighting to menace one part and to strike another. Read, I beg of you, Demosthenes or Cicero, or (if you do not care for pleaders whose aim is to speak plausibly rather than truly) read Plato, Theophrastus, Xenophon, Aristotle, and the rest of those who draw their respective rills of wisdom from the Socratic fountain-head. Do they show any openness? Are they devoid of artifice? Is not every word they say filled with meaning? And does not this meaning always make for victory? Origen, Methodius, Eusebius, and Apollinaris write at great length against Celsus and Porphyry. Consider how subtle are the arguments, how insidious the engines with which they overthrow what the spirit of the devil has wrought. Sometimes, it is true, they are compelled to say not what they think but what is needful; and for this reason they employ against their opponents the assertions of the Gentiles themselves. I say nothing of the Latin authors, of Tertullian, Cyprian, Minutius, Victorinus, Lactantius, Hilary, lest I should appear not so much to be defending myself as to be assailing others. I will only mention the Apostle Paul, whose words seem to me, as often as I hear them, to be not words, but peals of thunder. Read his epistles, and especially those addressed to the Romans, to the Galatians, and to the Ephesians, in all of which he stands in the thick of the battle, and you will see how skilful and how careful he is in the proofs which he draws from the Old Testament, and how warily he cloaks the object which he has in view. His words seem simplicity itself: the expressions of a guileless and unsophisticated person — one who has no skill either to plan a dilemma or to avoid it. Still, whichever way you look, they are thunderbolts. His pleading halts, yet he carries every point which he takes up. He turns his back upon his foe only to overcome him; he simulates flight, but only that he may slay. He, then, if any one, ought to be calumniated; we should speak thus to him: The proofs which you have used against the Jews or against other heretics bear a different meaning in their own contexts to that which they bear in your epistles. We see passages taken captive by your pen and pressed into service to win you a victory which in the volumes from which they are taken have no controversial bearing at all. May he not reply to us in the words of the Saviour: I have one mode of speech for those that are without and another for those that are within; the crowds hear my parables, but their interpretation is for my disciples alone? Matthew 13:10-17 The Lord puts questions to the Pharisees, but does not elucidate them. To teach a disciple is one thing; to vanquish an opponent, another. My

mystery is for me, says the prophet; my mystery is for me and for them that are mine.

14. You are indignant with me because I have merely silenced Jovinian and not instructed him. You, do I say? Nay, rather, they who grieve to hear him anathematized, and who impeach their own pretended orthodoxy by eulogizing in another the heresy which they hold themselves. I should have asked him, forsooth, to surrender peaceably! I had no right to disregard his struggles and to drag him against his will into the bonds of truth! I might use such language had the desire of victory induced me to say anything counter to the rule laid down in Scripture, and had I taken the line — so often adopted by strong men in controversy — of justifying the means by the result. As it is, however, I have been an exponent of the apostle rather than a dogmatist on my own account; and my function has been simply that of a commentator. Anything, therefore, which seems a hard saying should be imputed to the writer expounded by me rather than to me the expounder; unless, indeed, he spoke otherwise than he is represented to have done, and I have by an unfair interpretation wrested the plain meaning of his words. If any one charges me with this disingenuousness let him prove his charge from the Scriptures themselves.

I have said in my book, If 'it is good for a man not to touch a woman,' then it is bad for him to touch one, for bad, and bad only, is the opposite of good. But, if though bad it is made venial, then it is allowed to prevent something which would be worse than bad, and so on down to the commencement of the next chapter. The above is my comment upon the apostle's words: It is good for a man not to touch a woman. Nevertheless, to avoid fornication, let every man have his own wife, and let every woman have her own husband. 1 Corinthians 7:1-2 In what way does my meaning differ from that intended by the apostle? Except that where he speaks decidedly I do so with hesitation. He defines a dogma, I hazard an inquiry. He openly says: It is good for a man not to touch a woman. I timidly ask if it is good for a man not to touch one. If I thus waver, I cannot be said to speak positively. He says: It is good not to touch. I add what is a possible antithesis to good. And immediately afterwards I speak thus: Notice the apostle's carefulness. He does not say: 'It is good for a man not to have a wife,' but, 'It is good for a man not to touch a woman'; as if there is danger in the very touching of one — danger which he who touches cannot escape. You see, therefore, that I am not expounding the law as to husbands and wives, but simply discussing the general question of sexual intercourse — how in comparison with chastity and virginity, the life of angels, It is good for a man not to touch a woman.

Vanity of vanities, says the Preacher, all is vanity. Ecclesiastes 1:2 But if all created things are good, as being the handiwork of a good Creator, how comes it that all things are vanity? If the earth is vanity, are the heavens vanity too?— and the angels, the thrones, the dominations, the powers, and the rest of the virtues? No; if things which are good in themselves as being the handiwork of a good Creator are called vanity, it is because they are compared with things which are better still. For example, compared with a lamp, a lantern is good for nothing; compared with a star, a lamp does not shine at all; the brightest star pales before the moon; put the moon beside the sun, and it no longer looks bright; compare the sun with Christ, and it is darkness. I am that I am, God says; Exodus 3:14 and if you compare all created things with Him they have no existence. Give not your sceptre, says Esther, unto them that be nothing Esther 14:11 — that is to say, to idols and demons. And certainly they were idols and demons to whom she prayed that she and hers might not be given over. In Job also we read how Bildad says of the wicked man: His confidence shall be rooted out of his tabernacle, and destruction as a king shall trample upon him. The companions also of him who is not shall abide in his tabernacle. This evidently relates to the devil, who must be in existence, otherwise he could not be said to have companions. Still, because he is lost to God, he is said not to be.

Now it was in a similar sense that I declared it to be a bad thing to touch a woman— I did not say a wife — because it is a good thing not to touch one. And I added: I call virginity fine grain, wedlock barley, and fornication cow-dung. Surely both grain and barley are creatures of God. But of the two multitudes miraculously supplied in the Gospel the larger was fed upon barley loaves, and the smaller on grain bread. You, Lord, says the psalmist, shall save both man and beast. I have myself said the same thing in other words, when I have spoken of virginity as gold and of wedlock as silver. Again, in discussing the one hundred and forty-four thousand sealed virgins who were not defiled with women, I have tried to show that all who have not remained virgins are reckoned as defiled when compared with the perfect chastity of the angels and of our Lord Jesus Christ. But if any one thinks it hard or reprehensible that I have placed the same interval between virginity and wedlock as there is between fine grain and barley, let him read the book of the holy Ambrose On Widows, and he will find, among other statements concerning virginity and marriage, the following: The apostle has not expressed his preference for marriage so unreservedly as to quench in men the aspiration after virginity; he commences with a recommendation of continence, and it is only subsequently that he stoops to mention the remedies for its opposite. And although to the strong he has pointed out the prize of their high calling, Philippians 3:14 yet he suffers none to faint by the way; Matthew 15:32 while he applauds those who lead the van, he does not despise those who bring up the rear. For he had himself learned that the Lord Jesus gave to some barley bread, lest they should faint by the way, but offered to others His own body, that they should strive to attain His kingdom; and immediately afterwards: The nuptial tie, then, is not to be avoided as a crime, but to be refused as a hard burden. For the law binds the wife to bring forth children in labor and in sorrow. Her desire is to be to her husband that he should rule over her. Genesis 3:16 It is not the widow, then, but the bride, who is handed over to labor and sorrow in childbearing. It is not the virgin, but the married woman, who is subjected to the sway of a husband. And in another place, You are bought, says the apostle, with a price; be not therefore the servants of men. Ephesians 6:6 You see how clearly he defines the servitude which attends the married state. And a little farther on: If, then, even a good marriage is servitude, what must a bad one be, in which husband and wife cannot sanctify, but only mutually destroy each other? What I have said about virginity and marriage diffusely, Ambrose has stated tersely and pointedly, compressing much meaning into a few words. Virginity is described by him as a means of recommending continence, marriage as a remedy for incontinence. And when he descends from broad principles to particular details, he significantly holds out to virgins the prize of the high calling, yet comforts the married, that they may not faint by the way. While eulogizing the one class, he does not despise the other. Marriage he compares to the barley bread set before the multitude, virginity to the body of Christ given to the disciples. There is much less difference, it seems to me, between barley and fine grain than between barley and the body of Christ. Finally, he speaks of marriage as a hard burden, to be avoided if possible, and as a badge of the most unmistakable servitude. He makes, also, many other statements, which he has followed up at length in his three books On Virgins.

15. From all which considerations it is clear that I have said nothing at all new concerning virginity and marriage, but have followed in all respects the judgment of older writers — of Ambrose, that is to say, and others who have discussed the doctrines of the Church. And I would sooner follow them in their faults than copy the dull pedantry of the writers of today. Let married men, if they please, swell with rage because I have said, I ask you, what kind of good thing is that which forbids a man to pray, and which prevents him from receiving the body of Christ? When I do my duty as a husband, I cannot fulfil the requirements of continence. The same apostle, in another place, commands us to pray always.
1 Thessalonians 5:17 But if we are always to pray we must never yield to the claims of wedlock for, as often as I render her due to my wife, I incapacitate myself for prayer. When I spoke thus it is clear that I relied on the words of the apostle: Defraud ye not one the other, except it be with consent for a time, that you may give yourselves to . . . prayer. 1 Corinthians 7:5 The Apostle Paul tells us that when we have intercourse with our wives we cannot pray. If, then, sexual intercourse prevents what is less important — that is, prayer— how much more does it prevent what is more important — that is, the reception of the body of Christ? Peter, too, exhorts us to continence, that our prayers be not hindered.
1 Peter 3:7 How, I should like to know, have I sinned in all this? What have I done? How have I been in fault? If the waters of a stream are thick and muddy, it is not the river-bed which is to blame, but the source. Am I attacked because I have ventured to add to the words of the apostle these words of my own: What kind of good thing is that which prevents a man from receiving the body of Christ? If so, I will make answer briefly thus: Which is the more important, to pray or to receive Christ's body? Surely to receive Christ's body. If, then, sexual intercourse hinders the less important thing, much more does it hinder that which is the more important.

I have said in the same treatise that David and they that were with him could not have lawfully eaten the show-bread had they not made answer that for three days they had not been defiled with women — not, of course, with harlots, intercourse with whom was forbidden by the law, but with their own wives, to whom they were lawfully united. Moreover, when the people were about to receive the law on Mount Sinai they were commanded to keep away from their wives for three days. Exodus 19:15 I know that at Rome it is customary for the faithful always to receive the body of Christ, a custom which I neither censure nor endorse. Let every man be fully persuaded in his own mind. Romans 14:5 But I appeal to the consciences of those persons who after indulging in sexual intercourse on the same day receive the communion — having first, as Persius puts it, washed off the night in a flowing stream, and I ask such why they do not presume to approach the martyrs or to enter the churches. Is Christ of one mind abroad and of another at home? What is unlawful in church cannot be lawful at home. Nothing is hidden from God. The night shines as the day before Him. Let each man examine himself, and so let him approach the body of Christ. 1 Corinthians 11:28 Not, of course, that the deferring of communion for one day or for two makes a Christian any the holier or that what I have not deserved today I shall deserve tomorrow or the day after. But if I grieve that I have not shared in Christ's body it does help me to avoid for a little while my wife's embraces, and to prefer to wedded love the love of Christ. A hard discipline, you will say, and one not to be borne. What man of the world could bear it? He that can bear it, I reply, let him bear it; Matthew 19:12 he that cannot must look to himself. It is my business to say, not what each man can do or will do, but what the Scriptures inculcate.

16. Again, objection has been taken to my comments on the apostle in the following passage: But lest any should suppose from the context of the words before quoted (namely, 'that you may give yourselves...to prayer and come together again') that the apostle desires this consummation, and does not merely concede it to obviate a worse downfall, he immediately adds, 'that Satan tempt you not for your incontinency.' 1 Corinthians 7:5 'And come together again.' What a noble indulgence the words convey! One which he blushes to speak of in plainer words, which he prefers only to Satan's temptation, and which has its root in incontinence. Do we labor to expound this as a dark saying when the writer has himself explained his meaning? I speak this, he says, 'by way of permission, and not as a command.' Do we still hesitate to speak of wedlock as a thing permitted instead of as a thing enjoined? Or are we afraid that such permission will exclude second or third marriages or some other case? What have I said here which the apostle has not said? The phrase, I suppose, which he blushes to speak of in plainer words. I imagine that when he says come together, and does not mention for what, he takes a modest way of indicating what he does not like to name openly — that is, sexual intercourse. Or is the objection to the words which follow — which he prefers only to Satan's temptation, and which has its root in incontinence? Are they not the very words of the apostle, only differently arranged — that Satan tempt you not for your incontinency? Or do people cavil because I said, Do we still hesitate to speak of wedlock as a thing permitted instead of as a thing enjoined? If this seems a hard saying, it should be ascribed to the apostle, who says, But I speak this by way of permission, and not as a command, and not to me, who, except that I have rearranged their order, have changed neither the words nor their meaning.

17. The shortness of a letter compels me to hasten on. I pass, accordingly, to the points which remain. I say, remarks the apostle, to the unmarried and widows, It is good for them if they abide even as I. But if they cannot contain, let them marry; for it is better to marry than to burn. 1 Corinthians 7:8-9 This section I have interpreted thus: When he has granted to those who are married the use of wedlock, and has made clear his own wishes and concessions, he passes on to those who are unmarried or widows, and sets before them his own example. He

calls them happy if they abide even as he, 1 Corinthians 7:8 but he goes on, 'if they cannot contain, let them marry.' He thus repeats his former language, 'but only to avoid fornication,' and 'that Satan tempt you not for your incontinence.' And when he says, 'If they cannot contain, let them marry,' he gives as a reason for his words that 'it is better to marry than to burn.' It is only good to marry, because it is bad to burn. But take away the fire of lust, and he will not say 'it is better to marry.' For a thing is said to be better in antithesis to something which is worse, and not simply in contrast with what is admittedly good. It is as though he said, 'It is better to have one eye than none.' Shortly afterwards, apostrophizing the apostle, I spoke thus: If marriage is good in itself, do not compare it with a conflagration, but simply say, 'It is good to marry.' I must suspect the goodness of a thing which only becomes a lesser evil in the presence of a greater one. I, for my part, would have it not a lighter evil but a downright good. The apostle wishes unmarried women and widows to abstain from sexual intercourse, incites them to follow his own example, and calls them happy if they abide even as he. But if they cannot contain, and are tempted to quench the fire of lust by fornication rather than by continence, it is better, he tells them, to marry than to burn. Upon which precept I have made this comment: It is good to marry, simply because it is bad to burn, not putting forward a view of my own, but only explaining the apostle's precept, It is better to marry than to burn; that is, it is better to take a husband than to commit fornication. If, then, you teach that burning or fornication is good, the good will still be surpassed by what is still better. But if marriage is only a degree better than the evil to which it is preferred, it cannot be of that unblemished perfection and blessedness which suggest a comparison with the life of angels. Suppose I say, It is better to be a virgin than a married woman; in this case I have preferred to what is good what is still better. But suppose I go a step further and say, It is better to marry than to commit fornication; in that case I have preferred, not a better thing to a good thing, but a good thing to a bad one. There is a wide difference between the two cases; for, while virginity is related to marriage as better is to good, marriage is related to fornication as good is to bad. How, I should like to know, have I sinned in this explanation? My fixed purpose was not to bend the Scriptures to my own wishes, but simply to say what I took to be their meaning. A commentator has no business to dilate on his own views; his duty is to make plain the meaning of the author whom he professes to interpret. For, if he contradicts the writer whom he is trying to expound, he will prove to be his opponent rather than his interpreter. When I am freely expressing my own opinion, and not commenting upon the Scriptures, then any one that pleases may charge me with having spoken hardly of marriage. But if he can find no ground for such a charge, he should attribute such passages in my commentaries as appear severe or harsh to the author commented on, and not to me, who am only his interpreter.

18. Another charge brought against me is simply intolerable! It is urged that in explaining the apostle's words concerning husbands and wives, Such shall have trouble in the flesh, I have said: We in our ignorance had supposed that in the flesh at least wedlock would have rejoicing. But if married persons are to have trouble in the flesh, the only thing in which they seemed likely to have pleasure, what motive will be left to make women marry? For, besides having trouble in spirit and soul, they will also have it even in the flesh. 1 Thessalonians 5:23 Do I condemn

marriage if I enumerate its troubles, such as the crying of infants, the death of children, the chance of abortion, domestic losses, and so forth? Whilst Damasus of holy memory was still living, I wrote a book against Helvidius On the Perpetual Virginity of the Blessed Mary, in which, duly to extol the bliss of virginity, I was forced to say much of the troubles of marriage. Did that excellent man — versed in Scripture as he was, and a virgin doctor of the virgin Church — find anything to censure in my discourse? Moreover, in the treatise which I addressed to Eustochium I used much harsher language regarding marriage, and yet no one was offended at it. Nay, every lover of chastity strained his ears to catch my eulogy of continence. Read Tertullian, read Cyprian, read Ambrose, and either accuse me with them or acquit me with them. My critics resemble the characters of Plautus. Their only wit lies in detraction; and they try to make themselves out men of learning by assailing all parties in turn. Thus they bestow their censure impartially upon myself and upon my opponent, and maintain that we are both beaten, although one or other of us must have succeeded.

Moreover, when in discussing digamy and trigamy I have said, It is better for a woman to know one man, even though he be a second husband or a third, than several; it is more tolerable for her to prostitute herself to one man than to many, have I not immediately subjoined my reason for so saying? The Samaritan woman in the Gospel, when she declares that her present husband is her sixth, is rebuked by the Lord on the ground that he is not her husband. For my own part, I now once more freely proclaim that digamy is not condemned in the Church— no, nor yet trigamy — and that a woman may marry a fifth husband, or a sixth, or a greater number still just as lawfully as she may marry a second; but that, while such marriages are not condemned, neither are they commended. They are meant as alleviations of an unhappy lot, and in no way redound to the glory of continence. I have spoken to the same effect elsewhere. When a woman marries more than once — whether she does so twice or three times matters little — she ceases to be a monogamist. 'All things are lawful...but all things are not expedient.'
1 Corinthians 6:12 I do not condemn digamists or trigamists, or even, to put an impossible case, octogamists. Let a woman have an eighth husband if she must; only let her cease to prostitute herself.

19. I will come now to the passage in which I am accused of saying that — at least according to the true Hebrew text — the words God saw that it was good Genesis 1:10 are not inserted after the second day of the creation, as they are after the first, third, and remaining ones, and of adding immediately the following comment: We are meant to understand that there is something not good in the number two, separating us as it does from unity, and prefiguring the marriage-tie. Just as in the account of Noah's ark all the animals that enter by twos are unclean, but those of which an uneven number is taken are clean. Genesis 7:2 In this statement a passing objection is made to what I have said concerning the second day, whether on the ground that the words mentioned really occur in the passage, although I say that they do not occur, or because, assuming them to occur, I have understood them in a sense different from that which the context evidently requires. As regards the non-occurrence of the words in question (viz., God saw that it was good), let them take not my evidence, but that of all the Jewish and

other translators — Aquila namely, Symmachus, and Theodotion. But if the words, although occurring in the account of the other days, do not occur in the account of this, either let them give a more plausible reason than I have done for their non-occurrence, or, failing such, let them, whether they like it or not, accept the suggestion which I have made. Furthermore, if in Noah's ark all the animals that enter by twos are unclean, while those of which an uneven number is taken are clean, and if there is no dispute about the accuracy of the text, let them explain if they can why it is so written. But if they cannot explain it, then, whether they will or not, they must embrace my explanation of the matter. Either produce better fare and ask me to be your , or else rest content with the meal that I offer you, however poor it may be.

I must now mention the ecclesiastical writers who have dealt with this question of the odd number. They are, among the Greeks, Clement, Hippolytus, Origen, Dionysius, Eusebius, Didymus; and, among ourselves, Tertullian, Cyprian, Victorinus, Lactantius, Hilary. What Cyprian said to Fortunatus about the number seven is clear from the letter which he sent to him. Or perhaps I ought to bring forward the reasonings of Pythagoras, Archytas of Tarentum, and Publius Scipio in (Cicero's) sixth book Concerning the Common Weal. If my detractors will not listen to any of these I will make the grammar schools shout in their ears the words of Virgil:

Uneven numbers are the joy of God.

20. To say, as I have done, that virginity is cleaner than wedlock, that the even numbers must give way to the odd, that the types of the Old Testament establish the truth of the Gospel: this, it appears, is a great sin subversive of the churches and intolerable to the world. The remaining points which are censured in my treatise are, I take it, of less importance, or else resolve themselves into this. I have, therefore, refrained from answering them, both that I may not exceed the limit at my disposal, and that I may not seem to distrust your intelligence, knowing as I do that you are ready to be my champion even before I ask you. With my last breath, then, I protest that neither now nor at any former time have I condemned marriage. I have merely answered an opponent without any fear that they of my own party would lay snares for me. I extol virginity to the skies, not because I myself possess it, but because, not possessing it, I admire it all the more. Surely it is a modest and ingenuous confession to praise in others that which you lack yourself. The weight of my body keeps me fixed to the ground, but do I fail to admire the flying birds or to praise the dove because, in the words of Virgil, it

Glides on its liquid path with motionless swift wings?

Let no man deceive himself, let no man, giving ear to the voice of flattery, rush upon ruin. The first virginity man derives from his birth, the second from his second birth. The words are not mine; it is an old saying, No man can serve two masters; Matthew 6:24 that is, the flesh and the spirit. For the flesh lusts against the spirit, and the spirit against the flesh; and these are contrary the one to the other, so that we cannot do the things that we would. Galatians 5:17 When, then, anything in my little work seems to you harsh, have regard not to my words, but to the Scripture, whence they are taken.

21. Christ Himself is a virgin; and His mother is also a virgin; yea, though she is His mother, she is a virgin still. For Jesus has entered in through the closed doors, John 20:19 and in His sepulchre — a new one hewn out of the hardest rock — no man is laid either before Him or after Him. John 19:41 Mary is a garden enclosed...a fountain sealed, Song of Songs 4:12 and from that fountain flows, according to Joel, the river which waters the torrent bed either of cords or of thorns; of cords being those of the sins by which we were beforetime bound, Proverbs 5:22 the thorns those which choked the seed the goodman of the house had sown. Matthew 13:7 She is the east gate, spoken of by the prophet Ezekiel, always shut and always shining, and either concealing or revealing the Holy of Holies; and through her the Sun of Righteousness, Malachi 4:2 our high priest after the order of Melchizedek, Hebrews 5:10 goes in and out. Let my critics explain to me how Jesus can have entered in through closed doors when He allowed His hands and His side to be handled, and showed that He had bones and flesh, thus proving that His was a true body and no mere phantom of one, and I will explain how the holy Mary can be at once a mother and a virgin. A mother before she was wedded, she remained a virgin after bearing her son. Therefore, as I was going to say, the virgin Christ and the virgin Mary have dedicated in themselves the first fruits of virginity for both sexes. The apostles have either been virgins or, though married, have lived celibate lives. Those persons who are chosen to be bishops, priests, and deacons are either virgins or widowers; or at least when once they have received the priesthood, are vowed to perpetual chastity. Why do we delude ourselves and feel vexed if while we are continually straining after sexual indulgence, we find the palm of chastity denied to us? We wish to fare sumptuously, and to enjoy the embraces of our wives, yet at the same time we desire to reign with Christ among virgins and widows. Shall there be but one reward, then, for hunger and for excess, for filth and for finery, for sackcloth and for silk? Lazarus, Luke 16:19-25 in his lifetime, received evil things, and the rich man, clothed in purple, fat and sleek, while he lived enjoyed the good things of the flesh but, now that they are dead, they occupy different positions. Misery has given place to satisfaction, and satisfaction to misery. And it rests with us whether we will follow Lazarus or the rich man.

LETTER XLIX

To Pammachius

Jerome encloses the preceding letter, thanks Pammachius for his efforts to suppress his treatise against Jovinian, but declares these to be useless, and exhorts him, if he still has any hesitation in his mind, to turn to the Scriptures and the commentaries made upon them by Origen and others. Written at the same time as the preceding letter.

1. Christian modesty sometimes requires us to be silent even to our friends, and to nurse our humility in peace, where the renewal of an old friendship would expose us to the charge of self-seeking. Thus, when you have kept silence I have kept silence too, and have not cared to remonstrate with you, lest I should be thought more anxious to conciliate a person of influence than to cultivate a friend. But, now that it has become a duty to reply to your letter, I will endeavor always to be beforehand with you, and not so much to answer your queries as to write independently of them. Thus, if I have shown my modesty hitherto by silence, I will henceforth show it still more by coming forward to speak.

2. I quite recognize the kindness and forethought which have induced you to withdraw from circulation some copies of my work against Jovinian. Your diligence, however, has been of no avail, for several people coming from the city have repeatedly read aloud to me passages which they have come across in Rome. In this province, also, the books have already been circulated; and, as you have read yourself in Horace, Words once uttered cannot be recalled. I am not so fortunate as are most of the writers of the day — able, that is, to correct my trifles whenever I like. When once I have written anything, either my admirers or my ill-wishers — from different motives, but with equal zeal— sow my work broadcast among the public; and their language, whether it is that of eulogy or of criticism, is apt to run to excess. They are guided not by the merits of the piece, but by their own angry feelings. Accordingly, I have done what I could. I have dedicated to you a defense of the work in question, feeling sure that when you have read it you will yourself satisfy the doubts of others on my behalf; or else, if you too turn up your nose at the task, you will have to explain in some new manner that section of the apostle 1 Corinthians vii in which he discusses virginity and marriage.

3. I do not speak thus that I may provoke you to write on the subject yourself — although I know your zeal in the study of the sacred writings to be greater than my own — but that you may compel my tormentors to do so. They are educated; in their own eyes no mean scholars; competent not merely to censure but to instruct me. If they write on the subject, my view will be the sooner neglected when it is compared with theirs. Read, I pray you, and diligently consider the words of the apostle, and you will then see that — with a view to avoid misrepresentation — I have been much more gentle towards married persons than he was disposed to be. Origen, Dionysius, Pierius, Eusebius of Cæsarea, Didymus, Apollinaris, have used great latitude in the interpretation of this epistle. When Pierius, sifting and

expounding the apostle's meaning, comes to the words, I would that all men were even as I myself, 1 Corinthians 7:7 he makes this comment upon them: In saying this Paul plainly preaches abstinence from marriage. Is the fault here mine, or am I responsible for harshness? Compared with this sentence of Pierius, all that I have ever written is mild indeed. Consult the commentaries of the above-named writers and take advantage of the Church libraries; you will then more speedily finish as you would wish the enterprise which you have so happily begun.

4. I hear that the hopes of the entire city are centred in you, and that bishop and people are agreed in wishing for your exaltation. To be a bishop is much, to deserve to be one is more.

If you read the books of the sixteen prophets which I have rendered into Latin from the Hebrew; and if, when you have done so, you express satisfaction with my labors, the news will encourage me to take out of my desk some other works now shut up in it. I have lately translated Job into our mother tongue: you will be able to borrow a copy of it from your cousin, the saintly Marcella. Read it both in Greek and in Latin, and compare the old version with my rendering. You will then clearly see that the difference between them is that between truth and falsehood. Some of my commentaries upon the twelve prophets I have sent to the reverend father Domnio, also the four books of Kings — that is, the two called Samuel and the two called Malâchim. If you care to read these you will learn for yourself how difficult it is to understand the Holy Scriptures, and particularly the prophets; and how through the fault of the translators passages which for the Jews flow clearly on for us abound with mistakes. Once more, you must not in my small writings look for any such eloquence as that which for Christ's sake you disregard in Cicero. A version made for the use of the Church, even though it may possess a literary charm, ought to disguise and avoid it as far as possible; in order that it may not speak to the idle schools and few disciples of the philosophers, but may address itself rather to the entire human race.

LETTER L

To Domnio

Domnio, a Roman (called in Letter XLV. the Lot of our time), had written to Jerome to tell him that an ignorant monk had been traducing his books against Jovinian. Jerome, in reply, sharply rebukes the folly of his critic and comments on the want of straightforwardness in his conduct. He concludes the letter with an emphatic restatement of his original position. Written in 394 A.D.

1. Your letter is full at once of affection and of complaining. The affection is your own, which prompts you unceasingly to warn me of impending danger, and which makes you on my behalf

Of safest things distrustful and afraid.

The complaining is of those who have no love for me, and seek an occasion against me in my sins. They speak against their brother, they slander their own mother's son. You write to me of these — nay, of one in particular — a lounger who is to be seen in the streets, at crossings, and in public places; a monk who is a noisy news-monger, clever only in detraction, and eager, in spite of the beam in his own eye, to remove the mote in his neighbor's. Matthew 7:3-5 And you tell me that he preaches publicly against me, gnawing, rending, and tearing asunder with his fangs the books that I have written against Jovinian. You inform me, moreover, that this home-grown dialectician, this mainstay of the Plautine company, has read neither the Categories of Aristotle nor his treatise On Interpretation, nor his Analytics, nor yet the Topics of Cicero, but that, moving as he does only in uneducated circles, and frequenting no society but that of weak women, he ventures to construct illogical syllogisms and to unravel by subtle arguments what he is pleased to call my sophisms. How foolish I have been to suppose that without philosophy there can be no knowledge of these subjects; and to account it a more important part of composition to erase than to write! In vain have I perused the commentaries of Alexander; to no purpose has a skilled teacher used the Introduction of Porphyry to instruct me in logic; and — to make light of human learning — I have gained nothing at all by having Gregory of Nazianzum and Didymus as my catechists in the Holy Scriptures. My acquisition of Hebrew has been wasted labor; and so also has been the daily study which from my youth I have bestowed upon the Law and the Prophets, the Gospels and the Apostles.

2. Here we have a man who has reached perfection without a teacher, so as to be a vehicle of the spirit and a self-taught genius. He surpasses Cicero in eloquence, Aristotle in argument, Plato in discretion, Aristarchus in learning, Didymus, that man of brass, in the number of his books; and not only Didymus, but all the writers of his time in his knowledge of the Scriptures. It is reported that you have only to give him a theme and he is always ready — like Carneades — to argue on this side or on that, for justice or against it. The world escaped a great danger, and civil actions and suits concerning succession were saved from a yawning gulf on the day when, despising the bar, he transferred himself to the Church. For, had he

been unwilling, who could ever have been proved innocent? And, if he once began to reckon the points of the case upon his fingers, and to spread his syllogistic nets, what criminal would his pleading have failed to save? Had he but stamped his foot, or fixed his eyes, or knitted his brow, or moved his hand, or twirled his beard, he would at once have thrown dust in the eyes of the jury. No wonder that such a complete Latinist and so profound a master of eloquence overcomes poor me, who — as I have been some time away (from Rome), and without opportunities for speaking Latin — am half a Greek if not altogether a barbarian. No wonder, I say, that he overcomes me when his eloquence has crushed Jovinian in person. Good Jesus! What! even Jovinian that great and clever man! So clever, indeed, that no one can understand his writings, and that when he sings it is only for himself — and for the muses!

3. Pray, my dear father, warn this man not to hold language contrary to his profession, and not to undo with his words the chastity which he professes by his garb. Whether he elects to be a virgin or a married celibate — and the choice must rest with himself — he must not compare wives with virgins, for that would be to have striven in vain against Jovinian's eloquence. He likes, I am told, to visit the cells of widows and virgins, and to lecture them with his brows knit on sacred literature. What is it that he teaches these poor women in the privacy of their own chambers? Is it to feel assured that virgins are no better than wives? Is it to make the most of the flower of their age, to eat and drink, to frequent the baths, to live in luxury, and not to disdain the use of perfumes? Or does he preach to them chastity, fasting, and neglect of their persons? No doubt the precepts that he inculcates are full of virtue. But if so, let him admit publicly what he says privately. Or, if his private teaching is the same as his public, he should keep aloof altogether from the society of girls. He is a young man — a monk, and in his own eyes an eloquent one (do not pearls fall from his lips, and are not his elegant phrases sprinkled with comic salt and humor?)— I am surprised, therefore, that he can without a blush frequent noblemen's houses, pay constant visits to married ladies, make our religion a subject of contention, distort the faith of Christ by misapplying words, and — in addition to all this — detract from one who is his brother in the Lord. He may, however, have supposed me to be in error (for in many things we offend all, and if any man offend not in word he is a perfect man James 3:2). In that case he should have written to convict me or to question me, the course taken by Pammachius, a man of high attainments and position. To this latter I defended myself as best I could, and in a lengthy letter explained the exact sense of my words. He might at least have copied the diffidence which led you to extract and arrange such passages as seemed to give offense; asking me for corrections or explanations, and not supposing me so mad that in one and the same book I should write for marriage and against it.

4. Let him spare himself, let him spare me, let him spare the Christian name. Let him realize his position as a monk, not by talking and arguing, but by holding his peace and sitting still. Let him read the words of Jeremiah: It is good for a man that he bear the yoke in his youth. He sits alone and keeps silence, because he has borne it upon him. Lamentations 3:27-28 Or if he has really the right to apply the censor's rod to all writers, and fancies himself a man of learning because he alone

understands Jovinian (you know the proverb: Balbus best knows what Balbus means); yet, as Atilius reminds us, we are not all writers. Jovinian himself — an unlettered man of letters if ever there was one — will with most justice proclaim the fact to him. That the bishops condemn me, he says, is not reason but treason. I want no answers from nobodies, who, while they have authority to put me down, have not the wit to teach me. Let one write against me who has a tongue that I can understand, and whom to vanquish will be to vanquish all.

'I know full well: believe me, I have felt
The hero's force when rising o'er his shield
He hurls his whizzing spear.'

He is strong in argument, intricate and tenacious, one to fight with his head down. Often has he cried out against me in the streets from late one night till early the next. He is a well-built man, and his thews are those of an athlete. Secretly I believe him to be a follower of my teaching. He never blushes or stops to weigh his words: his only aim is to speak as loud as possible. So famous is he for his eloquence that his sayings are held up as models to our curly-headed youngsters. How often, when I have met him at meetings, has he aroused my wrath and put me into a passion! How often has he spat upon me, and then departed spat upon! But these are vulgar methods, and any of my followers can use them. I appeal to books, to those memorials which must be handed down to posterity. Let us speak by our writings, that the silent reader may judge between us; and that, as I have a flock of disciples, he may have one also — flatterers and parasites worthy of the Gnatho and Phormio who is their master.

5. It is no difficult matter, my dear Domnio, to chatter at street corners or in apothecaries' shops and to pass judgment on the world. So-and-so has made a good speech, so-and-so a bad one; this man knows the Scriptures, that one is crazy; this man talks glibly, that never says a word at all. But who considers him worthy thus to judge every one? To make an outcry against a man in every street, and to heap, not definite charges, but vague imputations, on his head, is nothing. Any buffoon or litigiously disposed person can do as much. Let him put forth his hand, put pen to paper, and bestir himself; let him write books and prove in them all he can. Let him give me a chance of replying to his eloquence. I can return bite for bite, if I like; when hurt myself, I can fix my teeth in my opponent. I too have had a liberal education. As Juvenal says, I also have often withdrawn my hand from the ferule. Of me, too, it may be said in the words of Horace, Flee from him; he has hay on his horn. But I prefer to be a disciple of Him who says, I gave my back to the smiters...I hid not my face from shame and spitting. Isaiah 50:6 When He was reviled He reviled not again. 1 Peter 2:23 After the buffeting, the cross, the scourge, the blasphemies, at the very last He prayed for His crucifiers, saying, Father, forgive them, for they know not what they do. Luke 23:34 I, too, pardon the error of a brother. He has been deceived, I feel sure, by the art of the devil. Among the women he was held clever and eloquent; but, when my poor writings reached Rome, dreading me as a rival, he tried to rob me of my laurels. No man on earth, he resolved, should please his eloquent self, unless such as commanded respect rather than sought it, and showed themselves men to be feared more than favored. A man of consummate address, he desired, like an old soldier, with one

stroke of the sword to strike down both his enemies, and to make clear to every one that, whatever view he might take, Scripture was always with him. Well, he must condescend to send me his account of the matter, and to correct my indiscreet language, not by censure but by instruction. If he tries to do this, he will find that what seems forcible on a lounge is not equally forcible in court; and that it is one thing to discuss the doctrines of the divine law amid the spindles and work-baskets of girls and another to argue concerning them among men of education. As it is, without hesitation or shame, he raises again and again the noisy shout, Jerome condemns marriage, and, while he constantly moves among women with child, crying infants, and marriage-beds, he suppresses the words of the apostle just to cover me — poor me — with odium. However, when he comes by and by to write books and to grapple with me at close quarters, then he will feel it, then he will stick fast; Epicurus and Aristippus will not be near him then; the swineherds will not come to his aid; the prolific sow will not so much as grunt. For I also may say, with Turnus:

Father, I too can launch a forceful spear,
And when I strike blood follows from the wound.

But if he refuses to write, and fancies that abuse is as effective as criticism, then, in spite of all the lands and seas and peoples which lie between us, he must hear at least the echo of my cry, I do not condemn marriage, I do not condemn wedlock. Indeed — and this I say to make my meaning quite clear to him — I should like every one to take a wife who, because they get frightened in the night, cannot manage to sleep alone.

'St. Jerome', woodcut 1492, Albrecht Durer

www.ingramcontent.com/pod-product-compliance
Lightning Source LLC
Chambersburg PA
CBHW060230030426
42335CB00014B/1398